Practical Ideas for Teaching Primary Science

CW00555167

Practical Ideas for Teaching Primary Science is a fun and interactive guide which supports teachers to design and deliver enjoyable science lessons. Peter Loxley explores different scientific topics – from growing plants and nutrition to forces and magnetism – with an emphasis on story-telling and art to help children share their ideas and work collaboratively in the classroom. This practical guide uses a three-stage framework design to encourage and guide sociocultural practice across three levels: KS1 (5–7), lower KS2 (7–9) and upper KS2 (9–11). The ideas for practice are placed in engaging and significant contexts to encourage curiosity and enquiry and, most importantly, promote feelings of pleasure and satisfaction from science learning. Teachers are guided through hands-on puzzles and activities such as role-play and design and technology tasks both inside and outside of the classroom, with health and safety aspects highlighted throughout, to inspire children's interest in how the world works from an early age and provide them with the skills to apply their new-found scientific thinking in other contexts.

Extended subject knowledge for all topics covered in this book can be found in *Teaching Primary Science*.

A companion website is available for both books. Features include:

- web links to external sites with useful teaching information and resources
- an interactive flashcard glossary to test students' understanding
- an image bank with downloadable pictures for use in the classroom

Practical Ideas for Teaching Primary Science is an invaluable teaching resource for both trainee and qualified teachers.

Peter Loxley taught in both primary and secondary schools for many years, including in the UK, Australia and Jamaica. He was previously Subject Leader of Science Education at the University of Northampton, UK.

'A great resource to support the teaching of the National Curriculum's programmes of study… it provides enrichment ideas for science enquiry that go beyond this minimum requirement. Each topic has some practical "hooks", such as poetry, photographs and quotes, to set the scene at the start of each new topic. There are many ideas for Key Stage 1, Lower and Upper Key Stage 2. Each topic is clearly introduced, with the working scientifically focus clearly defined. It is rich in ideas, questions to ask and science enquiry to do.'

From the **Association for Science Education** Green Tick Award Evaluation Report

'A comprehensive range of exciting practical ideas to support the teaching of science in primary schools. A must-have companion to *Teaching Primary Science* by the same author.'

Christine Khwaja, Associate Professor, Middlesex University, UK

'This text is engaging with an enthusiasm for the themes within it that is quite infectious. The ideas are so well explained and sequenced that they serve as a valuable aid to planning for a beginner teacher or for one who lacks confidence in science. Consistent with key theories of learning and teaching, the text incorporates a range of approaches, styles and strategies whilst also giving a wealth of background information and support for the teacher's content knowledge, in ways that most other texts do not.'

Deborah Holt, BEd Primary Programme Director, University of Edinburgh, UK

'A very useful resource for everyone, with a wide range of topics and themes. This book is particularly novel in its approach as it links science content (and sometimes stories!) with practical ideas which are realistic and engaging. The material will inspire scientists of the future.'

Karen Kerr, Lecturer in Education, Queen's University Belfast, UK

Practical Ideas for Teaching Primary Science

Inspiring Learning and Enjoyment

Peter Loxley

Routledge
Taylor & Francis Group

LONDON AND NEW YORK

First published 2018
by Routledge
2 Park Square, Milton Park, Abingdon, Oxon OX14 4RN

and by Routledge
711 Third Avenue, New York, NY 10017

Routledge is an imprint of the Taylor & Francis Group, an informa business

British Library Cataloguing in Publication Data
A catalogue record for this book is available from the British Library

Library of Congress Cataloging in Publication Data
Names: Loxley, Peter.
Title: Practical ideas for teaching primary science : inspiring learning and enjoyment / Peter Loxley.
Description: New York : Routledge, 2017. | Includes bibliographical references and index.
Identifiers: LCCN 2016048528| ISBN 9781138659636 (hardback: alk. paper) | ISBN 9781138659650 (pbk. : alk. paper)
Subjects: LCSH: Science—Study and teaching (Elementary) | Curriculum planning.
Classification: LCC LB1585 .L678 2010 | DDC 372.35/044—dc23
LC record available at https://lccn.loc.gov/2016048528

ISBN: 978-1-138-65963-6 (hbk)
ISBN: 978-1-138-65965-0 (pbk)
ISBN: 978-1-135-62008-4 (ebk)

Typeset in Frutiger
by Fish Books Ltd.

Printed and bound by CPI Group (UK) Ltd, Croydon, CR0 4YY

Visit the companion website: www.routledge.com/cw/loxley

CONTENTS

CONTENTS BY TOPIC

Topics	Key scientific ideas	Links to subject knowledge chapters in *Teaching Primary Science*, 3e
CHAPTER 1: INTRODUCTION		
The introduction provides an overview of the nature of the teaching and learning promoted by the *Ideas for practice* contained in the book.		Learning theory which underpins the *Ideas for practice* can be found in Part 1 of the Core book.
CHAPTER 2: GROWING PLANTS		
Yrs 5–7: Growing plants from seeds Yrs 7–9: Growing healthy plants Yrs 9–11: Bulbs and cuttings propagating plants	Germination of seeds Conditions for healthy plant growth Different ways of	Ch. 13: Interdependence Ch. 14: Diversity
CHAPTER 3: FLOWERING PLANTS		
Yrs 5–7: Flowering plants Yrs 7–9: Pollination Yrs 9–11: Adaptation	Plant structure and variety Structure of flowers Pollination Life cycles Adaptation	Ch. 14: Diversity Ch. 15: Adaptation and evolution
CHAPTER 4: WOODLAND HABITATS		
Yrs 5–7: Autumn in the woodland Yrs 7–9: Spring in the woodland Yrs 9–11: Habitats and food chains	Seasons Habitats Food chains Interdependence Adaptation	Ch. 13: Interdependence Ch. 15: Adaptation and evolution
CHAPTER 5: ROCKS AND FOSSILS		
Yrs 5–7: Micro-habitats Yrs 7–9: Rocks and fossils Yrs 9–11: Fossil hunters	Habitats Structure of rocks Fossils Evolution	Ch. 11: The Earth and beyond Ch. 15: Adaptation and evolution

Topics	Key scientific ideas	Links to subject knowledge chapters in *Teaching Primary Science*, 3e
CHAPTER 6: LIVING THINGS		
Yrs 5–7: Living or non-living? Yrs 7–9: Body parts Yrs 9–11: Life cycles	Characteristics of living things Digestive system Skeleton and muscles Life cycles Changes as humans develop	Ch. 14: Diversity Ch. 16: Health and well-being
CHAPTER 7: DECOMPOSERS		
Yrs 5–7: What have woodlice ever done for us? Yrs 7–9: What have mushrooms ever done for us? Yrs 9–11: What has mould ever done for us?	Habitats Detritivores Nature's recyclers Decomposers: mushrooms and mould Microbes and science's fight against disease	Ch. 13: Interdependence Ch. 15: Adaptation and evolution Ch. 16: Health and well-being
CHAPTER 8: NUTRITION		
Yrs 5–7: Five a day Yrs 7–9: Eating the right kinds of food Yrs 9–11: The circulatory system	Balanced diet Benefits of exercise Sugar and obesity Circulatory system History of medicine Links between diet and performance	Ch. 16: Health and well-being
CHAPTER 9: THE MATERIAL WORLD		
Yrs 5–7: Everyday materials Yrs 7–9: Fabrics Yrs 9–11: Plastic waste	Properties of materials and their uses Natural materials: properties and uses Man-made materials: properties and uses	Ch. 17: The particle nature of materials

Topics	Key scientific ideas	Links to subject knowledge chapters in *Teaching Primary Science*, 3e
CHAPTER 10: CHANGING MATERIALS		
Yrs 5–7: In the kitchen Yrs 7–9: The water cycle Yrs 9–11: Solutions and suspensions	Temporary change Melting and freezing Evaporation and condensation Mixtures Permanent change	Ch. 17: The particle nature of materials Ch. 18: Changing materials
CHAPTER 11: EARTH AND SPACE		
Yrs 5–7: Journey to the Moon Yrs 7–9: Mission to Mars Yrs 9–11: In search of Goldilocks Planets	Conditions on the Moon Conditions on Mars NASA missions Solar System Beyond the Solar System	Ch. 11: The Earth and beyond
CHAPTER 12: ELECTRICITY		
Yrs 5–7: Introducing electric circuits Yrs 7–9: Electric circuit challenge Yrs 9–11: Saving energy	Electrical components Simple series circuits Conductors and insulators Electrical current Using electrical circuits	Ch. 19: Electricity and magnetism
CHAPTER 13: FORCES AND MAGNETISM		
Yrs 5–7: Forces in action Yrs 7–9: Gravity and magnetism Yrs 9–11: What has gravity ever done for us?	Actions of forces: pushes, pulls and twists Links between force and motion Gravity and magnetism Weight Universal effects of gravity	Ch. 19: Electricity and magnetism Ch. 20: Forces and motion

Topics	Key scientific ideas	Links to subject knowledge chapters in *Teaching Primary Science*, 3e
CHAPTER 14: LIGHT		
Yrs 5–7: Night animals Yrs 7–9: Reflections and shadows Yrs 9–11: Chasing shadows	Light and dark Light and vision Reflecting light Blocking light Light travels in straight lines	Ch. 15: Adaptation and evolution Ch. 21: Light
CHAPTER 15: SOUND		
Yrs 5–7: How noisy is our world? Yrs 7–9: Elephants: the ultimate sound machine Yrs 9–11: How marine animals use sound	Noise Creating sounds Vibrations, frequency, pitch and volume Detecting sound Sound in solids and liquids	Ch. 15: Adaptation and evolution Ch. 22: Sound

LIST OF FIGURES

LIST OF TABLES

ACKNOWLEDGEMENTS

I would like to thank Routledge for publishing the book, and for the help and support they have provided throughout. Special thanks go to Emma Hudson who organised the work of the reviewers, and enthusiastically guided me through the writing and publication of the book.

I should also mention the valuable contributions made by educationalists from universities in the UK and overseas who reviewed the initial drafts of the book. Their advice was thoughtful, critical and always constructive. I hope they will recognise how the book has benefited from their recommendations.

Finally, I would like to say a very special thank you to my wife, Anna, for her patience, support and creativity. Although her ideas are never referenced, you can be sure they feature prominently in practically every page of the book.

PUBLISHER'S ACKNOWLEDGEMENTS

"Woolly Saucepan" by Michael Rosen (©Michael Rosen, 2000) is printed by permission of United Agents (www.unitedagents.co.uk) on behalf of Michael Rosen.

In some instances we have been unable to trace the owners of copyright material and we would appreciate any information that would enable us to do so.

Chapter 1
Introduction

Science is about exploring, and the only way to uncover the secrets of the universe is to go and look.

Brian Cox, scientist (b. 1968)

The purpose of this book is to provide practical ideas for teaching science which promote the value of scientific understanding. The book is written as a companion to a core text entitled *Teaching Primary Science: Promoting Enjoyment and Developing Understanding,* co-authored by Peter Loxley, Lyn Dawes, Linda Nicholls and Babs Dore. The approaches to teaching described in both books are complementary and influenced by sociocultural views on learning, which recognise language as an important tool for shaping understanding (Vygotsky, 1962).

The core book is designed principally as a text for education students learning to teach primary science. It is arranged in two parts. Part 1 explores learning theory, which provides insights into effective teaching practices. Part 2 presents the scientific knowledge students need to teach the subject confidently, and in addition provides *ideas for practice* based on a three-stage framework for science learning.

This companion book has been written to extend and enrich the range of *ideas for practice* set out in the core text, and is supported by the same learning theory and subject knowledge. The book can also be used as a standalone teaching resource by both trainee and qualified teachers.

Views on learning

Views on learning which underpin the *ideas for practice* set out in this book can be described as sociocultural. Put simply, this means children learn best by sharing ideas and working collaboratively towards common goals in contexts which are familiar and meaningful. The role of the teacher is that of an active participant who guides, models and assists the children's learning. As the expert, the teacher takes a central role by organising learning tasks, modelling and demonstrating good practice and assisting the children to think, talk and act in ways which support effective learning. Detailed accounts of the learning theory on which this book is based can be found in Chapters 1, 2, 4 and 5 in the core book, Loxley *et al.* (2017).

Organising science learning

Ideas for practice set out in this book are structured in the same way as the core book, using a three-stage framework designed to encourage and guide sociocultural practices. The three stages are the *exploration stage*, the *re-describing stage* and the *application stage*.

In the *exploration stage* the scene is set for science learning when a puzzle sets children off on a trail of enquiry in search of an answer. In this stage learning involves sharing ideas and working scientifically to solve problems.

In the *re-describing stage*, children are encouraged to re-think their ideas from a scientific point of view. Introducing scientific ideas at this stage provides children with alternative ways of talking and thinking about the things they discussed in the *exploratory stage*. The term *re-describing stage* is used to emphasise the role language plays in helping children re-think their ideas when working on their understanding of the scientific point of view. The role of the teacher is to assist children's learning by helping them talk about and mentally engage with the scientific view (Alexander, 2008). This involves the use of stories, models, analogies, role-play, and image-rich resources such as video clips.

In the *application stage* children have opportunities to develop their understanding and appreciation of the scientific ideas by re-using them in other contexts. By making use of scientific ideas for specific purposes, children have opportunities to assimilate them into their own way of thinking and hence adopt them as their own. The contexts are diverse, including problem-solving in real-life situations, Design and Technology tasks, historical settings, STEM careers and the arts.

A full description of the three-stage framework and the theory behind it can be found in the core book, Loxley *et al.* (2017).

Ideas for practice are theme-based

Each chapter provides theme-based *ideas for practice* at three age-related levels: key stage 1 (5–7 years), lower key stage 2 (7–9 years) and upper key stage 2 (9–11 years). Topics for each age group are consistent with the requirements of the primary school science curricula in England, Wales, Scotland and Northern Ireland. They are also applicable to the curriculum in The Republic of Ireland.

The *ideas for practice* are not designed as specific teaching programmes or lesson plans to be followed step by step in the classroom. Their purpose is to exemplify how a range of topics can be taught using the three-stage framework. It is envisaged that teachers will adapt and extend the activities to suit their resources, their curriculum and the needs of their children.

Structure of ideas for practice

Introduction: Provides a brief outline of the nature of the intended learning, including activities in the application stage.

Scientific view: Provides a description of the scientific ideas which the children are expected to learn.

Working scientifically: Outlines the enquiry skills children require to find answers to questions.

Health and safety: Highlights some issues related to health and safety and provides guidance about how to keep children safe.

Exploration stage: Presents a range of teaching and learning strategies designed to support collaborative learning and to enable children to voice their ideas.

Re-describing stage: Presents a range of teaching and learning strategies which can be used to help children make sense of the scientific view.

Application stage: Presents opportunities for children to make use of their newly acquired scientific knowledge in different contexts.

STEM education

In schools around the world the term 'STEM education' is used as a call to action to make science, technology, engineering and mathematics more relevant to pupils' lives and open them up as career options. Developing long-lasting positive attitudes to science is a central theme of STEM education and is also the overarching objective for the *ideas for practice* presented in this book.

The *ideas for practice* support teaching styles which value collaboration, communication, creativity, critical thinking, curiosity and problem-solving as important elements of science learning. These are skills which are considered necessary for children to participate successfully in our twenty-first century global society. In the future children will be required to continually update their knowledge and skills to keep pace with new technological developments and therefore develop a capacity for life-long learning. Scientific ways of working, using both primary and secondary sources of information, underpin the *ideas for practice* and set children on the road to developing the active learning skills they need to manage their own learning in the future. Where appropriate, children's learning involves real-world issues which serve to illustrate the relevance of science, and the value of the ideas they are expected to learn.

Talk for science learning

It is the link between speaking, listening, thinking and learning which makes spoken language so important in the science classroom. We can provide children with fascinating experiences and thoughtful resources. But, unless we provide them with opportunities to discuss what they are doing and talk about scientific ideas in ways that make sense to them, their learning will be diminished and less satisfying.

In addition to working scientifically, the *ideas for practice* introduce talk-based strategies and resources to guide the way children engage with the scientific ideas. Effective practice includes the teacher and children together exploring and sharing ideas. Progression involves carrying the children's thinking forward until there is a need for a scientific explanation. Talking about scientific ideas in different ways and in different contexts helps children work on their under-standing of them and make sense of the views of nature they represent. Effective talk enables children to share their thinking and to collaborate so that the group does better than each child could have done alone. However, it is the teacher's job to model and guide the way children interact with each other. Classes benefit from devising a set of rules which help everyone to remember that talk is crucial for learning. Children can be asked what rules they would use to ensure a good discussion and can be helped to formulate their own ground rules.

Some rules which have been shown to promote effective talk

- Listen attentively.
- Include everyone in the discussion.
- Ask questions.
- Share all relevant information openly.
- Challenge one another's ideas and opinions with respect.
- Ask for and give reasons for ideas.
- Seek to reach a group agreement before proceeding.
- Support one another during subsequent whole-class discussion.

A particular resource which can promote talk is *talking points*. *Talking points* are designed to provide starting points for discussion. Children who are familiar with the ground rules for talk can be asked to work with others, to decide if they agree or disagree with the *talking points* or if they are unsure. Subsequent whole-class discussion orchestrated by the teacher helps everyone to consider a range of points of view, share their thinking, establish areas of uncertainty for further work and generally develop their vocabulary and ideas. *Talking points* as a strategy to promote effective talk is an idea developed by my colleague Lyn Dawes (2012). More detailed information on talk for learning science can be found in Chapter 5 in the core book, Loxley *et al.* (2017).

Narrative and story-telling

Each chapter begins with a *narrative* which includes the voice of the author. Narrative is used in the wider sense of the word, providing a contextualised account of the science from the author's point of view. Besides describing the science, the *narrative* serves a number of other purposes:

- It provides a context involving ideas, objects and events which children can progressively engage with at different levels.

- The story-line provides direction and continuity in children's learning across the age groups.

- It helps teachers of all age groups to visualise the bigger picture and understand where their children's learning is heading conceptually, and therefore helps them manage progression.

- Puzzling events and problem-solving scenarios can be drawn out of the *narrative* to arouse children's curiosity and engage them in a quest for knowledge.

- The *narrative* also provides a model for the nature of the children's story-telling which is intrinsic to the approach to science learning fostered by the *ideas for practice*.

Structured contexts, talk activities, story-telling and scientific ways of working enable children to interact with the scientific ideas and to develop the narrative through their own voices. Children's story-telling is a key part of learning science because it features the children's voices as opposed to the authoritative voice of the teacher. It enables children to talk about the science in their own words; hence it can capture the nature of the children's understanding and reveal its influence on the way they think and feel. Children's stories can provide valuable formative assessment information which can inform the basis of self and peer assessment and so the children can have a say in what they need to do next.

Children's learning needs

Essentially, the purpose of formative assessment is to gather information about children's ideas and to use it to help create new and appropriate learning opportunities. In science classrooms, development is dependent on finding out, and addressing, the difference between a child's existing ideas and a more scientific point of view. The ideas in question may concern understanding natural phenomena or events, or they may be to do with attitudes, or ways of working scientifically. The difference between the children's way of thinking, and ways of thinking from a scientific point of view can be defined as their *learning needs* (Leach and Scott, 2002). The concept of *learning needs* helps us to target teaching strategies for different children, to identify next steps and to hold focused discussions with classes and individuals.

Opportunities for formative assessment arise whenever children engage in discussion about scientific ideas. Well-judged questions enable teachers to probe children's thinking and assess their understanding of the scientific ideas. *Talking points* can be useful for assessment, as the process lays bare the limitations of the children's thinking. Misconceptions can be identified and addressed as part of group or whole-class discussions. *Talking points* also provide opportunities for peer and self-assessment. Working in small groups allows children to compare and evaluate ideas, and enables them to identify weaknesses in their own understanding.

Other opportunities for formative assessment are provided when children engage in solving puzzles, scientific enquiry, modelling through drama, story-telling and describing their ideas through drawings. Listening to children's talk, challenging their ideas and probing the reasons for their thinking enables teachers to identify their *learning needs*, and assess their understanding of the scientific ideas. Strategies which promote talk for learning, and provide assessment opportunities are discussed in the core book, Loxley *et al.* (2017), Chapter 7.

Summative assessment

The purpose of summative assessment is to summarise children's achievements at particular points in time, such as at the end of topics or terms. Outcomes of summative assessment are recorded, and used for various purposes including planning, reporting to children, reporting to parents and governors and reporting to other teachers during transition from class to class or school to school.

The Nuffield Foundation (2012) published a report which argues that there is no need for separate types of assessment for formative and summative purposes. It suggests that the rich and extensive descriptions of each child's achievements which are provided by effective formative assessment practices can be summarised and used to create a narrative-style annual report to parents. The report should indicate the child's progress regarding the learning outcomes for the year, and indicate where support is being provided to ensure the expected learning can be achieved by the end of the key stage. The transfer from formative data to summative judgements at the end of each key stage should be subject to internal moderation, and referenced to national exemplars.

The Teacher Assessment in Primary Science (TAPS) project team worked with schools and other professional organisations to consider how the Nuffield model would work in practice. As a result, they produced a comprehensive model of school assessment with its foundations firmly embedded in shared understanding of good classroom practice. The model provides a structure containing examples from a wide range of schools, which can be used as a source of ideas for teachers or as a whole school self-evaluation tool to identify strengths and areas for development. The resource is especially rich in ideas which exemplify the many ways formative assessment practices can be integrated into the curriculum. The TAPS pyramid and reports are available for download from the Primary Science Teachers Trust website.

Supporting children's learning

Group work is a key feature of the *ideas for practice*. For younger children effective group work requires the support of a trained adult, be it the teacher, a classroom assistant or a parent with relevant expertise. All adults supporting group work need to understand their role in the children's learning. They should be provided with clear instructions for each activity and trained so that they understand how to help children work collaboratively.

For visits away from school children are usually organised in small groups, each with a responsible adult. Each of these adults should be clear about their role in relation to the children's safety and well-being, and also given instruction on how to help children engage with the experience. Many sites have an education officer who can help plan school visits. However, the teacher remains in charge of the children's learning during the visit and should ensure the nature of the children's learning is consistent with learning in the classroom.

Visitors to the classroom

Visiting experts are an important part of science education as they provide role models to which children can aspire. Children look forward to having visitors, who often bring with them exciting new resources, experiences and ideas. STEM ambassadors are volunteers who have been trained to support the teaching of the subjects in schools. They are able to actively support the teaching of the subjects in normal classroom situations, on STEM days and in STEM clubs. Ambassadors cross all ages and backgrounds, representing thousands of different employers across the UK. Information about STEM ambassadors can be found on the STEMNET website.

Every neighbourhood has its local industries and people with STEM skills. These include the local doctor, vet, farmer, engineering and energy companies, college, university or gardener. There are people in every community who can help bring science and the other STEM subjects alive for children. Professionals can open children's minds to a world of opportunities and possibilities which come from pursuing STEM subjects and related careers.

Health and safety

Each chapter highlights some of the key health and safety issues, but this information is not exhaustive. It remains the teacher's duty to assess classroom management, hygiene and hazard risks. Teachers need to know that the science activities which they plan for their children are inherently safe. Danger to children's health is often due to misbehaviour and misuse of science equipment. Children need to be instructed how to behave when working with scientific equipment, and to be made aware of any risks involved when performing practical work.

Equipment used in primary science is inherently safe when used with care and bought from established suppliers. However, there are some situations in which specific precautions need to be taken, for example, when handling certain types of plants or using iron filings. As part of the planning of any science lesson teachers need to assess the risks involved with the help of suitable information sources. The ASE publication *Be Safe!* (2011) provides extensive guidance on health and safety matters for science and other STEM subjects. Guidelines provided by CLEAPPS and SSERC can also be consulted. Teachers should also take account of school policies. Technology and the internet are useful classroom tools, but they can be open to abuse and place children in danger. Teachers should be aware of the potential problems and should follow their school guidance in relation to e-safety.

Summary

The book provides a wide range of *ideas for practice* which trainees and qualified teachers can use to guide the way children develop their understanding of science. Activities are set in a wide range of contexts and foster learning through collaboration, communication, creativity, critical thinking, curiosity and problem-solving. Sharing ideas, story-telling and working scientifically are key elements of each topic, and they provide opportunities for children to develop understanding through their own voices. Where appropriate, children's learning involves real-world issues which serve to illustrate the value of learning scientific skills and ideas.

References

Alexander, R. (2008) 'Culture, dialogue and learning: Notes on emerging pedagogy.' In N. Mercer and S. Hodgkinson (eds), *Exploring talk in school*, London: Sage.

Dawes, L. (2012) *Talking points: Discussion activities in the primary classroom*, London: Routledge.

Leach, J. and Scott, P. (2002) 'Designing and evaluating science teaching sequences: An approach drawing upon the concept of learning demand and a social constructivist perspective on learning.' *Studies in Science Education*, 28: 115–42.

Loxley, P., Dawes, L., Nicholls, L. and Dore, B. (2018) *Teaching primary science: Promoting enjoyment and developing understanding*, London: Routledge.

Nuffield Foundation (2012) *Developing policy, principles and practice in primary school science.* www.nuffieldfoundation.org/primary-science-assessment

TAPS (2015) on the Primary Science Teachers Trust website. https://pstt.org.uk/

The Association for Science Education (ASE) (2011) *Be Safe!* (4th ed.), Hatfield: ASE.

Vygotsky, L. S. (1962) *Thought and language,* Cambridge MA: MIT.

Websites

CLEAPSS. www.cleapss.org.uk/primary/primary-resources
Primary Science Teachers Trust. https://pstt.org.uk/
SSERC. www.sserc.org.uk
STEM Centre. www.stem.org.uk
STEMCLUBS. www.stemclubs.net
STEMNET. www.stemnet.org.uk

Further reading – ASE Journals

Emergent Science 10 (Winter 2015/2016) *Using Prediction–Observation–Explanation–Revision to structure young children's learning about floating and sinking* by Tang Wee Teo, Yaw Kai Yan and Mei Ting Goh.

Primary Science 144 (Sept/Oct 2016) *Developing 'argumentation' with the 4–11 age group* by Terry Russell and Linda McGuigan.

Primary Science 139 (Sept/Oct 2015) *Integrating STEM into the primary school curriculum* by Asima Qureshi.

Primary Science 136 (Jan/Feb 2015) *An exploration of whole-school assessment systems* by Sarah Earle.

Chapter 2
Growing plants

One who plants a garden plants happiness.

Chinese proverb

Growing plants is a pleasure we can share with our children. It takes time to grow plants from seeds, but the delight and satisfaction children feel when the plants burst into flower makes it all worthwhile. After all, what could be more rewarding than giving nature a hand in creating some of the most beautiful things on the planet? This chapter presents *ideas for practice* which focus on growing plants in different ways. Young children start by growing plants from seeds and exploring the concept of germination. Later topics focus on growing plants from bulbs and cuttings, and the role nutrients play in producing healthy crops. Ideas for how to start a gardening club are featured in the final topic.

Topics in this chapter:

● Growing plants from seeds

● Growing healthy plants

● Bulbs and cuttings

Subject knowledge to support the teaching of these topics can be found in the core book, Loxley, P., Dawes, D., Nicholls, L. and Dore, B. (2018) *Teaching primary science: Promoting enjoyment and developing understanding*, Abingdon: Routledge, Chapter 13: Interdependence and Chapter 14: Diversity.

Gardening: giving nature a hand

And Spring arose on the garden fair,
Like the Spirit of Love felt everywhere;
And each flower and herb on Earth's dark breast
Rose from the dreams of its wintry rest.

Percy Bysshe Shelley, 'The Sensitive Plant'

Growing plants from seeds is a magical experience. They are so small and unremarkable, yet can grow into some of the biggest and most beautiful life-forms on the planet.

When children are asked to draw what they imagine to be inside a seed, they often draw a capsule containing a fully formed baby plant. In reality the embryo from which a new plant grows is only a tiny part of a seed. Besides containing the embryo, a seed also stores the food it needs to grow. To germinate, the embryo uses the food to grow small roots and shoots. Once its first leaves are formed, it is able to produce its own food through photosynthesis, grow into a mature plant and produce flowers and seeds for the next generation.

One way for children to grow more of their favourite plants is to take cuttings by removing non-flowering stems and planting them in damp compost. After a few weeks, new roots develop and a new plant is produced. Taking cuttings is a way of cloning a plant, which means the new plants (offspring) will be genetically identical to the parent plant. The appearance of plants grown from seeds is less predictable because they can inherit physical characteristics from more than one parent plant. So if children want identical plants, take cuttings!

Gardening is all about patience and optimism. Plants can take a long time to grow, especially bulbs which are planted in autumn and do not emerge until the spring sunlight warms up the soil. They lie dormant and conserve their energy through the dark cold winter days waiting for the right environmental conditions to burst into life. Snowdrops are often first to show. Not long after, crocuses, daffodils and then tulips fill gardens with colour which raises our spirits, delights our senses and helps us feel good about the world.

Like Shelley, children can be romantics. They love beautiful things and benefit emotionally from participating in their creation. According to a report commissioned by the Royal Horticultural Society, gardening activities boost child development, teach life skills and make children healthier and happier.[1] After all, what could be more rewarding for children than giving nature a hand in making its annual rebirth a spectacular affair?

Ideas for practice

Topic: Growing plants from seeds

Age group: 5–7 years

Introduction

The purpose of the activities is to raise children's interest in growing plants and make them aware of the conditions they need to germinate and grow. Plants take time to grow so children will need to take care of them and record data over a prolonged period. Their patience will be rewarded when their plants flower and produce seeds. The application stage introduces children to the variety of plants found at a garden centre and provides opportunities to make a small garden of their own.

Scientific view

Seeds are living things in a state of dormancy waiting for the right conditions to grow. Seeds contain food (starch) to fuel the growth of the embryo plant. To germinate, seeds require water and the right soil temperature. Once they produce roots and leaves, seedlings need light and water to continue to grow. They also use nutrients from the soil to keep themselves healthy.

Working scientifically

In these activities children will:

● ask simple questions;

● observe closely using simple equipment;

● perform simple tests;

● learn to identify different plants;

● use their own ideas and scientific ideas to answer questions;

● gather and record data to help answer questions.

Health and safety

Plan all gardening activities to include appropriately sized tools and equipment, as well as considerations of safety and hygiene. Risk assess any outside visits. For guidance refer to *Be Safe!* (2011).

Exploration stage

Children's talk involves trying out their own ideas

Setting the scene

Start by reading *The Little Gardener* by Emily Hughes which portrays the joys and frustrations of gardening. Listen to children's stories about gardens and plants they have at home.

Choose a range of seeds for fast growing flowering plants. Remove seeds from their packets and put them in different coloured bags. Tell the children you have something very special inside each bag and ask them to guess what it might be. Show pictures of the flowers produced by the seeds. Would they believe that all these lovely flowers are inside the bags? How can that be? Discuss what children know about seeds. Did they know the little seeds could grow into such beautiful plants? Talk about how the seeds are alive. They are resting (dormant) waiting to grow. Make a display of the names and pictures of the plants from the packets.

Puzzle

How could the children 'wake the seeds up' and help them to grow?

Produce your own puzzle cartoon. Children can talk about the ideas in groups or as a whole class. Encourage them to provide reasons for their responses to the puzzle points.

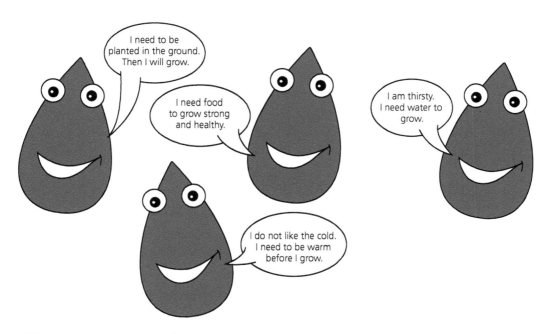

Figure 2.1   Seeds cartoon

More puzzle points for children to consider:

- Shouting at the seeds would wake them up.
- Seeds have their own food.
- Music will help the seeds to grow.
- Seeds only grow during the day.
- Seeds only grow in a garden.
- Seeds need water to bring them alive.
- There are baby plants inside the seeds.

Alter the puzzle points to suit your children. Encourage them to justify their responses. Use children's ideas to assess their understanding of the conditions seeds need to grow.

Scientific enquiry

The challenge is to find the best way to 'wake up' the seeds. Children choose to grow seeds in different light, temperature and water conditions using seed trays and a suitable compost mix. Once the plants start growing, they should observe and record their progress over a suitable time period. Record the growth of the plants by making observational drawings and taking photographs. Once the seedlings are established pot-on the healthy ones into bigger pots to give them room to grow. Potting-on provides opportunity for children to observe and talk about the purpose of the roots. Plants grown in the dark should be left for long enough after germination to compare with those growing in the light.

Children use data from their enquiry to re-think their responses to the talking points and try to establish a consensus regarding how to grow plants. Compare ideas and work towards establishing common knowledge on the subject.

Formative assessment

Provide opportunities for children to voice what they have learnt in the exploratory stage. Use evidence from their responses to the puzzle, puzzle points and other activities to assess differences between children's ideas and the scientific view. Plan how you will use the re-describing stage to help the children address their *learning needs* (see Chapter 1). You may need to modify the activities depending on the collective and individual needs of your children.

Re-describing stage

Children's talk involves making sense of scientific ideas

Teacher-led discussion

Children might not think of seeds as living things and imagine they only come alive once they have been planted. Focus on the puzzle and reinforce the idea that seeds are living things waiting for the right conditions to grow. Discuss how the children interpreted the data from the enquiry and what they have learnt. Establish that seeds need water to grow and how their growth is affected by temperature and light. Introduce scientific terms such as dormant (resting) and germination (starting to grow). Make it clear that germinated plants (seedlings) require light and water to help them grow strong and healthy. Use video clips and animations to help children understand how plants grow from seed.

Scientific enquiry

Choose the best plants for growing-on in bigger pots in school or at home. Children make care labels describing how to look after the plants as they mature and produce their flowers. Continue to introduce scientific vocabulary as they need it. Seeds can be collected from the mature plants and children design their own packaging. The seeds can be sold at a school fete and the proceeds used to buy new plants to grow in the school garden.

Art work

Show children a range of plant portraits. The Royal Botanical Gardens Kew website has a stunning collection. Discuss the main parts of the plants and compare the variety of shapes and colours. Children paint pictures of their fully grown plants, and talk about the different parts. They can compare their pictures, identifying similarities and differences in form and colour.

Story-telling

Sam Goodwin's book, *A seed in need*, has been popular in schools since it was published in 1998. Share the book with the children. Children can create a cartoon strip with the same title, which tells their own story of how they looked after their seeds until they grew into healthy plants. Encourage them to tell their stories using scientific language. After listening to their stories address any outstanding *learning needs*.

Information and teaching resources

BBC Bitesize:

● What does a plant need to grow? *www.bbc.co.uk/guides/zxxsyrd*

Other websites:

● Marianne North online gallery. Royal Botanical Gardens.
  www.kew.org/mng/gallery/plant-groups.html

● Get growing. *www.youtube.com/watch?v=I8-_WsvzDY8*

Figure 2.2 Botanical illustration of tobacco and nigella plants

Source: iStock

Application stage

Children's talk involves trying out scientific ideas

Create a garden

Figure 2.3 **Sunflowers and marigolds attract insects and brighten up the garden**

Source: Photos by Anna Loxley

Regardless of the size of the school grounds, it is usually possible to create a garden. Take children on a visit to a garden centre to see the variety of plants on show. Arrange for an expert to show you around and talk about the different types of plants. Children should prepare questions in advance, including:

● Which plants are easiest to grow?

● How tall do the plants grow?

● Which plants like to grow in the sun?

● Which like to grow in shade?

● Which plants flower for longest and when?

● Which flowers have a strong scent?

● Which plants attract insects and birds?

A selection of easy care plants which flower at different times of the year can provide continuous colour to the garden. If there is room, a small tree can provide a good focal point and something which will always be there for the children to remember.

Back at school children design their garden and decide how to arrange the plants regarding colour combinations and size. Which plants go where for maximum visual impact? A video of children planting the garden can be made in the style of a television programme like the BBC's *Gardeners' World*, with the children taking the role of the experts. What advice would they give to novice gardeners?

Topic: Growing healthy plants

Age group: 7–9 years

Introduction

The purpose of the activities is to build on children's understanding of plant growth by exploring the role compost and manufactured fertilisers play in producing healthy plants. In the application stage children investigate farming strategies used in the developing world to grow healthy crops.

Scientific view

Plants need air, light, water, nutrients from the soil and room to grow. Plants make their own food through the process of photosynthesis using water from the ground, carbon dioxide from the air and energy from the sun. The nutrients they take from the ground such as nitrogen, phosphorus and potassium make crops grow faster and bigger so that crop yields are increased. Fertilisers contain these essential nutrients and when added to the soil dissolve in water and are taken up by the roots.

Working scientifically

In these activities children will:

- set up practical enquiries to answer questions;
- record findings appropriately;
- use results to draw conclusions;
- use scientific evidence and ideas for problem-solving;
- apply scientific ideas to real-life situations.

Health and safety

Use horticultural sand and chemicals which are available from garden centres or DIY stores. Maintain hygiene safety and wash food crops before eating them. Follow ASE guidance in *Be Safe!* (2011) on gardening and composting.

Exploration stage

Children's talk involves trying out their own ideas

Setting the scene

Figure 2.4 **Desert landscape**

Source: iStock

Figure 2.5 **Garden landscape**

Source: iStock

On the IWB show children pictures of desert landscapes and contrast with large garden landscapes. Compare the different environments and the types of plants. Find out what children know about the problems of growing plants in a desert environment.

Puzzle

Why do plants not grow so well in a sandy desert? Is it just the lack of water?

Talking points: true, false or not sure?

- The desert is too hot for most plants to grow.
- Plants that grow without water can live in a desert.
- In a desert plants cannot find enough to eat.
- Plants live beneath the sand in a desert.
- Plants will not grow well in sand if there are no nutrients.
- When it rains in the desert plants start to grow.
- Plants will grow in sand if they have enough water.
- Plants will grow anywhere given enough water.

Discuss children's reasons for their responses and assess what they know about growing plants. Ask groups to summarise what they think plants need to grow and to keep healthy.

Scientific enquiry

Children plan experiments to find the best way to grow grass in sand. They plan comparative tests and justify why their tests are fair.

Things to consider:

- Does grass grow well in sand with the right amount of light and water?
- Does it grow better in warm or cool conditions?
- Does it grow better if fertiliser is added to the sand?
- Does adding organic matter (compost) to the sand make a difference?
- Any additional questions children would like to answer.

Use fast growing grass, horticultural sand and soluble fertiliser recommended for grass. Children keep a diary to record germination and rate of growth of grass for each experiment. The class can combine their data on a chart to compare how well the grass grew in different conditions. Talk about the best conditions for growing grass. Would it be possible to turn a desert into a meadow? What would need to be done?

Scientific enquiry

Composting is an amazing process through which nutrient-rich waste plant material can be broken down and returned to the ground. The science of composting is fascinating because it sheds light on the unfamiliar and hidden world of the decomposers such as fungi and bacteria, as well as the lives of more familiar organisms such as worms, woodlice and beetles. Children can use information sources to find out how to compost waste organic materials from the school kitchens and grounds. If need be, parents can be asked to bring in materials from home. Only plant material should be composted, for example potato peelings, leaves, grass, etc. Once set up the compost heap can become a valuable resource when studying mini-beast habitats and food chains.

Scientific enquiry

Ornamental grasses are a favourite with gardeners because they add to the structure of the garden, while edible grasses such as rice, corn and wheat are grown by farmers all over the world as sources of food. Children use information sources to research different types of grasses, where they can be found, how they reproduce and their uses. They can compare the structure of ornamental grasses with crop grasses and explore variation.

Focusing on crop plants, children can compare the uses of different grasses. Bring in a range of food products made from different types of grasses. Children compare their properties including colour, texture, taste and how they change when mixed with a liquid. Help children match the properties of the products to the types of plants. Are there any patterns?

Art work

Figure 2.6 **Watercolour of *Spring Grasses* by Carolyn Ritchie Bedford**

Source: © Carolyn Ritchie Bedford

Bring in pots of grasses so children can observe and explore their structure closely. Use them to create a still life for children to paint. The grasses can be used on their own, or combined with stunning flowers. Be aware of children's allergies.

Formative assessment

Provide opportunities for children to voice what they have learnt in the exploratory stage. Use evidence from their responses to the puzzle, talking points and other activities to assess differences between children's ideas and the scientific view. Plan how you will use the re-describing stage to help the children address their *learning needs* (see Chapter 1). You may need to modify the activities depending on the collective and individual needs of your children.

Re-describing stage

Children's talk involves making sense of scientific ideas

Teacher-led discussion

Help children summarise what they discovered from their grass enquiry. Talk about how grass and other plants grow best when they have light, water and the right nutrients. Discuss how compost and fertilisers contain nutrients which help plants to grow bigger and stronger. Without these nutrients plants can struggle to survive.

A common misconception is that plants obtain the food they need to grow from the soil. To address this misconception children need to understand that plants make their own food, as well as take up water and nutrients from the soil. Use video clips and other illustrations to demonstrate how each part of the plant has a job to do in its growth. Roots anchor the plant and take water and nutrients up through the stems to the leaves. Leaves are where the food is made for the plant to grow by combining water, nutrients and air (carbon dioxide) using light energy from the sun. Remind children that in their enquiry, the grass grew best when all these elements were present.

Story-telling

Groups use data from their enquiry to write illustrated science articles about how to plant and grow a lawn on sandy soil. They should research on the web the most appropriate type of grass seeds, and also explain why their chosen fertiliser and compost are suitable for the job. Discuss how a scientific article should contain ideas which can be justified with reasons and evidence. Groups come together to present their articles. Identify and address any outstanding *learning needs*.

Information and teaching resources

BBC Bitesize:

- Healthy plant growth. *www.bbc.co.uk/education/clips/zctmhyc*
- What do plants need to grow? *www.bbc.co.uk/education/clips/z9f87hv*
- What do plants need to grow? *www.bbc.co.uk/education/clips/z3m76sg*
- Why do plants have leaves? *www.bbc.co.uk/education/clips/z2k4d2p*
- Why do plants need roots? *www.bbc.co.uk/education/clips/z6w8q6f*
- Why do plants need water? *www.bbc.co.uk/education/clips/zhqw2hv*

Application stage

Children's talk involves trying out scientific ideas

Pit cultivation

Figure 2.7 **Watering a pumpkin grown on a sandbar**

Source: Practical Action Bangladesh

Practical Action is a charity which uses technology to enable poor communities in the developing world to feed themselves and improve their lives. Every year in Bangladesh monsoon rains wash away fertile land and destroy homes and livelihoods. The rains wash over the land leaving the soil barren, without the nutrients to grow crops.

Practical Action worked with communities in the Rangpur District to help them make the land productive again by using the technique of pit cultivation for growing pumpkins and other crops. Pit cultivation involves digging out pits in poor soil or sand and filling up the hole with compost. Pumpkins and other vegetables can then be grown in the nutrient-rich compost. Children can visit the *Practical Action* website to find out about the work they do in Bangladesh.

Children evaluate the pit cultivation technique by growing crops in compost and horticultural sand. Compare the difference between growing plants with and without the nutrients contained in composted soil.

The following hints from the Royal Horticultural Society on how to grow vegetables in containers could be useful:

TABLE 2.1 Growing vegetables in containers

When to grow vegetables in containers	Timings vary depending on the crop, but the main growing season is from early spring to autumn.
Container choice	Pots, troughs and grow-bags can all be used. Smaller containers can result in a lack of moisture and nutrients for plant roots. Aim for containers with a depth and width of at least 45cm (18in), otherwise frequent watering and feeding will be needed.
Compost choice	Use sterile proprietary potting composts to obtain best results. Compost in grow-bags is often both good value and reasonable quality.
Further care	Aftercare should involve provision of a constant water supply, but take care to avoid prolonged waterlogging. A feed of general-purpose liquid fertiliser can be applied every two weeks. If frost is likely, cover the plants with horticultural fleece and move the pots to a warm, sheltered spot.
Crop selection	Most vegetables such as beetroot, carrots, potatoes, beans and peas can be grown in containers. Salad leaves like rocket, coriander, lettuce, chicory and spinach are tasty choices. Harvest by pinching off the top few salad leaves, leaving a stump to re-sprout for follow-on crops. Mini lettuces such as *Little Gem* and *Tom Thumb* are ideal, and herbs such as basil and parsley make tasty additions to any salad.

For further information visit the RHS website.

Information and teaching resources

- *Practical Action* – pit cultivation.
  http://practicalaction.org/schools/search/pit%20cultivation
- *Practical Action. http://practicalaction.org/schools*
- RHS School gardening. *https://schoolgardening.rhs.org.uk/home*
- Growing vegetables in containers. *www.rhs.org.uk/advice/profile?pid=527*

Topic: Bulbs and cuttings

Age group: 9–11 years

Introduction

This topic builds on children's understanding of germination and the conditions required to grow healthy plants to produce crops, flowers and seed. They should also have some understanding of pollination. The activities explore different methods of propagation and introduce the concepts of inheritance and variation. The *application stage* looks at the wider benefits of gardening for children, and provides suggestions about setting up a gardening club.

Scientific view

Beans are seeds which contain an embryo and food to germinate. A bulb is not a seed. Bulbs are made from rings, which are modified leaves that store food. The plant lies dormant until the growing season when it uses the food stored in the bulb to grow and produce green leaves above the ground. The green leaves enable it to create its own food through photosynthesis which it uses to grow. It also produces food which it stores in its bulb for next year's growth. Plants that grow from bulbs can reproduce either from seed or by their bulbs splitting and forming smaller bulbs called bulblets.

Working scientifically

In these activities children will:

- make detailed scientific observations;
- take measurements over an extended time period;
- record data and use graphs to compare results;
- present findings in written form;
- use evidence to support or refute arguments.

Health and safety

Children use disposable gloves when handling soil and bulbs. Some bulbs can be toxic. Because they look like onions, children may be tempted to taste bulbs. Make it clear that bulbs can be poisonous and should not be tasted. Refer to the ASE publication *Be Safe!* (2011) for guidance on plants and gardening.

Exploration stage

Children's talk involves trying out their own ideas

Setting the scene

> I wandered lonely as a cloud
> That floats on high o'er vales and hills,
> When all at once I saw a crowd,
> A host, of golden daffodils;
> Beside the lake, beneath the trees,
> Fluttering and dancing in the breeze
>
> *William Wordsworth, 'I wandered lonely as a cloud'*

Read Wordsworth's poem. Talk about the Romantic poets and how they lyrically described feelings invoked by nature.

Puzzle

What are daffodils? How do they grow? Start with a bag of broad beans and a bag of daffodil bulbs. Hand them out and see if the children can identify them. Compare similarities and differences. Are daffodils and broad beans different types of seeds?

Scientific enquiry

To help resolve the puzzle children dissect a bean and a bulb, and use magnifiers to compare their structures. They should produce detailed drawings of their findings. Warn children to take care when cutting, and refer to ASE guidance for handling bulbs.

Things to consider:

- Similarities and differences of internal structures
- Evidence of an embryo (baby plant)
- Evidence of any roots or other parts of a plant
- Evidence of how a new plant would grow
- Evidence of stored food for a new plant to grow
- Evidence of how the bean and the bulb were produced

Based on their observations children draw pictures of how they imagine new plants would grow from both the bean and the bulb.

Groups prepare arguments to resolve the puzzle based on reasoning and evidence. Groups share their ideas and discuss which are most persuasive. At the end of the debate children use information sources to find out more about the difference between seeds and bulbs.

Scientific enquiry

Both broad beans and daffodils can be planted outside in autumn in the same plot or container. Children record, graph and compare their growth until they produce flowers and fruit. Keep them well watered and fertilised during the growing season. Plant enough of them so children can remove some at intervals from the soil to see how the whole plant has developed and compare with their drawings. In addition, broad beans can be germinated quite quickly on damp kitchen paper in a warm dark place in the classroom.

Story-telling

Children use diaries, photographs and video camera to record the life cycles of the beans and the bulbs. They can tell the life stories of 'bean to bean', and 'bulb to bulb' in a display or in cartoon form. They could produce an illustrated story book for 5–7 year olds in their school, which they can read to them.

Scientific enquiry

If you want to grow bulbs for Christmas, both amaryllis and hyacinth varieties can be bought to grow indoors. Buy hyacinths which can be grown in water, perhaps in a see-through container so that children can watch and record the whole plant growing. Take advice from your local plant-centre so the bulbs will flower before the Christmas holidays. Children can draw inspiration from the flowers for making Christmas cards.

Formative assessment

Provide opportunities for children to voice what they have learnt in the exploratory stage. Use evidence from their responses to the puzzle and other activities to assess differences between children's ideas and the scientific view. Plan how you will use the re-describing stage to help the children address their *learning needs* (see Chapter 1). You may need to modify the activities depending on the collective and individual needs of your children.

Re-describing stage

Children's talk involves making sense of scientific ideas

Teacher-led discussion

Discuss the difference between a seed and a bulb. The difference becomes clear when comparing their life cycles. Seeds germinate and grow into plants, which produce their own seeds to keep the cycle going. Bulbs are not seeds. They are basically the leaves of a plant waiting to grow. A bulb is a way of storing a plant's energy when it is not growing. The plant lies dormant until the growing season when it uses the food stored in the bulb to grow and produce green leaves above the ground. The green leaves enable it to create its own food through photosynthesis which it uses to grow into a mature plant. After flowering, the plant produces food in its leaves which it stores in its bulb for next year's growth. Plants that grow from bulbs can reproduce either by producing seed, or by their bulbs splitting and forming smaller bulbs called bulblets.

Figure 2.8   **Amaryllis: bulb to flowering plant**

Source: Photos by Anna Loxley

Use diagrams, animation and video to illustrate and compare the life cycles of plants grown from seeds and bulbs. Focus on inheritance. Seeds which have two parents inherit characteristics from both, which means offspring will not be identical to either of the parents. This can result in variation in the colour of the flowers produced by the same kind of seeds. On the other hand, a plant grown from a bulblet has only one parent and will be genetically identical. It is therefore a clone of its parent.

Scientific enquiry

Children can produce clones of plants by taking cuttings. Find out how to grow plants from cuttings from RHS publications and other gardening books and websites.

The challenge is to discover the best conditions for growing plants from cuttings by setting up fair tests. Possible variables include: levels of moisture, nutrients, temperature and light. Some cuttings can be grown in water until roots are established. Having done their research, children can decide their own tests. The most promising cuttings can be planted out in the garden or in containers until they grow to maturity. Compare the offspring which survive with their parents.

Story-telling

Children design and create illustrated gardening books. The books should provide guidance for growing plants from seeds, bulbs and cuttings, as well as illustrations of different stages of growth. Let children look through modern gardening books to see how authors use a combination of story-telling and technical information to interest the readers. Children can explore some of the works of the romantic poets and pen their own poems to put in the book. Probe children's understanding of the science content of their books and address any outstanding *learning needs*.

Information and teaching resources

BBC Bitesize:

- Root and shoot growth. *www.bbc.co.uk/education/clips/zb4rkqt*
- The life cycle of a dandelion. *www.bbc.co.uk/education/clips/zs9c87h*
- The life cycle of a plant. *www.bbc.co.uk/education/clips/zgqyrdm*
- Time-lapse footage of a seed growing. *www.bbc.co.uk/education/clips/zs89wmn*
- Why do plants have leaves? *www.bbc.co.uk/education/clips/z2k4d2p*

Application stage

Children's talk involves trying out scientific ideas

Gardening

Gardening is an all-year-round activity and there is not enough time in a normal school curriculum for children to create and maintain a garden. To inspire and develop interest in gardening many schools have formed gardening clubs which organise lunch time and after school activities. The Royal Horticultural Society (RHS) campaigns for school gardening and provides wide ranging information and guidance on its website to support clubs in primary schools.

The list of benefits of gardening for children include:

- Improving physical and mental well-being.
- Building life skills such as confidence, teamwork and communication.
- Enhancing literacy, numeracy and oracy skills.
- Enriching the entire curriculum from science, maths and geography, to art, design and languages.
- Encouraging a better and healthier life style.
- Teaching about environment and sustainability.
- Helping young people engage with their surroundings and develop a sense of responsibility.

Creating a garden

Rural schools do not necessarily have any more space for a garden than urban ones. Even if the school grounds are paved, gardens can be created from raised beds, containers, dump bags, hanging baskets and window boxes. Growing plants is exciting no matter where they are grown.

Think small! Gardens need to be maintained. Watering, feeding, weeding and mulching are crucial parts of garden maintenance and can become unmanageable for children if the garden is too big. Propagate using seeds, cuttings and bulblets from plants in the garden, or package and sell them. Cut flowers and vegetables can be used in school, taken home or sold to boost the garden club funds.

Science seminars

Do not forget the science. Hold regular meetings and discuss the science of the garden. When planning which plants to grow, children research the best conditions, types of soil and nutrients they need for strong growth, as well as the birds and insects they are likely to attract. Invite local gardeners and STEM ambassadors to talk to the club. Visit the STEMNET website to find out about the support available for gardening clubs in your area.

News sheets

The club can produce news sheets to inform and entertain, which can be distributed in school to encourage children to join the club. News sheets can contain tips for growing plants at home, and keep parents up-to-date with initiatives going on in school.

Young Gardeners' Question Time

There is a BBC television programme called *Gardeners' Question Time* where a panel of experts answer questions on gardening from the studio audience. Set up a classroom or school hall as a studio and re-create the show using a panel of 'experts' from the club. Non-members of the club including parents can form the audience. Restrict the topics to what is grown in the garden. A teacher or local gardener should be part of the panel to help answer difficult questions.

Information and teaching resources

- STEM ambassadors. *www.stemnet.org.uk*
- STEM clubs. *www.stemclubs.net*
- Kids gardening. *www.kidsgardening.org*
- Beginning gardening. *www.rhs.org.uk/advice/beginners-guide*
- School gardening. *https://schoolgardening.rhs.org.uk/home*
- STEM Centre. *www.nationalstemcentre.org.uk*

Note

1   Passy, R., Morris, M., and Reed, F. (2010) 'Impact of school gardening on learning.' Final report submitted to the Royal Horticultural Society. www.nfer.ac.uk/publications/RHS01/RHS01_home.cfm

Chapter 3
Flowering plants

It seems to me that the natural world is the greatest source of excitement; the greatest source of visual beauty; the greatest source of intellectual interest. It is the greatest source of so much in life that makes life worth living.

David Attenborough, broadcaster and naturalist (b. 1926)

This chapter presents *ideas for practice* which can be used to help children explore the structure of flowering plants. It examines the way plants are adapted to form mutually beneficial relationships with animals such as bees and butterflies. A feature of this chapter is the exploration of the beauty of plants and whether scientific knowledge enhances or diminishes their aesthetic appeal.

Topics in this chapter:

● Flowering plants

● Pollination

● Adaptation

Subject knowledge to support the teaching of these topics can be found in the core book, Loxley, P., Dawes, D., Nicholls, L. and Dore, B. (2018) *Teaching primary science: Promoting enjoyment and developing understanding*, Abingdon: Routledge, Chapter 14: Diversity and Chapter 15: Adaptation and evolution.

The beauty of flowers

Richard Feynman, one of the most brilliant scientists of modern times, was accused by an artist friend of destroying the beauty of flowers. This is what he wrote about the encounter:

I have a friend who's an artist and he's sometimes taken a view which I don't agree with very well. He'll hold up a flower and say 'Look how beautiful it is,' and I'll agree. And he says – 'you see, I as an artist can see how beautiful this is, but you as a scientist, oh, you take it all apart and it becomes a dull thing.' And I think that he's kind of nutty. First of all, the beauty that he sees is available to other people and to me, too, I believe, although I might not be quite as refined aesthetically as he is; but I can appreciate the beauty of the flower. At the same time I see much more about the flower than he sees. I can imagine the cells in there, the complicated actions inside which also have beauty. I mean it's not only beauty of the whole thing, there is beauty at smaller dimensions, the inner structure. Also the processes, the fact that the colours in the flower evolved in order to attract insects to pollinate it is fascinating – it means that insects see colour. It adds a question: Does this aesthetic sense also exist to bees, butterflies and other animals which may be attracted to the flower. What is it about a flower which makes it beautiful? All kinds of interesting questions which shows that scientific knowledge only adds to the excitement and mystery and awe of a flower. It only adds: I don't understand how science subtracts.

It is not just the beauty of the flower's form and colour that Feynman sees, but he is also affected by feelings of awed wonder at the part its beauty plays in nature. Charles Darwin described pollination as acts of contrivance between plants and animals. It is no accident that animals such as bees and butterflies are attracted to particular flowers. Without knowing it the animals are seduced by the flowers into helping the plant reproduce. In the case of bees, they are made to work for their dinner. To reach the nectar they have to push past the male organs of the flower, collecting pollen as they go. Off they fly to another flower and complete the sexual act by rubbing against the female organ, coating it with the sticky pollen.

For over 140 million years animals have helped flowering plants to sexually reproduce. The first flowering plants appeared on earth when dinosaurs still existed and it is generally assumed that from the start the function of the flowers was to help the plant reproduce. When transporting pollen between plants, animals are in fact exporting the plant's genes. The seeds which are produced and the new plants which grow from them contain two sets of genes, one set from each of their parents. The mixing of genes has created the wealth and diversity of plants that populate our planet.

Today there are over 400,000 types of flowering plants around the world, each with its own unique beauty. We only have to look in our gardens, woodlands and meadows to find a vast variety of colours, shapes and scents. Bees are one of the most common pollinators. They are attracted to brightly coloured flowers because they know they will find pollen and nectar inside. Scientists believe that bees seek out certain colours such as blue and violet, not only because they expect to find more nectar in those flowers but because they are warm flowers which bees use to heat their bodies.

Different types of plants have developed their own special ways of attracting pollinators. Some orchids, for example, produce pheromones to attract insects. Bee orchids are fascinating and beautiful plants with flowers that resemble a female bee. The petals also smell like female bees emitting an enticing fragrance. When male bees land on them thinking they have found a mate they are covered with pollen, and consequently pollinate the next orchid they visit.

The point of Feynman's anecdote is that the beauty of nature goes far deeper than just its appearance. Seeing things through 'scientific eyes' enables us to not only recognise their aesthetic beauty, but also be captivated by their wondrous behaviour.

References and information sources

- Feynman, Richard P. (1999) *The pleasure of finding things out*, London: Penguin.
- Naked Scientist: 'How Flowers Are Turning Up the Heat.' *www.thenakedscientists.com/HTML/interviews/interview/355/*

Ideas for practice

Topic: Flowering plants

Age group: 5–7 years

Introduction

Whether the children live in an urban or rural environment, they will have some experience of flowering plants. Especially in spring and summer, flowers can be seen growing in gardens, parks, woodlands and public spaces such as verges and roundabouts. The purpose of this topic is to open children's eyes to the variety of flowering plants in their neighbourhood, to help them identify common varieties and to talk about the plants in scientific ways.

Scientific view

Many plants have a common structure which includes roots, stems, leaves and flowers. Some flowers serve a special purpose by attracting insects and providing them with food. Roots also serve a special purpose. It is through the roots that plants take up the water they need to grow and stay alive.

Health and safety

Be aware of children with sensitivities or allergies particularly to pollen. Teach children hygiene rules when handling soil and plants. Choose materials and tools appropriate to the age and capability of the children in making activities. Follow ASE guidance in *Be Safe!* (2011) for gardening and visits outside the classroom.

Working scientifically

In these activities children will:

- ask questions;
- observe using simple equipment;
- perform simple tests;
- gather and record data to help answer questions.

Exploration stage

Children's talk involves trying out their own ideas

Setting the scene

Figure 3.1 *Dr Seuss* by **William Huggin, acrylic on canvas**

Source: Getty Images

Start by showing the children a picture of a painting of flowers like William Huggin's *Dr Seuss*. Without any initial comment ask the children to describe the painting and explain what they think the colours and shapes represent. What do they like and dislike about it? Discuss whether the children think the painting is realistic or not. Does it represent real flowers? Encourage the children to justify their responses.

Scientific enquiry

Ask children if they would like to make their own paintings of flowers. Provide each group with a vase of different coloured flowers and art equipment to paint their own still life. You need to be aware of children's sensitivities and allergies to plants when planning this activity. Children should wear protective gloves when handling the plants.

Before they start, ask the children to look closely at the flowers and compare the different types. They start by counting the number of petals on the different flowers. Let the children touch and smell them. Help them choose words to describe the texture and scent of the petals compared to the stems and leaves. Which flowers have the strongest scent and the most intense colour? Do different coloured flowers have different scents? Help children find words to describe and compare the flowers. What things are similar and what things are different about them? Provide them with magnifying glasses so they can look closely at their structure and compare the shape of the petals. Help them distinguish between the petals that make up the flower and the leaves which are connected to the stem.

Children can paint their still lifes of the vase of flowers paying attention to form and colour. Ask children to compare their paintings to the real thing. Help them identify the different types of flowers. Create a display using the vases of flowers and the children's paintings. Pin photographs of the flowers alongside the paintings.

Puzzle

When discussing their paintings focus children's attention on the colours and the fragrances of the flowers. Do they know why some flowers are so brightly coloured? Why do they have their own scent? Can they think of any reasons?

> ## Talking points: true, false or not sure?
>
> - Flowers have bright colours so we can see them in the dark.
> - Flowers smell nice to make us happy.
> - Bees and butterflies are attracted to many flowers.
> - Bees and butterflies are attracted to flowers which provide them with food.
> - Not all plants have flowers.

Discuss the talking points and encourage children to talk about their experiences. If they have gardens at home, they can talk about their favourite flowers and whether they have seen any bees or butterflies flying around. Encourage children to elaborate and talk about why they think bees might be attracted to flowering plants. Ask them to think of two things which they know about bees. Did they know that bees have five eyes and like to dance? Talk about how honey bees use the food they find in flowers to make honey in their hives.

Figure 3.2 **Bee collecting food (pollen) from the flower**

Source: iStock

Figures 3.3 Cabbage White butterfly feeding on a verbena flower, with a Red Admiral resting on a post

Source: Photos by Anna Loxley

Scientific enquiry

Organise a walk around the local neighbourhood to explore the types of flowers being grown in gardens, in containers and hanging baskets. Also look out for insects such as bees and butterflies.

Include the local park to have a look at their bedding. Arrange for a park gardener to talk about the different flowers, and explain why they have been chosen. Take photographs of a wide range of plants and any insects flying around them. Focus children's attention on the range of colours and shapes of their flowers and leaves, and the types of insects. Which are the most popular colours for spring/summer flowers? Which are the most popular insects?

Back in the classroom print some of the photographs and make a display of the flowering plants in your neighbourhood. Group them in the display according to the shape of their flowers and name the different types.

Story-telling

In speech and writing children tell their own stories about their flower walk. What were their favourite flowers and what insects did they see? Why do they think bees and butterflies were attracted to the flowers? With support, children can make 'thank you' cards to send to the park gardener. They decorate their cards with line drawings of their favourite flowers. Ask children to pay attention to detail regarding the number of petals and their shape. If need be they can get pictures of their flowers on the web.

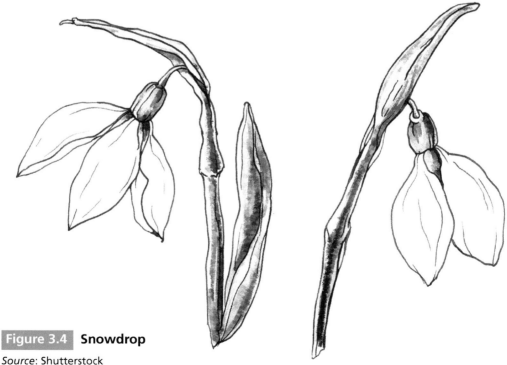

Figure 3.4 **Snowdrop**

Source: Shutterstock

Scientific enquiry

For this activity you will need a range of bedding plants, containers, potting compost and appropriate tools. Purchase a range of colourful bedding plants from your local garden centre or supermarket. With the help of an adult children can plant them in containers and look after them until they produce their flowers. When transplanting, talk about the names and different parts of the plants, and let the children look carefully at the roots. Ask them to explain what they know about roots.

Children keep diaries in which they record how often they water their plants, and make observations about how they grow. At intervals, let the children carefully take a plant out of the compost and view the development of the roots with magnifiers. They should carefully repot their plant and water it. Probe their understanding of why plants need water.

Puzzle

Encourage the children to hypothesise about what happens to the water after it is poured into the container. Children may know that plants need water to survive, but not know how it is taken up by the roots. Ask groups to place a clear plastic bag over one of their plants. Next day they inspect the bag to find it has misted up with water droplets. The puzzle is: how did the water get there? Children discuss the puzzle in groups and then as a whole class. Help them share ideas, and construct a reasoned explanation.

Photographs can be taken at different stages as the plants grow, then added to the display. The photographs of the plants can be grouped on the display according to the shape of the flowers.

Formative assessment

Provide opportunities for children to voice what they have learnt in the exploratory stage. Use evidence from their responses to the puzzles, talking points and other activities to assess differences between children's ideas and the scientific view. Plan how you will use the re-describing stage to help the children address their *learning needs* (see Chapter 1). You may need to modify the activities depending on the collective and individual needs of your children.

Re-describing stage

Children's talk involves making sense of scientific ideas

Teacher-led discussion

Start by discussing children's responses to the second puzzle concerning the purpose of the roots. Use pictures and video clips to elaborate on their ideas, showing how water taken up by the roots travels through stems to the leaves where some of it escapes into the air.

Modelling

Children can role-play how a plant takes up water through its roots. In the playground draw a giant picture of a plant in chalk. The plant needs to have huge roots, leaves and stems. Draw a line to represent the surface of the soil, with the roots on one side and the rest of the plant on the other. Make it clear which sides of the line represent the soil and the air. Children imagine they are rain drops falling on the soil. They then travel through the roots, up the stems, into the leaves and back out into the air. Discuss how some water stays in the plant to help it grow. Back in class children can draw cartoons which represent the model.

Teacher-led discussion

Return to the first puzzle. Reinforce and elaborate on the ideas from the exploratory stage by showing them a video of a bee collecting nectar from a flower. Make the point that flowers which attract bees have food inside for them to eat. Bees, butterflies and other animals love flowers which have sweet sticky nectar inside to eat. What else would they like to find out about bees?

Information and teaching resources

BBC Bitesize:

- What are the parts of a plant? *www.bbc.co.uk/guides/z3wpsbk#zg8tpv4*
- Why are butterflies and bees attracted to plants? *www.bbc.co.uk/education/clips/zmrb4wx*
- Why do plants need roots to grow? *www.bbc.co.uk/education/clips/zxdkjxs*
- What does a plant need to grow? *www.bbc.co.uk/guides/zxxsyrd*

Other websites:

- Bee feeding on a flower. *www.youtube.com/watch?v=Loucm_92Yl4*
- Growing a sunflower animation. *http://bpes.bp.com/primary-resources/science/ages-4-to-7/plants/planning-an-experiment/*

Application stage

Children's talk involves trying out scientific ideas

Fabulous flowers

With adult help, children design and make their own 'fabulous flowers' from a range of materials such as card, paper, fabric, art straws and pipe cleaners. The model flowers should have all the characteristics of real plants. They can be used to enhance the displays created in the exploratory stage.

Other activities:

- Design and make a flower badge which can be pinned to their clothes.
- Design and make a hat decorated with artificial flowers.
- Design and make a vase to display their artificial flowers.
- Make an attractive cover for a plain vase to display real flowers.

Poetry

Children can compose their own sense poems about flowers.

Flowers smell like …

Flowers feel like …

Flowers looks like …

Flowers sound like …

Information and teaching resources

● Fabulous flowers. *www.stem.org.uk/elibrary/resource/25920/designing-and-making-with-textiles-at-mid-key-stage-two-fabulous-flowers*. This project can be adapted for younger children.

● Sense poetry. *www.youngwriters.co.uk/sense-poetry*

Topic: Pollination

Age group 7–9 years

Introduction

Children are likely to have their own ideas about why bees and other insects are attracted to flowers. Often children imagine animals see the world as they do, so if they think the flowers are pretty, they may imagine the bees will feel the same way. The purpose of this topic is to open children's eyes to the way flowering plants have evolved a mutually beneficial relationship with animals such as bees to help them reproduce. The puzzling concept of whether bees can appreciate the beauty of flowers is left open to question. This topic is best done in spring or early summer.

Scientific view

Attracted by the reward of a meal, animals unintentionally help plants reproduce. To reach the nectar they have to push past the stamen, the male part of the flower, collecting pollen as they go. Off they go to another flower and complete the sexual act by rubbing against the carpel, the female part, coating the stigma with the sticky pollen. Pollination is part of the process through which seeds are produced.

Health and safety

Remember to check for children with sensitivities or allergies to pollen or plants. Pollen can stain clothes, so it is advisable for children to wear protective gloves and aprons when dissecting flowers. When working outside the classroom, be prepared for stings from wasps, bees and nettles. In some cases, these may need first aid treatment. When planning the activities in this topic follow guidance in the ASE publication *Be Safe!* (2011).

Working scientifically

In these activities children will:

- ask questions;
- make systematic and careful observations;
- gather, record, classify and present data;
- report on findings from enquiry;
- use scientific evidence to answer questions.

Exploration stage

Children's talk involves trying out their own ideas

Setting the scene

Find a picture of a bee foraging for nectar and pollen like the one shown in the previous topic. Look for a bee with a full pollen sac on its leg. Ask the children what they think has attracted the bee to the flower.

Puzzle

What is the bee doing inside the flower? What is it looking for? What is it carrying on its leg?

Talking points: true, false or not sure?

- The bee is just resting on the flower.
- It's the beauty of the flower which the bee can't resist.
- The bee is looking for small insects to eat.
- Bees eat the petals of the flower.
- Bees collect food from inside the flower.
- It's the smell of the flower which attracts them.
- Bees wash in the water that collects in flowers.
- Flowers protect bees from the cold and wind.

In groups children discuss the talking points. Encourage them to share and justify their ideas and try to reach agreement on each point. Not every point has a clear-cut answer. Use the talking points to start a conversation about bees. Children can share their stories. Do they know why bees are so important?

Scientific enquiry and art

In this activity groups explore the structure of a flower to see what could interest a bee. You will need simple dissection kits and magnifiers. Children should wear protective gloves and aprons. Follow safety advice in *Be Safe!* (2011). Use flowers which have large reproductive parts such as tulips, daffodils and gladioli.

Figure 3.5 **Drawing of a lily**

Source: Shutterstock

Children start by making a pencil drawing of their flower. Stress that detail is important. Encourage them to pay attention to the shape and number of petals, and the shape and number of the reproductive parts inside the flower.

Next, groups dissect the flowers and look carefully at the parts using magnifiers. They can make individual drawings of the main parts of the flower. Encourage children to talk about what the bee might be looking for inside the flower. Can they explain why bees get covered in pollen?

Using information sources, groups can discover the names and the reproductive purposes of each part of their flower. Groups come together to present and share their ideas. Display their drawings.

Scientific enquiry

Scientists have found that bees are attracted to certain types of flowers. Does this mean, as Feynman suggests, that bees could possibly have an aesthetic sense; in other words, do they like one colour better than another? Children can investigate which types of flowers bees visit most often and evaluate whether there is a colour they seem to prefer. Start in the school grounds. Each day for a week go out and record the number of bees and the flowers they visit. Ask children to continue the survey at home. Involve parents. Send a note home asking parents to take part in the survey. If possible, extend the survey by taking the class to a local park or woodland. Children collate and record their data on charts in the classroom, along with any photographs that children have taken. Draw conclusions and compare with the scientific view that bees prefer blue and violet coloured flowers.

It would be interesting to see if it is possible to trick bees into visiting artificial flowers. Children can set up different coloured artificial flowers in the school grounds to see if bees are attracted to them. Groups can investigate whether the colour alone is enough to interest the bees, or whether bees can be enticed to the flowers by attaching small amounts of food such as sugar or honey to replace the nectar, and flour to replace the pollen.

Different types of scent could be applied to the flowers to see whether the fragrance of a flower makes a difference. Also flowers with different structures can be tested. The tests need to be set up in a part of the school grounds which is likely to attract insects, and can also be monitored throughout the day. Children need to make sure their investigations are fair and that the data can be used to draw reliable conclusions.

Story-telling

Children report the outcomes of their enquiries in the style of a documentary (David Attenborough style) made in the outdoor settings. Groups work collaboratively to create their own stories about why bees are attracted to certain flowers.

Formative assessment

Provide opportunities for children to voice what they have learnt in the exploratory stage. Use evidence from their responses to the puzzle, talking points and other activities to assess differences between children's ideas and the scientific view. Plan how you will use the re-describing stage to help the children address their *learning needs* (see Chapter 1). You may need to modify the activities depending on the collective and individual needs of your children.

Information and teaching resources

BBC Bitesize:

● Why are bees and butterflies attracted to plants?
www.bbc.co.uk/education/clips/zmrb4wx

Other websites:

● Fake electric flowers reveal surprising bee seduction technique.
http://sitn.hms.harvard.edu/flash/2014/fake-electric-flowers-reveal-surprising-bee-seduction-technique/

Re-describing stage

Children's talk involves making sense of scientific ideas

Teacher-led discussion

Return to the puzzle. Draw children's attention to the pollen sac on the bee's leg. Does this provide a clue to what it is going on? From the scientific perspective, the bee is on a mission to collect nectar and pollen to be taken back to its nest or hive. When dissecting a flower, children can see the pollen on the ends of the stamens and have a good look at it with their magnifiers. They might find it harder to see the nectar, but they can have a look for it. Use diagrams and video clips to help children identify the main parts of the flower such as the stigma, style and ovary which form the carpel, the female part of the flower. The stamen is the male part of the flower consisting of the anther, filament and pollen.

Discuss how, in its search for food, the bee pollinates by carrying pollen from one plant to another. As it searches for nectar it rubs pollen off the filament inside the flower and carries it to the next plant it visits. It then transfers the pollen to the stigma on top of the carpel enabling fertile seeds to be produced in the ovary. Focus on the pollen sac and explain its purpose and how the bee 'fills it up'. Provide opportunities for children to find out more information using secondary sources.

Modelling

Children model pollination by taking on the role of the bee and parts of the flower. Out in the playground, draw two huge outlines of flowers using chalk. Children representing the reproductive parts can arrange themselves inside the flowers. Others can take on the role of bees. When planning the activity, children need to think carefully about the process of pollination and use their imaginations to narrate and perform the interactions between the flowers and the bees. Provide them with opportunities to make and use suitable props. Use the role modelling activity to assess children's understanding of pollination and address any outstanding *learning needs*.

Scientific enquiry and art

Ask children what they think happens to flowers after they have been pollinated. Show them pictures of the seed heads of different plants. Why have they lost their flowers? Bring in some seed heads so children can observe them using magnifiers. Discuss which part of the flower forms the seed head. What happens to the seeds inside the heads? Discuss children's responses.

Figure 3.6 *Starry, Starry Night* **by Sarah Hough, 2005 (digital)**

Source: Hough, Sarah / Private Collection / Bridgeman Images

Figure 3.7 *Bean Painting, Specimens from the Leguminosae Family* by
Rachel Pedder-Smith

Explore how plants have been traditionally recorded by artists. Show children paintings of seeds and flowers from the Kew Botanical Prints website. Focus on the work of Rachel Pedder-Smith, who uses seeds to create visually striking images. Children can use her work and other botanical art to inspire them to observe and produce both stunning and scientifically accurate paintings of their seeds.

Story-telling

Children use information sources to explore the different ways seeds are dispersed. Each group can tell the story of the life cycle of one type of flowering plant. Encourage children to think of creative ways of presenting their story to the class using role-play, drama, music, video, animation, puppets or even mime.

Information and teaching resources

BBC Bitesize:

- Life cycles. *www.bbc.co.uk/schools/scienceclips/ages/9_10/life_cycles.shtml*

- Seed dispersal. *www.bbc.co.uk/education/clips/znvfb9q*
- Seed spreading in autumn and making a winter bird-feeder. *www.bbc.co.uk/education/clips/zwhcwxs*
- The life cycle of a dandelion. *www.bbc.co.uk/education/clips/zs9c87h*
- The life cycle of a plant. *www.bbc.co.uk/education/clips/zgqyrdm*
- How plants produce seeds. *www.bbc.co.uk/education/clips/zfx76sg*

Other websites:

- Rachel Pedder-Smith. *http://prints.kew.org/category/botanical-art/pedder-smith*
- Botanical art. *http://prints.kew.org/category/botanical-art*

Application stage

Children's talk involves trying out scientific ideas

Figure 3.8   **Sedums are easy to grow and attract bees**

Source: Photo by Anna Loxley

Flowers to attract bees

Children can grow plants which attract bees in containers or in a small garden in the school grounds. Lavender and sedums are easy to grow and are favourite plants for honey bees. You can find lots of advice on the RHS website for growing bee- and butterfly-friendly plants.

Designing wind-pollinated plants

Children need to know that not all plants are pollinated by animals. Ask them whether they can think of another way that pollen could be transferred from one plant to another. Challenge them to design a plant which is pollinated by the wind. Remind them that the wind will need to carry pollen from the male part of one plant to the female part of another. Groups start by creating design drawings of their plants, which show how the process of pollination will take place. They can then make 3D models. Children can use information sources to compare their designs with wind-pollinated plants created by nature.

Perfume from plants

Children design and make their own perfume from plants. Start by exploring different types of commercial perfume and scents. Talk about the qualities of a good perfume. Children can plan their own tests to compare different brands and fragrances.

Groups explore ways of extracting the scent from plants such as lavender, sage, rosemary, roses and other plants with strong fragrances. They can mix the fragrances to design their own perfume.

'Perfumer' and 'cosmetic scientist' are terms used to describe an expert who creates cosmetic products such as perfumes, lipsticks, creams and toiletries. Children can use information sources to find out about the work of cosmetic scientists, and about some of the products which they help to produce.

Information and teaching resources

- Positive potions. *www.edenproject.com/learn/schools/lesson-plans/positive-potions*

- From plants to perfume. *www.telegraph.co.uk/gardening/how-to-grow/how-perfume-is-made-plants/*

- Making perfume from your garden. *www.motherearthnews.com/diy/making-perfume-from-your-garden.aspx*

- Plants in our daily life. *https://schoolgardening.rhs.org.uk/resources/Info-Sheet/Plants-in-our-daily-life*

- Newspaper article about cosmetic scientists. *www.theguardian.com/money/2007/jul/21/careers.graduates1*

- Plants which attract bees. *www.rhs.org.uk/science/conservation-biodiversity/wildlife/encourage-wildlife-to-your-garden/plants-for-pollinators*

Topic: Adaptation

Age group: 9–11 years

Introduction

Not all flowering plants are pollinated by bees. Plants need to adapt to their environment in order to survive and develop devices to attract the pollinators that live in their habitat when they flower. Plants can go to great lengths to attract pollinators. The purpose of this topic is to introduce children to the ideas of adaptation using plants as the context.

Scientific view

Adapted plants survive because they have inherited characteristics which suit the environment in which they live. For example, the skunk cabbage is a native of North America and lives in areas where winters are often cold and wet. Skunk cabbages thrive in cold, wet conditions because they have the ability to create their own heat. This means they can warm up the freezing ground and air around them and attract pollinating insects in winter, when most other plants are still dormant. Their putrid smell also helps them survive by discouraging animals from eating their leaves.

Working scientifically

In these activities children will:

- present findings from enquiries using video and other electronic devices;
- use scientific evidence obtained from information sources to inform and develop their ideas.

Health and safety

The research activities in this topic provide a good opportunity for teaching children about the benefits and dangers of the internet and information technology. Follow school policy on e-safety.

Exploration stage

Children's talk involves trying out their own ideas

Setting the scene

The skunk cabbage of North America is an amazing plant. It is a perennial wildflower that grows in early spring when there is still snow covering the ground. What is intriguing about this plant is that it can create its own heat. Before it flowers, it warms up and melts the ice around it so pollinators can get a 'whiff' of its fragrance! All around the air is filled with the putrid smell of rotting flesh, horrible to us, but alluring to the bees, flies, wasps and other insects that pollinate it. What does this tell us about the idea that insects are attracted to the sweet scent of flowering plants?

Figure 3.9 **Skunk cabbage**

Source: iStock

Puzzle

Is the skunk cabbage well adapted to its environment?

> ### Talking points: true, false or not sure?
>
> - Insects are attracted to the beauty of the skunk cabbage flowers.
> - Insects are only interested in finding food.
> - It is the fragrance of a flower that attracts the insects.
> - The insects depend on the skunk cabbage to survive.
> - The skunk cabbage depends on the insects to survive.
> - The putrid smell indicates there is food available.
> - The putrid smell stops some animals from eating the plant.
> - It is not just the food that attracts insects to plants.

Working in groups children can share their ideas and justify their responses to the talking points. They use information sources to find out about the environment in which the skunk cabbage lives to help respond to the points and solve the puzzle.

Story-telling

1   Attracting pollinators

    The skunk cabbage shows that not all insects are attracted to colourful, sweet smelling plants. What devices do plants use other than their scent and colour to attract pollinators? Children use a range of information sources to research unusual ways flowering plants attract pollinators. Each group can choose a case study to explore in depth and tell their story to the class using video clips and power point presentations. In each case children should explain the challenges faced by the plants and pollinators in order to survive in their habitat.

2   3D model of super plant

    Children work in groups to design their own flowering plant adapted to living in a particularly harsh environment such as a desert, in the mountains or in very cold conditions. They make a 3D model of their plant and use it to explain how it is able to survive and reproduce in its environment.

3   Joseph Banks

    Joseph Banks (1743–1820) was an explorer and naturalist who became known throughout the world for his knowledge and love of plants. He was director of the Royal Botanic Gardens at Kew for 50 years, during which time he turned the garden into a paradise for both gardeners and scientists. Mainly due to him, Kew became the greatest botanic collection in the world. Banks was famously part of the expedition led by Captain James Cook which circumnavigated the globe. In the 1700s there were no cameras, so Banks took artist Sydney Parkinson with him to record nearly a thousand plants and animals which they discovered.

Figure 3.10 **Botanical engraving of the melaleuca cajuputi tree commonly found in Australia**

Source: iStock

Groups use information sources to explore how Banks travelled the world in search of new types of plants. Botanical illustrations of plants discovered on the Cook expedition can be found on the Natural History Museum website. Children can also explore the collection of Botanical Art on the Kew website.

Groups choose an area of the world visited by the Cook expedition, and explore the types of plants which can be found there. Ask them to research in detail one plant of special interest, and discover how it is adapted to its environment. Children should create their own scientifically accurate drawing of the plant. Organise a class conference on adaptation. Groups present their drawings and outcomes of their research at the conference. They should provide a brief summary of their ideas on paper, which can be displayed along with their drawings. Discuss why scientists present their work at conferences and in peer-reviewed journals.

Scientific enquiry

Figure 3.11 **Bottlebrush plant**

Source: Photo by Anna Loxley

A wide range of Australian plants such as banksia and bottlebrush (callistemon) are commonly grown in the UK from either seed or cuttings. Bring into school a range of Australian flowering plants together with packets of their seeds. Groups plan their own enquiries to discover the best conditions for growing the plants, and whether they are best propagated from cuttings or seeds.

Formative assessment

Provide opportunities for children to voice what they have learnt in the exploratory stage. Use evidence from their responses to the puzzle, talking points and other activities to assess differences between children's ideas and the scientific view. Plan how you will use the re-describing stage to help the children address their *learning needs* (see Chapter 1). You may need to modify the activities depending on the collective and individual needs of your children.

Information and teaching resources

BBC Bitesize:

- Bromeliad growth in the rain forest. *www.bbc.co.uk/education/clips/zkwkjxs*

- Comparing broad leaf and pine forest. *www.bbc.co.uk/education/clips/z3rdsg8*

- How cacti survive without water. *www.bbc.co.uk/education/clips/z69rkqt*

- Variation in plants. *www.bbc.co.uk/education/clips/zsdkjxs*

Other websites:

- Botanical Art. *http://prints.kew.org/category/botanical-art*

- Japanese flowers. *http://prints.kew.org/category/botanical-art/japanese-floral-prints*

- Natural History Museum. *www.nhm.ac.uk/our-science/departments-and-staff/library-and-archives/collections/cook-voyages-collection/endeavour-botanical-illustrations/*

Re-describing stage

Children's talk involves making sense of scientific ideas

Teacher-led discussion

Each case study in the exploration stage adds to the amazing story of how flowering plants have adapted to life on earth by developing mutually beneficial relationships with pollinators. This is the scientific beauty of flowering plants that Feynman was talking about in the story at the beginning of the chapter.

Talk with the children about how plants, like all living things, need to reproduce to survive. Most flowering plants achieve this by means of sexual reproduction which often requires the help of an animal to transfer pollen from the male part of a flower onto the female part of another plant. This involves competing for pollinators. Plants which are most attractive to pollinators are more likely to reproduce and survive. Talk about the skunk cabbage and how it out-competes other plants by producing its flowers in winter while other plants remain dormant. Review children's case studies as evidence of how plants are adapted to survive in their habitats.

Story-telling

Ask the children to imagine what would happen to the plants they researched if their pollinators died out. How could they adapt to attract other animals? Could they adapt to use other agents of pollination such as wind? Children can draw pictures to show how their plants would need to change in order to survive. Probe children's thinking and address any outstanding *learning needs.*

Application stage

Children's talk involves trying out scientific ideas

Can we survive without the insect pollinators?

Bees pollinate most of the fruit crops around the world. Together with other insects, bees pollinate the vast majority of crops grown around the world. Without them we would find it difficult to feed ourselves, as would many of the animals who share our planet. Plants and animals around the world are very much dependent on the animal pollinators for their survival.

Children can debate whether humans could survive without the pollinators. Provide time for them to collect evidence from information sources and to prepare their arguments carefully. They will need to find out which crops are not pollinated by animals, and what other methods of pollination are possible, including human agency.

Why are bees dying out?

Children research the behaviour of bees and their life cycle. In recent years the populations of bees in the developed world have been diminishing and scientists are not sure why. Considering their importance to the food supply, this is a worrying development. Children explore the literature available online using newspaper and magazine articles to find out about the extent of the problem. They can tell their stories in the form of a blog entry to be published on the school website.

Does science enhance or reduce the natural beauty of the world?

Children can discuss Feynman's views about the beauty of flowers set out in the narrative at the start of the chapter. A video of Feynman expressing this view can be found on YouTube. Children listen to the video and discuss his remarks. Do they agree that scientific knowledge only adds to the excitement and mystery and awe of a flower? Or do they think that by probing and dissecting, and by discovering a flower's secrets we destroy its beauty and take way its appeal? In groups children can debate the issues and make their own video to communicate their views.

Information and teaching resources

BBC Bitesize:

- Food groups and eating plants. *www.bbc.co.uk/education/clips/zqj8q6f*
- What do plants give us? *www.bbc.co.uk/education/clips/zyqw2hv*

Other websites:

- Are bees dying because of insecticide? *www.theguardian.com/environment/ 2014/may/09/honeybees-dying-insecticide-harvard-study*
- Disappearance of wild bees. *www.bbc.co.uk/nature/28290890*
- Honey bees. *www.bbc.co.uk/guides/zg4dwmn*
- Feynman talking about the beauty of a flower. *www.youtube.com/watch?v=ZbFM3rn4ldo*

Useful book:

- Tony Juniper (2013) *What has nature ever done for us?* London: Profile Books.

Chapter 4
Woodland habitats

We can't blame children for occupying themselves with Facebook rather than playing in the mud. Our society doesn't put a priority on connecting with nature. In fact, too often we tell them it's dirty and dangerous.

David Suzuki, scientist (b. 1936)

This chapter presents ideas for practice to guide the way children find out about the living things which inhabit the woodland and how they change throughout the seasons. Learning starts with the younger children exploring how the woodland changes in autumn and how animals and plants use this time to get ready for winter. The next topic provides opportunities for children to study woodland habitats in more detail and to explore how the animals and plants depend on each other to survive. In the final topic, children further develop their understanding of habitats and food chains by exploring the part played by detritivores and decomposers in the woodland's ecosystem. Further activities focus on the need to save and maintain native woodland and forest around the world. Children explore the problems caused to wildlife by deforestation and the introduction of non-native trees, and look into possible solutions.

Topics in this chapter:

- Autumn in the woodland
- Spring in the woodland
- Habitats and food chains

Subject knowledge to support the teaching of these topics can be found in the core book, Loxley, P., Dawes, D., Nicholls, L. and Dore, B. (2018) *Teaching primary science: Promoting enjoyment and developing understanding*, Abingdon: Routledge, Chapter 13: Interdependence and Chapter 15: Adaptation and evolution.

The woodland habitat

Woodlands are interesting places to visit at any time of the year. Spring is the time when the woodland wakes up from its winter's rest. With renewed vitality wild flowers burst out, taking advantage of the spring sunshine before the leaves on the trees grow big enough to steal the sun's energy. In summer, trees monopolise the sun's energy to grow and produce their fruit. However, some flowering plants such as dog rose and honeysuckle still provide colour on the edge of the woodland, and in glades where they find enough sunlight to survive. In autumn the woodland prepares for the coming winter. Fruits ripen and seeds are distributed in the hope of creating offspring to maintain the species into the future. As the days grow colder and as winter approaches, deciduous trees shed their leaves and take a rest in preparation for the year to come. Winter is the time for the woodland to tidy itself up. Leaves and dead wood that litter the ground are broken down by invertebrates such as woodlice, snails and worms, and decomposed by fungi and bacteria. Nothing is wasted. Having been returned to the soil the decomposed leaf litter provides nutrients for plants to grow when spring comes around.

Strolling through a woodland we can see how important different areas are to the wildlife living there. Each level of the woodland from soil to canopy has inhabitants suited to their environment. Just like the floors in a house, different levels in the woodland contribute to the home by providing different services for the inhabitants.

Taking a tour of a woodland 'house', we can start by looking underneath the floorboards into the basement or cellar. Here we see the roots, which are the foundations on which trees and other plants are built. The roots also provide the plumbing system, able to pump vast quantities of water to the ever-thirsty trees. The basement is also a source of food for invertebrates such as worms, and animals which prey on them. It also provides a home for burrowing animals such as badgers, keeping the hibernators warm and safe throughout the winter.

Like many homes the ground floor is used the most. It is often untidy, being covered in leaf litter much of the time, but when carpeted in wild flowers can be breathtakingly beautiful. The ground floor is home for a wide variety of animals such as hedgehogs, mice, deer and a large range of invertebrates. It also provides a plentiful supply of food for birds, foxes, badgers, weasels, stoats and squirrels.

The first floor is not so busy. This is the level in the woodland made up of young trees and shrubs which provide homes for insects and other invertebrates to feed and lay their eggs. Some birds build their nests in the first floor keeping their young safe from predators which live on the ground.

The canopy is the equivalent to the roof or attic in a house. It provides shelter from the weather for both animals and fragile plants. Each species is adapted to where it lives in the wood, and the canopy helps maintain a microclimate which suits all its inhabitants living below.

Finally, we cannot have a house over four levels without an interconnecting staircase. In the woodland, the trunks and branches of the trees not only provide pathways between levels, but also provide accommodation for animals such as owls and squirrels, and a multitude of invertebrates.

Woodlands are very special homes for a great diversity of living things and need looking after as do all our homes. Nobody likes to think their homes are in danger. They are places where we feel safe and secure. But in today's world many of our woodlands face threats from climate change, increasing numbers of pests and diseases, pollution, overgrazing, invasive non-native species and intensification of land use. There are never simple solutions to complex issues but if we value our woodlands we need to protect them. For more information, visit the Woodland Trust website (*www.woodlandtrust.org.uk*).

Ideas for practice

Topic: Autumn in the woodland

Age group: 5–7 years

Introduction

The purpose of this topic is to provide opportunities for children to explore how the changing seasons affect living things, with a focus on trees, shrubs and birds. The activities help children understand how autumn is the time animals and plants get ready for winter. The application stage highlights the problems birds have to survive in winter, and challenges the children to come up with some practical ideas which can help them get through.

Scientific view

Autumn is a time of change when the weather gets colder, and living things prepare themselves for the coming winter. Autumn brings a host of ripening fruit and seeds which are eaten by animals and harvested by humans. Animals, such as squirrels, can be seen gathering and storing food for winter. Deciduous trees lose their leaves which provide food for fungi and a range of tiny animals.

Working scientifically

In these activities children will:

- observe closely using simple equipment;
- identify and classify living things in the woodland;
- use their observations and ideas to answer questions;
- gather and record data to help answer questions.

Health and safety

When planning health and safety refer to the ASE book *Be Safe!* (2011) and follow the guidelines set out in the *SAFETY CODE for Studies Outside the Classroom* (p. 13). Children should wear protective gloves when collecting samples from the park or woodland. Warn children not to put anything in their mouths and not to pick mushrooms. Also ensure they do not pick or damage any wild flowers. Plan all design and make activities to provide appropriate materials, tools and supervision.

Exploration stage

Children's talk involves trying out their own ideas

Setting the scene

As autumn begins ask the children what they remember about the summer. Talk about the warm weather, the long days, going to bed when it was still light, the clothes they wore and what they did on their holidays. Ask them to paint a picture which tells a story of what their summer was like. Encourage them to use 'summer colours' when painting their pictures. Display and talk about the pictures to provide a starting point for this topic.

Puzzle

How do the children know when summer is over?

> **Talking points: true, false or not sure?**
>
> - Summer ends when they come back to school.
> - Summer ends when it starts to snow.
> - Summer ends when it is too dark to play out after school.
> - Summer ends when they need to wear their warm jumpers.
> - Summer ends when the trees lose their leaves.
> - Summer ends when the heating is put on at home.

Explore children's ideas. Do they know which season comes next after summer? Encourage children to describe the differences between the seasons.

Scientific enquiry

Take children on a walk to look for signs that summer has ended and autumn has begun. Include the local park or woodland on your walk.

Signs of autumn to look out for:

- Tinting of leaves on trees
- Trees shedding their leaves
- Ripe fruit on apple trees
- Ripe berries on bushes

- Conkers, acorns and sycamore seeds on the ground
- Clues of feeding activity of animals such as mice, hedgehogs and squirrels
- Fungi (mushrooms)
- Gardens losing their bloom
- Autumn colours
- People wearing warm clothing
- Sun low in the sky in the afternoon
- Cool air temperatures out of the sun

Figure 4.1 **Autumn in the woodland**

Source: Photos by Anna Loxley

Modify the list to suit your local environment. Use the list as an aide-memoire when on the walk and point things out to the children. Impress on the children they should work scientifically. This means they observe things carefully, ask questions and make sure they do not damage the woodland. Take photographs and collect leaves and seeds. Look out especially for ripe acorns and conkers.

Back in the classroom children can sort their finds, identify and classify them. They can use magnifiers to observe them more closely. Follow H&S guidelines in *Be Safe!* (2011).

Story-telling and art

In groups children create posters using the things they collected and the photographs of the local environment. Encourage them to talk about the things they put on their posters and tell stories of their autumn walk. Talk about signs of animal activity they observed.

Children choose one thing from their walk to paint which is a sign that summer has ended and autumn has begun. They should focus carefully on form and colour. Encourage them to talk about their object and why they think it is found in autumn.

Formative assessment

Provide opportunities for children to voice what they have learnt in the exploratory stage. Use evidence from their responses to the puzzle, talking points and other activities to assess differences between children's ideas and the scientific view. Plan how you will use the re-describing stage to help the children address their *learning needs* (see Chapter 1). You may need to modify the activities depending on the collective and individual needs of your children.

Re-describing stage

Children's talk involves making sense of scientific ideas

Teacher-led discussion

Re-focus children's attention on the puzzle. Talk together about the differences between summer and autumn. Extend the conversation to include winter and spring. Use video clips to

Figure 4.2 *Autumn breeze* **by Robin Moorcroft**

tell the story of how the environment changes across the four seasons. Suitable resources can be found on the BBC Bitesize website. Use photographs from the web to illustrate the key changes that take place which indicate that autumn has begun.

Story-telling

Together with the children create a giant collage which tells the story of how a deciduous tree in your neighbourhood changes in autumn as it prepares for its long winter rest. The story begins in summer and shows the changes that take place all the way through to winter. Children make models of leaves and fruit to stick on the collage. They can also add pictures

Figure 4.3 **Squirrel Collage**

Source: © Perkins & Morley Ltd; Illustration by Jill Perkins of relevant animals, for example, squirrels collecting fruit, and a hedgehog hibernating close by. Do any birds make their home in the tree over winter? Talk to children about the story behind the collage and identify any outstanding learning needs.

Scientific enquiry

Re-focus children's attention on their posters and talk about the conkers, acorns, other fruits and seeds which they found. Talk about how these seeds could grow into new plants. Oak trees are native to England and feature heavily in its history, legends and folklore. Ripe acorns collected on the walk can be grown at school. Advice for how to grow them can be found on the RHS and National Forest websites. Children can also try to grow other seeds found on their walk.

Often children don't think of trees as plants and might not think they are living things. Use these activities to address misconceptions by pointing out the similarities between trees and other plants. Remind them that trees are plants because they have leaves and roots. They are also living things because they grow their leaves, and produce seeds which grow into new plants. Use photographs taken on the walk to remind them of the names of the relevant deciduous trees. Use the term deciduous trees in conversation to describe trees which shed their leaves in autumn.

Information and teaching resources

BBC Bitesize:

- What are the seasons? *www.bbc.co.uk/guides/zcx3gk7*

- Landscapes through the seasons. *www.bbc.co.uk/education/clips/zp4gcdm*

- How autumn affects animals and plants. *www.bbc.co.uk/education/clips/zg7wq6f*

- How changing seasons affect hedgehogs. *www.bbc.co.uk/education/clips/z7kc87h*

- How squirrels collect nuts. *www.bbc.co.uk/education/clips/zwcb4wx*

- Seasonal changes 1. *www.bbc.co.uk/education/clips/zhfnvcw*

- Seasonal changes 2. *www.bbc.co.uk/education/clips/zrjd7ty*

- Life cycle and inhabitants of an oak tree. *www.bbc.co.uk/education/clips/ztg3cdm*

Other websites:

- National Forest website. *www.nationalforest.org/document/involved/tree_from_seed.pdf*

- Royal Horticultural Society. *www.rhs.org.uk/education-learning/gardening-children-schools/family-activities/grow-it/grow/oak*

- Woodland Trust. *www.woodlandtrust.org.uk*

- British trees. *www.woodlandtrust.org.uk/visiting-woods/trees-woods-and-wildlife/british-trees/*

● Oak trees. *www.woodlandtrust.org.uk/visiting-woods/trees-woods-and-wildlife/british-trees/native-trees/english-oak/*

Application stage

Children's talk involves trying out scientific ideas

How can I help nature?

The purpose of this activity is to encourage children to think about the problems birds have to survive through the winter, and to come up with some practical ideas about how they can help.

Start by talking about what there is for birds to eat in autumn. Use photographs from their autumn walks and video clips to remind them that there are plenty of berries and seeds for birds to eat at this time of the year. When the berries and seeds have gone, what is left for them to eat in winter when the weather is cold? Use video clips to show how birds can struggle to survive in winter. You could use the BBC Bitesize clip, *How the seasons affect blackbirds.*

Figure 4.4 **Robin looking for food**

Source: Photo by Anna Loxley

In groups children discuss what they could do to help birds that live near the school. The Royal Society for the Protection of Birds (RSPB) website, *Giving nature a home,* has lots of ideas for children to consider. For example, children could turn an area of the school grounds into a bird café which provides different types of food for birds to eat in winter. With support, children can decide the 'menu' the café offers its 'customers' and design and make their own bird feeders.

A more ambitious project is to create a 'bird hotel' which not only provides food but also offers shelter for the birds against the winter weather. There are lots of websites with ideas for how to make bird boxes, including the RSPB website.

Information and teaching resources

BBC Bitesize:

- How the seasons affect blackbirds. *www.bbc.co.uk/education/clips/ztqd7ty*

Other websites:

- Make a home for wildlife. *ww2.rspb.org.uk/makeahomeforwildlife/*
- Making bird cake. *www.rspb.org.uk/discoverandenjoynature/families/children/ makeanddo/activities/birdcake.aspx*
- Open a bird café. *ww2.rspb.org.uk/makeahomeforwildlife/givenatureahomeinyour- garden/gardenactivities/openabirdcafe/*
- Advice on how to make a home for wildlife. *www.rspb.org.uk/makeahomeforwildlife/ advice/helpingbirds/nestboxes/smallbirds/making.aspx*
- Forestry Commission. *www.forestry.gov.uk*

Topic: Spring in the woodland

Age group: 7–9 years

Introduction

The focus for this topic is living things in a woodland habitat. The activities provide opportunities for children to identify and classify animals in the habitat, and to explore their interdependency. In the application stage children focus on rain forest habitats, and look into the problems created by their exploitation and destruction.

Scientific view

A woodland habitat is home to a diverse range of living things which depend on each other to survive. Plants such as trees, shrubs and wildflowers provide food for animals to eat and places to shelter from predators and the weather. Animals commonly found in the woodland consist of vertebrates such as birds and mammals, and invertebrates such as insects, snails and spiders. There is a wide range of predators including owls and hawks, and predatory mammals such as foxes, badgers, bats and hedgehogs. Invertebrates such as spiders, millipedes, types of beetles and wasps prey on other tiny creatures, but in turn can themselves fall prey to other animals. Within the woodland the plants are the producers of food on which all the animals directly or indirectly depend. Children may find it difficult to believe that without green plants all the animals in the wood could not survive.

Working scientifically

In these activities children will:

- ask questions and use scientific enquiry to answer them;
- gather, record and classify data in ways to help answer questions;
- record findings using scientific language and drawings;
- report on findings from enquiries orally, and through presentations and displays;
- use results to draw conclusions and make predictions;
- use scientific evidence to answer questions and support their findings.

Health and safety

Follow ASE guidelines in *Be Safe!* (2011) when planning your woodland walk. Stress safety, hygiene and the protection of the environment.

Exploration stage

Children's talk involves trying out their own ideas

Setting the scene

Show children photographs of a deciduous woodland and talk about the types of plants and animals which live there. Let children tell their stories of what they know about woodland.

Modelling

As described in the opening narrative, we can compare the layers of a typical deciduous woodland to the floors of a house.

- The underground made up of soil and the roots of different plants is equivalent to a cellar or basement in a house.
- The woodland floor covered in leaf litter and small plants is the equivalent of the ground floor in a house.

Canopy
(roof/attic)

First
floor

Ground
floor

Underground
(cellar)

Figure 4.5 Levels in the woodland can be compared to the floors in a house

Source: iStock

- The space taken up by shrubs and young trees is equivalent to the first floor in a house.
- The space taken up by the canopies of the mature trees is the equivalent of the roof or attic.

Puzzle

Discuss the above model of the woodland home. The puzzle is, what kinds of animals and plants would we finding living on each level? Children start to solve the puzzle by brainstorming answers to the following questions:

- What trees and shrubs do they expect to find in a woodland?
- What ground floor plants do they expect to discover?
- What invertebrates do they expect to discover?
- What vertebrates do they expect to discover?

Working in groups children respond to the questions and predict at which level or levels in the woodland the animals and plants could be found. They record their ideas by drawing pictures of the woodland as a home over four floors. Examine the reasons why they think certain plants and animals would prefer to live on a particular floor.

Scientific enquiry

Organise a visit to a woodland. If possible travel to an area of managed natural woodland; otherwise, find a wooded area in the local park. Spring is a delightful time. Children will be amazed by the range of wild flowers which carpet the 'ground floor'. Remind them not to pick or damage any flora.

Things to do and talk about:

- Look for holes in the ground which provide animals with doorways to the 'basement'. Which animals may live down there? Look for signs of animal activity.
- On the 'ground floor' identify and take photographs of the wild flowers. Do many plants grow directly under the trees?
- The 'ground floor' is the level on which most animals live. Look for signs of activity of small mammals and invertebrates in the leaf litter. Provide equipment so children can safely collect, observe and identify mini-beasts. Return the mini-beasts safely to their habitats. Children should wear protective gloves when exploring the ground floor.
- Explore shrubs and young trees on the 'first floor' for signs of mammals, bird life and invertebrates who may live there. Look out for bees, wasps and moths, as well as squirrels and various types of birds. Remind children not to disturb any nests.
- Check where the 'roof' is leaking. Find areas of the woodland where the canopy blocks out much of the sunlight. Which plants grow in these shady areas? Compare with ones which prefer sunnier locations. Do bluebells grow in sunny areas, or do they prefer shade?

- Look out for birds which live in the 'roof'. Why would they prefer to build their nests so high up? What are advantages and the dangers? Children can use twigs and materials they find on the ground to build a nest. How difficult is it to make it strong, weather proof and comfortable for the chicks? Children should return the materials to the woodland before they leave.

- The trunk of a tree is its 'stair case' to the different levels. Look for evidence for how it is used by different types of animals.

Children explore and identify flora and fauna at different levels and compare it with their drawings. How accurate were their drawings? What changes do they need to make to resolve the puzzle? Children annotate their drawings, adding or deleting parts so that they more accurately represent the ecology of the woodland. Use video recorders, sound recorders and cameras to record data from the visit which can be reviewed in the classroom.

Throughout the visit encourage groups to talk about how the different animals and plants are able to survive in their habitat. Use a worksheet to scaffold their discourse. The following headings may prove useful for the animals: name, colour, size, body parts, diet, possible predators, description of habitat and reasons why they think the animal is able to survive. Encourage groups to choose one animal and 're-design it' so it would struggle to survive.

Story-telling and art

Figure 4.6 **Birch trees**

Source: iStock

Back in school children write stories about life in the woodland. They can create their own illustrations using water colours, or as part of an art project they could design and make an embroidery of a woodland scene. Children's stories can be recorded and, together with their drawings, photographs, sound recordings and video of the woodland, used to create an interactive display.

Formative assessment

Provide opportunities for children to voice what they have learnt in the exploratory stage. Use evidence from their responses to the puzzle and other activities to assess differences between children's ideas and the scientific view. Plan how you will use the re-describing stage to help the children address their *learning needs* (see Chapter 1). You may need to modify the activities depending on the collective and individual needs of your children.

Information and teaching resources

BBC Bitesize:

- How spring weather affects animals and plants. *www.bbc.co.uk/education/clips/zx3fvcw*

- Food chains. *www.bbc.co.uk/education/clips/zjshfg8*

Other websites:

- Woodland activities. *www.woodlandtrust.org.uk/naturedetectives/activities/search/*

- Identifying spring flowers.
  www.woodlandtrust.org.uk/naturedetectives/activities/2016/03/spring-flowers-id/

- Spring hunt activity.
  www.woodlandtrust.org.uk/naturedetectives/activities/2016/03/spring-hunt/

ASE journals:

- Primary Science 132 (March/April 2014) *Children go bonkers about bugs* by Sue Fielding and Meriel Jones.

- Primary Science 135 (Nov/Dec 2014) *Developing an APP-TITUDE for learning outdoors* by Emily Baker.

Re-describing stage

Children's talk involves making sense of scientific ideas

Teacher-led discussion

Tell children there was a lot going on in the woodland which they may not have seen. For example, they may not have seen any foxes, badgers, bats, hedgehogs, snakes, frogs, hawks or owls. These are all woodland creatures which may have been hiding while the children were there. Use video clips and pictures from the web to provide insights into the diversity of animals which live in woodland. Classify as vertebrates and invertebrates. Define vertebrates as animals like us whose bodies are built around a skeleton with a backbone. Woodland animals such as beetles, spiders and bees which do not have internal skeletons are classified as invertebrates.

Modelling

Children sort pictures of woodland animals into vertebrates and invertebrates. Use information sources to compare their body structure and the way that they move. Each group can case-study a vertebrate and an invertebrate, and produce models designed to portray their structures. For example, the vertebrate can be built around a wire frame which represents its skeleton. Invertebrates can be built in sections held together with string. Children discuss and research the advantages their vertebrate gains from having a skeleton and whether the invertebrate is better off without one.

Talking points: true, false or not sure?

- Birds could fly faster without a skeleton.
- A butterfly would need much bigger wings to fly if it had a skeleton.
- A deer could run faster without a skeleton.
- A fox needs a skeleton to catch its prey.
- Having a skeleton would help a worm dig a hole.
- A snail would need a skeleton if it had legs.
- A bee would need to be the size of a bird if it had a skeleton.

In groups children discuss the talking points. Encourage them to focus on whether having a skeleton is an advantage considering the way they live. For example, having a skeleton may not be an advantage to a butterfly because it would make it too big and heavy to land on a leaf. Groups present and share their ideas with the class.

Scientific enquiry

Children re-sort the woodland animals into predators and prey. Some of the predators may themselves be prey for other animals. To illustrate the complexity of the feeding relationships, children construct food webs for the woodland in spring. These should include the plants which produce food and the different types of consumers which directly or indirectly rely on plants for their nutrition. Challenge children to construct a food web without any plants in it. Can they explain how the animals would survive? Identify any outstanding *learning needs*.

If possible, organise for the children to make a return trip to the woodland in autumn and explore how it has changed. What benefits does autumn bring for the animals and plants which make the woodland their home? What new problems do they face? Children create autumn food webs and compare them with those they made in spring. Discussion of the webs provides opportunities to assess children's understanding of the woodland habitat and the interdependency of the animals and plants which live there.

Information and teaching resources

BBC Bitesize:

● Invertebrates. *www.bbc.co.uk/education/clips/zmj8q6f*

● Vertebrates. *www.bbc.co.uk/education/clips/ztfnvcw*

● How animal skeletons have adapted. *www.bbc.co.uk/education/clips/zwq6cwx*

● Food chains. *www.bbc.co.uk/education/clips/zjshfg8*

Other websites:

● Woodland animals. *www.woodlandtrust.org.uk/visiting-woods/trees-woods-and-wildlife/animals/*

● Photographs of wildlife. *www.bbc.co.uk/nature/19357078*

● Photographs of common mammals. *www.bbc.com/earth/story/20160406-winning-mammal-photographs*

● Activities to identify birds. *www.stem.org.uk/elibrary/collection/46209/big-schools-birdwatch*

● UK wildlife. *www.bbc.co.uk/nature/places/United_Kingdom*

● Woodland food chains. *www.stem.org.uk/elibrary/resource/34119/education-pack-food-chains*

● Information about habitats. *www.wildwoodtrust.org/files/ks2-habitats.pdf*

Application stage
Children's talk involves trying out scientific ideas

Rainforest

Rainforest covers only 6% of the Earth, but it contains more than half of its plants and animal species. Children use video clips and other resources to explore the diversity of life in a rainforest. They can identify different types of plants and the food they provide for the animals. Each group can produce a power point presentation which depicts the diversity of life and illustrates the feeding relationships.

Children also produce case studies of two mammals. One of the mammals lives high in the canopy and the other spends its time on the ground. Children use information sources to compare the structure of their skeletons to find out how they are suited to their habitat.

Use information sources to explore how rainforests are exploited for their natural materials. What are the advantages and disadvantages for the animals, plants and people who live in that part of the world, and for the well-being of the world generally? Children design 'SOS Posters' designed to alert people to the problems caused by the destruction of rainforests. They can also design and record their own 'SOS Alert' video clips as part of a campaign to save our rainforests.

Information and teaching resources

BBC Bitesize:

- Rainforest.
  www.bbc.co.uk/nature/habitats/tropical_and_subtropical_moist_broadleaf_forests

- Mexican rainforest. *www.bbc.co.uk/education/clips/z939jxs*

- Plants and animals in the rainforest. *www.bbc.co.uk/education/clips/zb2jmp3*

- Guyana's rainforest. *www.bbc.co.uk/education/clips/zq7r9j6*

- Threats to rainforests. *www.bbc.co.uk/education/clips/zfp34wx*

Other websites:

- *The Living Planet*, rainforest destruction. *www.bbc.co.uk/programmes/p00kznts*

Topic: Habitats and food chains

Age group: 9–11 years

Introduction

This topic provides opportunities for children to further develop their understanding of habitats and food chains. Activities start with a review of their existing knowledge, followed by problem-solving activities designed to introduce children to the part detritivores and decomposers play in the woodland's ecosystem. The application stage presents children with the problem of deciding what to do about maintaining native woodland. Children explore different types of woodland and look into the benefits of sustainable management of predominantly native trees.

Scientific view

The diversity of life-forms in a woodland contribute to the well-being of the habitat. Detritivores and decomposers play a crucial role in food chains and webs, and without them the ecosystem would not function. Detritivores such as earthworms, slugs, snails and woodlice feed on dead and decaying plant material and help break it down so that its nutrients can be returned to the soil. Fungi and bacteria assist in the decomposition by secreting enzymes into the organic materials causing them to decay into a liquid form which they can absorb. Once decomposed and returned to the soil, leaf litter provides nutrients for the woodland plants. Detritivores not only help sustain plant life in the woodland but also provide food for a variety of predators such a birds, hedgehogs and mice. In turn these consumers are preyed on by predators higher up the food chain.

Working scientifically

In these activities children will:

- use scientific enquiries to answer questions;
- record and classify data;
- report and present findings orally and in written form;
- use established scientific knowledge to support problem-solving and decision-making.

Health and safety

This topic is a good opportunity to teach children about responsible behaviour and hygiene in the environment. Follow ASE guidelines in *Be Safe!* (2011) when planning these activities.

Exploration stage

Children's talk involves trying out their own ideas

Setting the scene

Start by reviewing what children know about how the woodland changes from season to season. Discuss pictures and video clips taken in spring, summer, autumn and winter. Children use information sources to create a calendar designed to tell a story of how seasonal changes affect animals and plants. Calendars should be illustrated and designed to be hung on a wall. Use the activity to assess children's understanding of habitats and food chains.

Scientific enquiry

In late autumn arrange a visit to the woodland or a local park where children can observe how the deciduous trees are getting ready for winter. Identify the trees and photograph the signs that animals and plants are preparing for winter. Talk about the reasons why some animals hibernate, and why deciduous trees become dormant and shed their leaves. Take drawing equipment so children can make sketches of the woodland floor. They can use their sketches back in the classroom to produce paintings which capture the patterns and colours created by the leaf litter.

Puzzle

Focus children's attention on the leaf litter which carpets the floor of the woodland. Ask them what they believe will happen to it over the winter. Who is going to clear it up? Would it be a good idea if we all came back with brushes, shovels and bin bags and tidied the place up?

Talking points: true, false or not sure?

- If they are not collected the leaves will all pile up.
- People who work in the woodland will sweep up.
- We need to look after the woodland and keep it clean.
- Animals will collect the leaves to make nests.
- Leaves provide a habitat for tiny animals.
- Leaf litter provides food for trees and other plants.
- Leaf litter keeps the roots of the trees warm.

Figure 4.7 **Oak leaf litter**

Source: © Colin Varndell

Discuss the talking points with the children and explore whether nature is able to clean up after itself. Encourage children to think about the leaf litter as a habitat for invertebrates. In groups children explore the leaf litter and observe the invertebrates closely using magnifiers. Use information sources such as picture cards or apps on Tablets/iPads, to identify and then record the animals they find. Which ones feed on rotting leaves and twigs? Can they identify the detritivores? Before you leave the woodland photograph the fungi wherever you can find it. Warn children not to touch or collect the fungi. Make sure children wear protective gloves when exploring the leaf litter.

Story-telling

Back in the classroom children use information sources and keys to classify invertebrates which can be found in leaf litter. They can compare the structure of the invertebrates and classify them according to their number of legs and body parts. How do the insects differ from other types of invertebrates? Children identify the detritivores and discover their role in recycling the leaf litter. They can also discover how fungi and bacteria help to decompose dead leaves and wood, and return the nutrients to the ground. Children tell the story of how nature 'cleans up' the woodland floor by recycling dead leaves, fruits and wood, and returning the nutrients to the soil. They can publish their story in the style of a blog or newspaper article under the title 'Nature doesn't need telling to tidy up.'

Formative assessment

Provide opportunities for children to voice what they have learnt in the exploratory stage. Use evidence from their responses to the puzzle, talking points and other activities to assess differences between children's ideas and the scientific view. Plan how you will use the re-describing stage to help the children address their *learning needs* (see Chapter 1). You may need to modify the activities depending on the collective and individual needs of your children.

Information and teaching resources

BBC Bitesize:

- Beetles. *www.bbc.co.uk/education/clips/z6ynvcw*

- Mini-beasts. *www.bbc.co.uk/education/clips/zkkc87h*

- How twigs and leaves are broken down. *www.bbc.co.uk/education/clips/z2tnr82*

- Nature recycling an oak tree. *www.bbc.co.uk/education/clips/z3g3cdm*

- Decomposing fruit. *www.bbc.co.uk/education/clips/zwx76sg*

- Life cycles and inhabitants of an oak tree. *www.bbc.co.uk/education/clips/z6bvr82*

Other websites:

- Information and activities about habitats. *www.wildwoodtrust.org/files/ks2-habitats.pdf*

- Food webs. *www.tpspublishing.co.uk/download/sample_sciencepacka.pdf*

- Habitat explorer. *www.wildlifetrusts.org/wildlife/habitat-explorer*
- Woodland wild flowers. *www.woodlandtrust.org.uk/visiting-woods/trees-woods-and-wildlife/plants-and-fungi/woodland-wildflowers/*

ASE Journals:

- Primary Science 132 (March/April 2014) *Taking the new curriculum outdoors* by Katherine Forsey.
- Primary Science 132 (March/April 2014) *Outdoor learning can help children flourish in science and across the curriculum* by Hannah Rose and Anneke Kempton.

Re-describing stage

Children's talk involves making sense of scientific ideas

Teacher-led discussion

Talk about woodland pyramid diagrams which include producers and consumers. Ask children to explain why numbers in the food chain steadily decrease from the bottom to the top. What would happen if there were more predators than prey?

Focus on the role of the detritivores and decomposers as nature's recyclers. Children may be surprised to learn that mushrooms help decompose rotting plants. Children may think fungi such as mushrooms are plants. Discuss why they are not plants. Plants have leaves which they use to produce their own food through photosynthesis. Mushrooms do not have leaves and cannot produce their own food. They are therefore not plants. Mushrooms feed by breaking down decaying organic material.

Figure 4.8 **Pyramid diagram showing feeding relationships in the woodland**

Figure 4.9 **Mushrooms feeding on decaying vegetation**

Source: Photo by Anna Loxley

Scientific enquiry

Ask children to create a food chain starting with leaf litter. Challenge them to turn it into a food web which includes predatory invertebrates, as well as mammals and birds. As a class activity children create a giant food web which depicts feeding relationships in the woodland which depend on leaf litter as the primary source of food. The web should include primary, secondary, tertiary consumers and top predators. Children use what they have learnt from the topic to debate whether our local parks are just too tidy. Should we clear the leaf litter from our parks or should we leave it alone and let nature do the work? Children debate the pros and cons. Take an active part in the debates and challenge the children's reasoning. Use the debates, food chains and webs to assess their understanding, and identify any outstanding *learning needs*.

Application stage

Children's talk involves trying out scientific ideas

Protecting native woodland

The biodiversity of the woodland is affected by whether the main tree species are native or not. Often tree species introduced from other countries reduce the light available for wild flowers and other plants that grow on the woodland floor. They can also affect the diversity of invertebrates which have evolved to feed on native trees. Native invertebrates often find imported trees unpalatable.

Children can research the effects that planting non-native trees has on the biodiversity of the woodland. Often non-native coniferous trees such as pine and spruce are grown for their timber. These softwood trees are evergreen and quick to grow compared to native hardwood trees. Children explore different types of woodland, their locations and their uses, and look into the benefits of sustainable management of predominantly native woodlands.

Things to discover include how woodlands are used:

● as a source of timber

● for recreation

● for conservation.

Children can develop informed attitudes towards the preservation of our native woodland. How would they respond if developers wanted to build a housing estate on an area of native woodland? This is a consideration for both urban and rural communities as more and more 'green space' is being targeted for development. Children debate the issues and develop a class policy related to the preservation and development of native woodland in the twenty-first century.

Information and teaching resources

● Native and non-native British trees. *www.woodlandtrust.org.uk/visiting-woods/trees-woods-and-wildlife/british-trees/*

● Introduction to British woodland. *www.countrysideinfo.co.uk/woodland_manage/intro.htm*

● British woodland and their management. *www.countrysideinfo.co.uk/woodland_manage/woodbio2.htm*

● Offwell Woodland & Wildlife Trust. *www.countrysideinfo.co.uk/*

● Publications and downloads from The National Forest. *www.nationalforest.org/document/*

● Managing woodland for wildlife. *www.woodlands.co.uk/owning-a-wood/managing-your-woodland-for-wildlife/managing-your-woodland-for-wildlife.pdf*

● Woodland management in Scotland. *www.biodiversityscotland.gov.uk/advice-and-resources/woodland-management/*

Chapter 5

Rocks, habitats and fossils

Why are the bones of great fishes, and oysters and corals and various other shells and sea-snails, found on the high tops of mountains that border the sea, in the same way in which they are found in the depths of the sea?

Leonardo da Vinci (1452–1519)

Look under a rock and you never know what you will find. Lift one up and there could be a whole new world underneath; it's like visiting a zoo in your own backyard. Look inside a rock and you could find a whole lot more. Geologists have a saying: rocks remember! They remember what life was like many years ago. As Leonardo da Vinci discovered, they record geological change and contain fossil remains of animals and plants that once populated the earth. This chapter presents *ideas for practice* which help children understand the structure of rocks and their uses in the natural and made world. The focus on fossils in the final topic helps children appreciate how they provide important evidence for evolution. Issues related to women in science are also raised.

Topics in this chapter:

- Micro-habitats
- Rocks and fossils
- Fossil hunters

Subject knowledge to support the teaching of these topics can be found in the core book, Loxley, P., Dawes, D., Nicholls, L. and Dore, B. (2018) *Teaching primary science: Promoting enjoyment and developing understanding*, Abingdon: Routledge, Chapter 11: The Earth and beyond and Chapter 15: Adaptation and evolution.

Stones

I like stones
I like to touch
their shape and colour:
such, and such.
Lift one up
and you may find
tiny creatures
there confined
hidden safely
out of sight
in a small
private night.
Stones are quiet,
stones are cold
Some of them
are old – so old
that upon
their surface clings
a pattern of
the strangest things:
leaves, and fish,
and shells and seas
and birds from different
skies than these
when the Earth
had just begun.
Stones know more
than anyone.

'Stones' *by Jean Kenward*

Jean Kenward's poem provides an intriguing narrative to arouse children's curiosity and engage them in a quest for knowledge. Stones are more than lumps of rock; they are homes for a diverse animal community. Lift one up and children will find a whole new world underneath: beetles, worms, ants, woodlice and many other creatures hidden out of sight in the dark damp environment. It is almost like visiting a miniature zoo, and the best thing is, it is right outside our front door.

Stones can provide other surprises. Lift one up and children may find not only creatures living beneath, but also the remains of the strangest creatures that ever lived buried inside the rock. Fossils are patterns of animals and plants. The best of them provide us with details of animals such as flying reptiles and dinosaurs which populated our world many millions of years ago.

Topic: Micro-habitats

Age group: 5–7 years

Introduction

This topic introduces children to the idea that animals live in places which provide for their needs. Children engage with and develop the narrative by exploring creatures which live under stones and in other micro-habitats. In the *application stage* children choose other habitats to explore.

Scientific view

Habitat is the term used to describe the natural home of a group of plants and animals. It is a place where organisms live and reproduce. Organisms within a habitat depend on each other to survive. A micro-habitat is a very small habitat where specific types of organisms live. Food chains can be used to illustrate the feeding relationships within micro-habitats.

Working scientifically

In these activities children will:

- observe closely using simple equipment;
- identify and classify common animals;
- gather and record data to solve questions.

Health and safety

Plan all outside activities following guidance provided by the ASE publication *Be Safe!* (2011). Children should wear disposable gloves and use suitable equipment when searching through leaf litter. Animals should be handled with care and returned to the place where they were discovered.

Exploration stage
Children's talk involves trying out their own ideas

Setting the scene

Find some interesting stones to show the children and read the first 12 lines of the poem. Discuss what children know about stones. What other word could they use? Draw out that stones are also called rocks. Have children ever seen tiny creatures hiding underneath a rock? What did they look like?

Puzzle

Why do tiny creatures hide beneath rocks? What are they hiding from?

Discuss the puzzle with the children. Use it to stimulate conversation about habitats and invertebrates which are often referred to as mini-beasts.

Story-telling

Children draw pictures and talk about creatures which they imagine live underneath stones. Listen to their stories about the things they have found hidden safely out of sight beneath a rock or another object such as a leaf, a log or even a discarded brick.

Modelling

A tray of silver sand and a variety of small plastic animals are needed for this part. Hide each animal beneath a rock in the sand tray. Use models of beetles, ants, worms, slugs, spiders and snakes, but also include animals such cats, dogs and cows, even an elephant. Children look under the rocks to discover the animals. The challenge is to decide whether the animals are in the right habitats. Children classify the animals according to where they think they live, either under a rock or somewhere else. Listen to children's reasoning and assess their understanding of habitats.

Scientific enquiry

Take children on a hunt for tiny creatures which live underneath things. Start with the school grounds, and then organise a trip to a park or woodland, depending on where you live. Working in supervised groups children hunt for animals such as ants, woodlice, worms, slugs, snails, beetles and so on. Take photographs of the different types of micro-habitats. Use information sources to identify the animals and plants that house them. Look out for large animals such as birds, frogs, hedgehogs and squirrels.

Back in the classroom use the photographs to discuss where the tiny creatures were hiding and use talking points to generate debate.

Discuss the talking points in the light of what children learnt from their visit to the woodland or park. Encourage them to give examples and reasons for their responses. Use the photographs to create a display.

Talking points: true, false or not sure?

- Leaves can provide shelter and food for tiny creatures.
- Some animals eat the things they live under.
- Only shy animals hide underneath things.
- Underneath rocks is a safe place to live.
- Some tiny creatures do not like the sun.
- Some creatures hide their eggs underneath leaves.
- Worms hide underground to keep safe from birds.
- Spiders never hide.

Scientific enquiry

Discuss whether the tiny creatures could be hiding from other animals. Explore what the children know about possible predators.

To help children identify predators provide them with picture cards of a wide range of animals such as foxes, rabbits, cats, dogs, sheep, frogs, different types of birds, hedgehogs, mice and so on. Ask children to identify the ones they think might want to eat tiny creatures. Children should justify their thinking. Make a list of animals which feed on tiny creatures. Record the outcomes by adding the predators to the display. Reinforce the idea that the micro-habitats provide good places for the tiny creatures to live because they provide food, shelter and a place to keep safe from other animals who want to eat them.

Formative assessment

Provide opportunities for children to voice what they have learnt in the exploratory stage. Use evidence from their responses to the puzzle, talking points and other activities to assess differences between children's ideas and the scientific view. Plan how you will use the re-describing stage to help the children address their *learning needs* (see Chapter 1). You may need to modify the activities depending on the collective and individual needs of your children.

Re-describing stage

Children's talk involves making sense of scientific ideas

Teacher-led discussion

Use video clips and animations to introduce the concept of a woodland habitat and micro-habitats within it. Talk about how the habitat provides for the needs of animals that live there.

Use the display to create simple food chains, for example: leaves ➤ snails ➤ birds. Children create food chains involving different animals. If you think it appropriate, introduce terms such as herbivore, carnivore and omnivore.

Story-telling

Children create a painting which tells the story of their favourite tiny creature hiding in its micro-habitat. It is important that children use information sources to study the anatomy of their creatures carefully before they create their pictures. Although we do not expect the pictures to be identical representations of the creatures, we should expect them to have the right number of legs, antennae, eyes and so on. Children can expand their story verbally to describe the advantages the creature gains from living in its micro-habitat.

Children continue to tell their story through movement. They can use video to study how their favourite creatures move and choreograph a mini-beast dance. Fill the hall with objects underneath which the children can crawl. Finish the dance with a hot-seating activity in which the class have to guess each other's favourite creature. The class can only ask three questions about the creature to identify it. The hot-seater can only answer 'yes' or 'no' to their questions. Use the story-telling activities to identify any outstanding *learning needs.*

Information and teaching resources

BBC Bitesize:

- What is a woodland habitat? *www.bbc.co.uk/guides/zc42xnb*
- The insects living on a decomposing tree. *www.bbc.co.uk/education/clips/zg9g4wx*
- The life cycle and inhabitants of an oak tree. *www.bbc.co.uk/education/clips/zx3ygk7*
- Woodland, pond and ditch habitats. *www.bbc.co.uk/education/clips/znm76sg*

Other websites:

- Woodland animals. *www.woodlandtrust.org.uk/visiting-woods/trees-woods-and-wildlife/animals/*

Application stage

Children's talk involves trying out scientific ideas

Habitats around the world

Children will have seen television programmes which depict animals in a wide variety of habitats around the world. Listen to their stories about their favourite programmes and the animals which most interest them. There is a wide range of websites which provide remarkable video clips of different types of terrestrial, fresh water and marine habitats. Start by exploring some of the clips on the *BBC Nature Wildlife* site.

In groups children choose a habitat to research and decide what they would like to find out about the animals and plants that live there. Using suitable information sources, they can seek answers to their questions and discover feeding relationships between different organisms. They can tell stories about a day in the life of their favourite animals.

Children can also design and make a mobile which depicts a simple food chain from their chosen habitat.

Information and teaching resources

● BBC Nature Video Collections. *www.bbc.co.uk/nature/collections*

Topic: Rocks and fossils

Age group: 7–9 years

Introduction

These activities provide opportunities to explore the structure and properties of sedimentary rocks and find out how fossils are formed. The application stage focuses on the uses of rock (natural stone) for building purposes through the ages.

Scientific view

The terms stone and rock are both commonly used to describe materials from which the Earth's crust is made. There are different types of rock. Limestone and sandstone are sedimentary rocks usually formed at the bottom of lakes and oceans. Sedimentary rocks form layers called strata which can often be seen in exposed cliffs. Fossils which are remains of once-living organisms are mainly found in sedimentary rocks.

Working scientifically

In these activities children will:

● use different scientific enquiries to answer questions and solve a puzzle;

● set up simple comparative tests;

● make systematic observations;

● record findings using tables;

● use results and information to draw conclusions.

Health and safety

Risk assess all visits outside the classroom following school polices and ASE guidelines in *Be Safe!* (2011). Also, follow guidance on the use of mouldable materials and on sanding or chipping rocks.

Exploration stage

Children's talk involves trying out their own ideas

Setting the scene

You will need a sedimentary rock with a fossil in it. They are easily purchased or borrowed from a museum or the local secondary school. Fossils can often be found in natural stone products sold by building merchants.

Puzzle

Read the poem by Jean Kenward to the children. What do they think the author is saying? What does she mean by 'stones know more than anyone'? Let children respond to these questions and explore their thinking about the nature of stones.

Figure 5.1 **Fossil of a trilobite**

Source: iStock

Talking points: true, false or not sure?

- Buildings can be made from rocks.
- Rocks are made in factories.
- Rocks are natural parts of the earth.
- Rocks are found; they are not made.
- Some of the rocks found in our gardens may be older than the dinosaurs.
- Fossils are remains of dead animals which can be found in rocks.

Listen to the children's reasons for their arguments and assess what they know about rocks.

Scientific enquiry

To add to their knowledge of rocks, children explore their properties. Use identifiable rocks which they can observe with hand lenses and test in different ways. Children decide on their own tests, or use Table 5.1 as a guide. They can also bring their own rocks to be tested.

Focus on the properties of the sedimentary rocks such as chalk and sandstone. Can children imagine how they were made? Can they guess how old they are?

Story-telling

Children use information sources to tell the story of how sedimentary rocks are made. Groups present their stories to the class. As part of the story-telling show children the rock with a fossil in it. Ask how it could have got there.

Children use information sources to identify the fossil and explore other types. Can they find fossils of birds, fish, leaves and shells? The most common fossils are those of ancient shellfish which include clams, snails, ammonites and trilobites which are over 540 million years old. Groups create annotated posters to illustrate how fossils are formed, and use them as part of a presentation on the origins of fossils.

Formative assessment

Provide opportunities for children to voice what they have learnt in the exploratory stage. Use evidence from their responses to the puzzle, talking points and other activities to assess differences between children's ideas and the scientific view. Plan how you will use the re-describing stage to help the children address their *learning needs* (see Chapter 1). You may need to modify the activities depending on the collective and individual needs of your children.

TABLE 5.1 Rock testing

Type of rock	What is its colour?	Does it mark paper?	Is it easy to mark with a nail?	Can it be sanded?	Does it contain grains or crystals?	Does it float?	Children's questions
chalk							
sandstone							
shale							

Information and teaching resources

ASE Journal:

● Primary Science 129 (Sept/Oct 2013) *Earth science: It's all about the processes* by Chris King.

Re-describing stage

Children's talk involves making sense of scientific ideas

STEM ambassador

Organise a visit from a local expert or a STEM ambassador to talk about different types of rock and how fossils are formed. Alternatively organise a visit to the local natural history museum which provides talks on rocks and fossils. Children should make a list of the questions which they would like to ask the expert, including the puzzle from the poem. Share these questions with the expert in advance and discuss the things most likely to interest the children. Ask the expert to focus on how fossils are formed.

Teacher-led discussion

Following the visit, reinforce the key ideas by using animations and video to talk about how sedimentary rocks and fossils are formed. Address the puzzle by discussing how fossils provide evidence of animals and plants which lived long ago. Fossils help us understand how living things on the earth have changed over time.

Modelling

Children make their own mould and cast fossils of small shells. Visit the Eden Project Great Fossil Hunters website for information about how to make fossil casts.

Children re-think their posters and modify them in the light of what they now know about fossils. Display the posters and ask children to explain the changes. Assess their understanding of sedimentary rock and fossils. Address any outstanding *learning needs*.

Artwork

The shapes, colours and patterns created by fossils are fascinating. Children can use images of fossils available on the web as inspiration for their own work of art.

Figure 5.2 *Jurassic Coast by Sarah Hough, 2009 (digital)*

Source: Hough, Sarah / Private Collection / Bridgeman Images

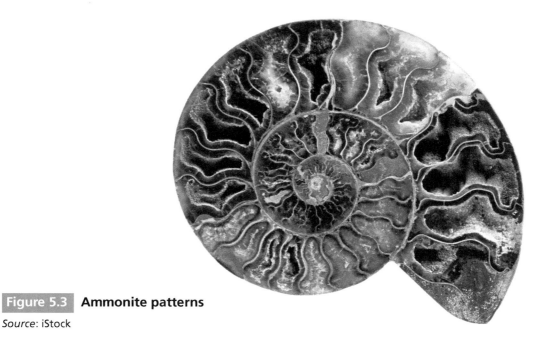

Figure 5.3 **Ammonite patterns**

Source: iStock

Information and teaching resources

BBC Bitesize:

- How dinosaurs' footprints get made in solid rock. *www.bbc.co.uk/education/clips/zwqqnbk*

- Formation of limestone and basalt rock. *www.bbc.co.uk/education/clips/z3b9jxs*

- How to calculate the height of a dinosaur. *www.bbc.co.uk/education/clips/z3kkxsg*

Other websites:

- The great fossil hunters. *www.edenproject.com/learn/schools/lesson-plans/great-fossil-hunters*

- Rocks. *http://bpes.bp.com/primary-resources/science/ages-7-to-9/rocks/*

- Nature – Prehistoric life. *www.bbc.co.uk/nature/fossils*

- Fossil hunting game. *www.ngkids.co.uk/games/dinosaurCove*

Application stage

Children's talk involves trying out scientific ideas

Using natural stone

Explore the local environment and take photographs of buildings and other objects which are made from stone. Distinguish between manufactured materials such as bricks and concrete, and natural materials such limestone, sandstone, granite and marble.

Children use information sources to find out how natural stone has been used through the ages for building purposes. Groups can choose different periods in history and research how civilisations around the world used stone as a building material. They should identify the type and structure of the stone used by each civilisation. They draw plans and make clay models of well known stone structures, and display them together with the findings of their research.

Topic: Fossil hunters

Age group: 9–11 years

Introduction

This topic builds on children's understanding of fossils. The activities focus on the work of the renowned fossil hunter Mary Anning, and explore how fossils can provide evidence of evolution. In the application stage children are asked to consider the role of women in science.

Scientific view

Fossils provide evidence for Darwin's theory of evolution. Pterosaurs lived among the dinosaurs and became extinct around the same time. Pterosaurs were flying reptiles. Modern birds did not descend from pterosaurs; their ancestors were small, feathered, terrestrial dinosaurs. It can be claimed that dinosaurs are not extinct; they are now covered in feathers, and can be found alive and well in our gardens!

Working scientifically

In these activities children will:

● plan different types of enquiries to answer questions;

● take measurements using scientific equipment;

● record data using line graphs;

● use test results to support or refute arguments;

● report findings of their enquiries in written and oral form;

● identify scientific evidence that has been used to support the theory of evolution.

Health and safety

Be aware of any children with allergies to feathers. Follow school policy on e-safety when children are using the internet for extensive research.

Exploration stage

Children's talk involves trying out their own ideas

Setting the scene

Mary Anning was one of the most successful fossil-collectors of all time. She was born in the seaside town of Lyme Regis in 1799 and made her living from selling fossils. During the nineteenth century, well-to-do tourists to Lyme, including Jane Austen, would often buy fossils as souvenirs of their visit.

Puzzle

In 1829 Mary found the first British fossil of a pterosaur, commonly known as a pterodactyl. Newspaper headlines gave it the nickname of the 'Flying Dragon'. When alive it was thought to have looked like the creature pictured in Figure 5.5.

Figure 5.4 **Mary Anning**

Source: Alamy

Figure 5.5 **Scientists' impression of a pterosaur**

Source: iStock

Scientists at the time puzzled over Mary's 'Flying Dragon'. They knew it had reptilian characteristics and because of its wings wondered if it provided an evolutionary link between reptiles and birds. It was later given the scientific name Dimorphodon Macronyx. Do the children think pterodactyls are extinct, or are they alive and well flying around their neighbourhood?

Scientific enquiry

In groups children debate whether Mary's 'Flying Dragon' provides evidence that birds evolved from a type of pterosaur. Start by listing the characteristics that define birds, mammals and reptiles, and compare them with the structure of the Dimorphodon Macronyx which they can research on the web. Was Mary's dragon more bat-like than bird-like? Do flying reptiles exist today? What evidence can they find that the Dimorphodon Macronyx was an evolutionary link between reptiles and birds? Is there enough evidence to draw convincing conclusions? Groups come together to share the outcomes of their research.

Story-telling

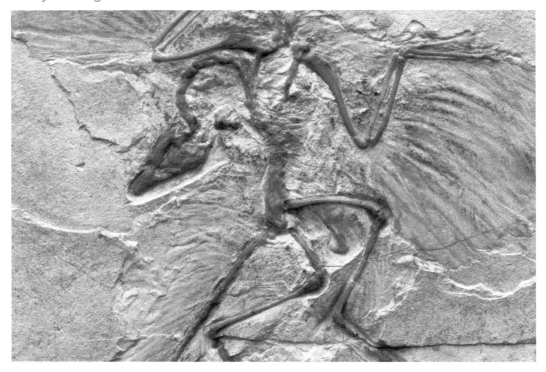

Figure 5.6 **Archaeopteryx**

Source: iStock

Archaeopteryx is considered to be a transitional fossil between dinosaurs and birds. It has a mixture of reptilian features such as a long bony tail and toothed jaws, along with avian features such as feathers and wings. Children explore how the first archaeopteryx fossil was discovered and how it was seized on as evidence of evolution by Darwin's supporters in the nineteenth century. They can explore up-to-date fossil records which provide evidence that birds are related to dinosaurs and tell the story of how this evidence supports Darwin's theory of evolution.

Scientific enquiry

Why did birds evolve feathers considering prehistoric reptiles could fly without them? Was flight the only reason? Groups can use information sources to research the advantages feathers provide for birds. They can devise experiments to test the properties of feathers.

Possible investigations include:

- the structure of feathers;
- the waterproof properties of feathers;

- the insulation properties of feathers;

- the aerodynamic properties of feathers;

- benefits of growing feathers rather than wool or hair.

Groups communicate the results, evidence and conclusions from their enquiries in a scientific paper which they present orally as part of a class conference on the evolution of birds. Suggest ways to ensure that presentations are clear, articulate and well organised. Discuss how scientists present their work at conferences and in peer-reviewed journals.

Scientific enquiry

Children can engage in reversing evolution! They start by making an x-ray drawing of a bird and then imagining how it would look if it evolved back into a dinosaur. Children draw annotated pictures to illustrate different stages in its evolution back to a dinosaur. Discuss their drawings and probe their understanding of evolution.

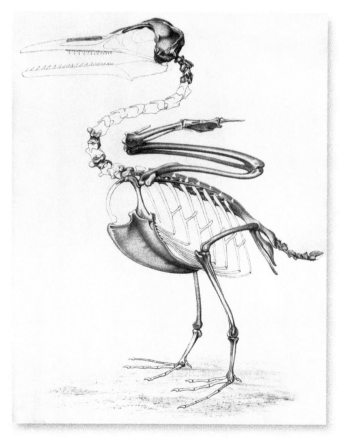

Figure 5.7 **Scientific drawing of toothed bird fossil**

Source: iStock

Formative assessment

Provide opportunities for children to voice what they have learnt in the exploratory stage. Use evidence from their responses to the puzzle and other activities to assess differences between children's ideas and the scientific view. Plan how you will use the re-describing stage to help the children address their *learning needs* (see Chapter 1). You may need to modify the activities depending on the collective and individual needs of your children.

Information and teaching resources

Website:

● Carnivora. *http://carnivoraforum.com/topic/9772230/1/*

ASE Journals:

● Primary Science 138 (May/June 2015) *Animals don't just grow feathers when they want to …* by Terry Russell and Linda McGuigan.

● Primary Science 136 (Jan/Feb 2015) *A fossil-based enquiry day stimulates children to think scientifically* by Denise Balmer.

● Primary Science 131 (Jan/Feb 2014) *Evolution in action* by Mike Dennis, Adrienne Duggan and Deb McGregor.

Re-describing stage

Children's talk involves making sense of scientific ideas

Teacher-led discussion

Use video clips and animations to illustrate the concept of evolution and how it has led to the diversity of life we have on the planet. Discuss how fossils provide evidence for believing evolution takes place. Explore the work of David Attenborough and show clips from his videos which illustrate evolution and the diversity of life on Earth.

Scientific enquiry

Did you know that Trafalgar Square in London is well known for its magnificent lions? I am not talking about the bronze statues which commemorate Nelson's victory, but real lions which roamed the area along the banks of the River Thames 125,000 years ago. They lived together with hippos, hyenas, elephants and rhinos. How do we know? Because their fossils have been found during building works.

Children go fossil hunting on the web to find animals that are now extinct in the UK but still live in other parts of the world. They report their finds on maps of the UK showing pictures of fossil evidence, and the locations of the habitats in which they lived. All information can be pooled and presented in a display.

Story-telling

The last lines in the poem claim that 'stones know more than anyone.' As the topic illustrates, fossils found in rock have a lot to tell us about life on Earth long ago and how our ancestors evolved into organisms that populate the Earth today. Ask children to write their own poems about fossils. Use their poems as starting points to probe their understanding of the evidence fossils provide for evolution. Identify any outstanding *learning needs*.

Information and teaching resources

BBC Bitesize:

- Timeline of life on Earth. *www.bbc.co.uk/education/clips/zyjqycw*
- Why did the brown bear evolve into the polar bear? *www.bbc.co.uk/education/clips/ztw8q6f*
- Why do giraffes have long necks? *www.bbc.co.uk/education/clips/z4ys34j*
- Why do tortoises look different in different parts of the world? *www.bbc.co.uk/education/clips/zfx2tfr*
- Why do panda bears eat bamboo? *www.bbc.co.uk/education/clips/zjcg9j6*

Other websites:

- Tree of life. *www.youtube.com/watch?v=H6lrUUDboZo*
- The Dino Directory. *www.nhm.ac.uk/discover/dino-directory/index.html*

Application stage

Children's talk involves trying out scientific ideas

Mary Anning

Children research the life of Mary Anning and the contribution she made to our understanding of fossils. Mary sold fossils of creatures such the ichthyosaurus and plesiosaur to prominent scientists who named and described them in science journals, while failing to mention Mary as the person who had discovered them.

Discuss whether Mary deserved to get more credit from the scientific community for her discoveries. It could be argued that she was not a trained scientist and the money she received for the fossils was reward enough. On the other hand, if science at the time progressed because of her activities, she surely deserved recognition for her contribution. Children debate whether scientists such as William Buckland should have given Mary more credit in their scientific publications. To inform the debate children research social and cultural attitudes to women in the nineteenth century. Science was dominated by a few prominent men who were members of the Royal Society in London. The Society was founded in 1660 and did not permit women to become fellows until 285 years later in 1945.

Talking points: true, false or not sure?

- Science is a man's thing.
- Mary wasn't clever enough to be a scientist.
- Mary never had an opportunity to become a scientist.
- Mary found important scientific evidence.
- William Buckland could have written his scientific papers without Mary's fossils.
- Mary did not contribute to the development of scientific knowledge.
- Knowledge without evidence is not worth having.

Children can add some talking points of their own which emerge from their debate. Try to arrive at an informed and well-reasoned consensus about Mary's contribution to science.

Women scientists

Children explore the lives and achievements of women scientists from the nineteenth century to the present day. Information is available on the Royal Society's website.

Even today, science is considered by some people to be a man's thing. Why is this? What opportunities are there for women? How many of the children are open to a STEM-related career? Invite women in science-related professions to talk to the children about their careers.

Information and teaching resources

- Influential women scientists. *https://royalsociety.org/news/2010/influential-british-women/*

Chapter 6
Living things

There are some four million different kinds of animals and plants in the world. Four million different solutions to the problems of staying alive.

David Attenborough, broadcaster and naturalist (b. 1926)

What is life? How can we tell one thing is alive and another is not? The dog next door which never stops barking is alive, and so is the tree which blocks out the sun. But my computer is not alive, and neither is the rain falling from the clouds. Children intuitively often know when something is alive, but may not be able to explain why. The *ideas for practice* presented in the chapter focus on characteristics of living things. Young children start by examining the behaviour of living things, compared to objects which have never lived. Later topics focus on how our bodies function in order to keep us alive, and also examine how different stages in an animal's life cycle help the species survive.

Topics in this chapter:

● Living or non-living?

● Body parts

● Life cycles

Subject knowledge to support the teaching of these topics can be found in the core book, Loxley, P., Dawes, D., Nicholls, L. and Dore, B. (2018) *Teaching primary science: Promoting enjoyment and developing understanding*, Abingdon: Routledge, Chapter 14: Diversity and Chapter 16: Health and well-being.

Talking about living things

'It was on a dreary night of November,' recalled Victor Frankenstein. 'I collected the instruments of life around me, that I might infuse a spark of being into the lifeless thing that lay at my feet… I saw the dull yellow eye of the creature open; it breathed hard, and a convulsive motion agitated its limbs.'

In its time the story of Frankenstein captivated and alarmed its readers, not only because he had created a 'monster', but because the possibility of resurrecting the dead seemed a real possibility at the time. It wasn't unusual for scientists to perform experiments on freshly hung convicts, making their limbs jerk and their backs arch using massive electrical currents.

In the nineteenth century, scientists were obsessed with discovering the nature of life. There were widespread reports that insects could be created by electrifying stones, and that it was possible for the spark of life to be spontaneously generated, to naturally spring out of non-living things, an action which could be attributed to God.

Today we know a lot more about the nature of life, but we still do not know for sure how it originated here on Earth. All known life on Earth consists of carbon-based compounds containing hydrogen, oxygen and nitrogen. Living things use energy to organise these chemicals into complex molecules, from which their parts are built. Cells are the most basic unit of living things. Organisms such as bacteria and yeast are made from single cells. In more complex organisms such as humans, cells combine to make tissue, organs and organ systems.

We can decide whether something is living or non-living by examining its behaviour. The key characteristics of living organisms are movement, reproduction, sensitivity, growth, respiration, excretion and nutrition. Non-living things can share some of the same characteristics but not all of them. For example, a robot uses energy to move and can sense the world around it, but it cannot grow, reproduce or nourish itself in the ways living things do. The desire to produce offspring in humans and other animals is very strong because of the need to reproduce to enable the species to survive.

During their life cycles humans and other animals go through various stages which include birth, growth and reproduction. Offspring of different animals begin their lives in different ways. Chicks burst out of their eggs where they have been kept warm and safe by their brooding parents during the incubation period. The parents watch over them, feed them and keep them warm and safe until they are ready to fend for themselves. On the other hand, most mammals give birth to live young who, in many cases, are able to stand and move unaided within minutes. It takes human babies up to 18 months to learn to walk, whereas a baby antelope is up and walking within minutes and has the strength to run with the herd within days. Running is an important survival skill for antelopes, and the sooner they can keep up with the herd, the safer they are.

As they grow and mature, animals develop skills allied to particular senses which help them survive. Predators such as owls learn to hunt using their keen sense of sight and hearing. Bats and dolphins learn how to use their 'in-built' sonar to locate and catch prey, while blind moles rely on their sense of smell to seek out worms in the darkness underground. Chameleons are amazing reptiles which are famed for their ability to change colour, though not all species can. In some cases, the colour change is used as camouflage, but more often it is actually a form of communication used to attract potential mates or warn off rivals. To keep safe, chameleons are able to revert to a default colour that merges with their habitat; green for a jungle species and beige for a desert one. Not so well known is their ability to rotate their eyes individually in their sockets, so they can see simultaneously both behind and in front of them. This natural skill helps them hunt their prey and at the same time avoid their predators.

As animals grow, their bodies change to enable them to cope with each phase of their lives. Young male deer develop by growing bigger and stronger, and by the time they are mature they have grown imposing antlers which they can use to compete for the females. As humans develop, they too compete for partners by the way they dress and act. Their bodies get bigger and stronger as they become more capable of looking after themselves, and a family. Most significant is the time they move from the childhood stage to adolescence. This is the time of puberty when they begin to change both physically and emotionally as their bodies prepare to be able to reproduce.

Ideas for practice

Topic: Living or non-living?

Age group: 5–7 years

Introduction

This topic provides opportunities for children to explore the characteristics of living things, and to learn to recognise whether something is living, dead or has never lived. Case studies and enquires in the application stage enable children to discover how animals rely on their senses, and also to evaluate how they use their own senses.

Scientific view

Living things behave in ways that are essential for keeping them alive and healthy. For example, animals grow, have babies, move, eat and drink, breathe, excrete their waste and sense the world. Non-living things may exhibit some of these characteristics, but not all of them.

Working scientifically

In these activities children will:

- ask and try to find answers to questions;
- perform simple tests;
- identify and classify objects as living, dead or never having lived;
- use their observations and ideas to answer questions;
- gather and record data to help in answering questions.

Health and safety

You may need to check with CLEAPPS or SSERC for advice on the safety of battery-operated toys. Adults should supervise all battery charging or changing. Check any toys you will be using for damage.

Environmental visits present excellent opportunities to teach children about common hazards, including hazardous litter, animal faeces, and irritant or poisonous plants, and to teach them about hygiene after handling soil or plant matter. Plastic gloves are recommended. As you risk assess these activities, always refer to the *Be Safe!* (2011) booklet.

Exploration stage

Children's talk involves trying out their own ideas

Setting the scene

Create a display of toys which can move and make sounds. Include some programmable and remotely operated toys. Demonstrate how the toys work. Children compare the toys with what humans and different animals can do. Can they think of two things a dog can do, which cannot be done by any of the toys? Ask them to decide whether the toys are living or non-living things. Some children might think a toy is living because it is able to move, or mimic other characteristics of living things. Encourage them to provide reasons for their views. Probe children's thinking and their understanding of the behaviour of living things.

Puzzle

How can we tell whether something is living? List all the things children think living things are able to do.

Scientific enquiry

Refer to the ASE publication *Be Safe!* (2011) for health and safety guidance when planning the activity. Take children into the school grounds or local park in search of living things. With care children can collect a range of small objects off the ground including seeds, leaves, stones and twigs. They can also take photographs of any animals they see, and of other objects including trees, plants, cars, buildings and so on. Talk together about which are living and which are not living. Help children distinguish between things which are dead and things which have never lived.

Back in the classroom children classify their objects and photographs as living, dead or have never lived. Working collaboratively, groups choose an example from each category and present the reasons for their choices to the rest of the class. Encourage them to justify their choices. Use the photographs and objects to make a display which represents the children's ideas.

Talking points: true, false or not sure?

- Everything in the world is living.
- Only animals are living.
- Toys that move are living.
- A tree is not living because it never moves.
- Plants are living because they grow.
- We know dogs are living because they have puppies.
- Teddy bears are not living things because they never eat anything, and never go to the toilet.

Discuss the talking points, encourage children to elaborate on their answers. Help them identify some basic characteristics of living things such as the need to eat, the ability to move, grow and produce offspring.

Story-telling

Ask the children to imagine they are space scientists who have been sent on a mission to a faraway alien planet. They arrive on the planet to find some very strange looking creatures living there. Although they look like frogs, they are much bigger and, surprisingly, are able to speak their language. It is possible that the frog creatures are not real animals; they may be robots sent from another world! Some clues to the nature of the frog creatures are:

1 They are all the same size.

2 There are no young frog creatures to be seen.

3 There is no food or water on the planet.

4 There are no other animals on the planet.

How could the children find out whether the frog creatures are living or non-living? What questions could they ask the frog creatures to find out what they are able to do? Of course, the frog creatures may not know whether they are living or non-living, so there is no point in asking them directly. Children could act out the story with some taking on the role of the frog creatures being questioned by others playing the space scientists.

Formative assessment

Provide opportunities for children to voice what they have learnt in the exploratory stage. Use evidence from their responses to the puzzle, talking points and other activities to assess differences between children's ideas and the scientific view. Plan how you will use the re-describing stage to help the children address their *learning needs*. You may need to modify the activities depending on the collective and individual needs of your children.

Re-describing stage

Children's talk involves making sense of scientific ideas

Teacher-led discussion

Children can be helped to recognise the characteristics of living things. Start, for example, with a focus on the ability to grow. Compare changes over time that happen to a baby with changes that are likely to happen to toys. The baby will grow and change – toys will remain the same, or become damaged in ways that they cannot repair themselves. Discuss what else a baby can do, including eating, hearing, seeing, smelling and feeling. How many of these things can non-living things such as a teddy bear or a doll do?

Talk about how living things reproduce by having babies or offspring. Use BBC Bitesize video clips to illustrate the life cycles of humans, and of common animals such as a butterfly and a frog. Reinforce the idea that having offspring which grow into adults is a characteristic of living things. Point out that the alien frog creatures were not living things because they did not eat and they did not grow, they were all made the same size, and they had no young frogs.

Together, develop a list of characteristics that living things have in common. Use the list to help children re-think their ideas from the exploration stage and, finally, to re-classify the objects in the display.

Story-telling

Ask children to consider the following scenario. In the corner of a field are a young oak tree and a car. No one goes near the field for many years. Children draw a picture to show the corner of the field. What has happened to the oak tree? What has happened to the car? Children compare and justify their pictures with reference to what they know about living and non-living things. Probe children's thinking and address outstanding *learning needs*.

Information and teaching resources

BBC Bitesize:

- The life cycle of animals. *www.bbc.co.uk/guides/zttckqt#zyyw7ty*
- Is it alive? *www.bbc.co.uk/guides/zs73r82#zcdf34j*
- Common characteristics of living things. *www.bbc.co.uk/education/clips/zcd9wmn*
- Growth and change. *www.bbc.co.uk/education/clips/z4tmhyc*

Application stage

Children's talk involves trying out scientific ideas

Walking home a child hears a noisy bus, feels the sun's heat, smells and tastes a cake from the bakery and sees a friend waiting by the door, and has used all five senses. All animals have similar senses, but most have developed a particularly keen sense or two to match their specific survival needs. In this stage children explore how living things rely on their senses, and discover how powerful their senses can be.

Dogs – Bloodhound

Figure 6.1 **Bloodhounds have very sensitive noses**

Source: iStock

Show children a picture of a bloodhound and talk about its ability to find things by smelling them out. The membrane in a bloodhound's nose which detects odours is fifty times bigger and a million times more sensitive than a human's. Listen to children's stories about their dogs.

Provide groups with containers of familiar liquids such as water, lime juice, vinegar, cola, tea, coffee, milk and so on. Have gauze and lids on the containers and label them A, B, C, etc. Without looking inside the containers, children take off the lids and use their sense of smell to describe what they think is inside. Groups try to agree on words to describe the smell of each liquid.

How sensitive are their noses? How far away can they smell the liquids? Help children plan their own tests to find out how far away they can smell a peeled lemon or an orange. How far away do they think a bloodhound could detect an orange? Help children use information sources to discover more about how bloodhounds and other animals rely on their sense of smell.

Cats and other pets

Figure 6.2 **Cat's eyes**

Source: iStock

Ask children to bring in photographs of their cats. Supplement them if need be with pictures of cats from the web. Ask children with cats at home to describe their behaviour. Do their cats ever go out at night? Listen to children's stories and probe their ideas about why cats are able to see in the dark better than we can.

Cats require only one-eighth of the light that we need to see by. Children can compare pictures of a cat's eyes with their own. Use pictures from the web which show how the shape of a cat's pupils changes. In the day they are narrow slits, but at night they open wide to help them see. Children work in groups to draw the shapes of each other's eyes. Focus their attention on the shape of their pupil, and compare with that of a cat. Discuss how animals which see well in the dark have big pupils in their eyes. Children re-design and re-draw their own eyes so they would be able to see better than a cat in the dark. Display their pictures, along with the photographs of the cats.

Talk together about other pets which the children have at home. What do their pets like doing? Compare children's pets with those displayed in the RSPCA picture gallery. Which of the pets from the gallery can the children recognise? Which do they think have eyes which enable them to see in the dark?

Talk about looking after pets. Working in groups, ask children to identify three things pets need to keep happy and healthy. Groups come together to share ideas. Between them, can the class think of five things pets need? Compare children's ideas with the five needs published by the RSPCA on their interactive website:

● Animals should live in a comfortable environment at the right temperature.

● Animals should have enough space and the right sort of toys and housing so they can behave normally.

● Most pets need company, but it must be the right sort of company. However, some animals prefer to be alone.

● Animals need to have access to fresh water all the time and should be fed the right amount and type of food to keep them fit and healthy.

● Animals should be protected from pain, suffering, injury and disease and should be treated by a vet if they are sick or injured.

Help children to make sense of the RSPCA statements, and to understand what they mean for how they should treat their pets. Children use pictures and words to describe the basic needs of animals we keep as pets. They could create a poster of an animal of their choice, with its picture and a description of its needs. Possible titles for the poster could be 'What makes me happy?' or 'Thanks for looking after me.'

To complete this part, children could imagine themselves to be their favourite pet animal. They design and make face masks, and imitate the movement of the animal. They can tell stories from the animal's point of view.

Bats

A bat is a mammal which can fly. It is not a bird because it has no feathers. Use video clips and other information resources to tell children its story. Explain how it cannot see very well and uses sound to find its way around at night. Look at the relative sizes of bats' ears.

Children investigate being a bat. Working in small groups, they find out what it is like to use echolocation to identify their prey. One of the group who does not mind wearing a blindfold takes on the role of the bat and the others become the prey. In the playground or other large

Figure 6.3 **Brown long-eared bat**

Source: iStock

space the prey spread out around the bat. One of the prey is chosen to respond to the beeps made by the bat. The game starts with the bat making beeping sounds and the prey providing the echo by beeping back. The bat uses its ears to detect where the echo is coming from and walks towards its prey. To start with the prey should stand in one place, but the game can be made more fun if the prey is allowed to slowly wander around. Children take turns to be bat and prey. Help children use information sources to discover other animals which depend on their sense of hearing.

Superhuman senses

Ask children to imagine what it would be like if they had a superhuman sense. Perhaps they could see at night like a cat, or smell things like a bloodhound or hear things like a bat? Would it be an advantage to have such powerful senses? Ask them to tell a story in which they used their superhuman power for a good purpose. They can orally record their story, and play it back to the class. Encourage children to respond respectfully to one another's stories. What did they like best about them?

You can do this next activity in the playground, the park or even better in the woodland. Tell children that they are going to find out which senses they use most. Children start by sitting apart in the chosen space and concentrate on all the things around them. Provide them with a clipboard and a piece of paper. Put a dot in the middle of the paper to represent where they are and draw symbols to represent the things they notice. What do they notice first? Is it a sound, a smell, something they feel or something they see? Can they use two or more senses at once? Talk about the things which the children sensed most and record them on a chart back in the classroom. Try to establish which of their senses the children relied on most. Try the same exercise in a different location and compare results. Ask children to imagine how they would live without their senses. What would they still be able to do? Discuss a range of points of view. Support or challenge their ideas by modelling reasoned arguments.

Information and teaching resources

BBC Bitesize:

- What are the senses? *www.bbc.co.uk/guides/zxy987h*

- The five senses. *www.bbc.co.uk/education/clips/zwh6n39*

- Habitats – where do different owls live? *www.bbc.co.uk/education/clips/zn84d2p*

- Nocturnal animals and birds. *www.bbc.co.uk/education/clips/zsshfg8*

Other websites:

- Night owls. *http://video.nationalgeographic.com/video/wd-ep2-owls*

- Animals with the best sense of smell. *http://largestfastestsmartest.co.uk/animals-with-the-best-sense-of-smell-in-the-world/*

- RSPCA Education. *http://education.rspca.org.uk/education/home*

- Picture gallery. *http://education.rspca.org.uk/education/teachers/gallery*

- The five needs for pets. *www.rspca-education.org.uk/the-five-needs*

Topic: Body parts

Age group: 7–9 years

Introduction

This topic provides children with opportunities to identify key organs inside their bodies and to describe the function of the digestive system. They also explore the purpose of their skeleton and how their muscles work. In the application stage children apply their understanding to the design of robots.

Scientific view

Humans are complex organisms made up of different parts which perform vital functions to keep us alive and healthy. The digestive system consists of a number of organs such as the mouth, oesophagus, stomach and small and large intestines. These parts work together to break down our food so it is small enough to be transported by our blood to different parts of our body. Our skeleton, together with our muscles, provides support for our bodies, helps us move and protects our vital organs.

113

Working scientifically

In these activities children will:

- use different types of scientific enquiries to answer questions;
- set up simple practical enquiries;
- take accurate measurements using standard units;
- record findings using tables and bar charts;
- use results to draw simple conclusions.

Health and safety

Consider all aspects of safety when using tools and materials by referring to the ASE booklet *Be Safe!* (2011). Choose appropriate materials, glues and tools. Classroom management and supervision of all cutting and making activities are vital.

Exploration stage

Children's talk involves trying out their own ideas

Setting the scene

Start this topic by telling a child-friendly version of Mary Shelley's classic tale of *Frankenstein*. Usborne Young Readers has published a version suitable for this age group. Discuss the story with the children. Would Frankenstein's creation have had the same body parts as themselves?

Puzzle

What parts do they have inside their bodies?

Scientific enquiry

Working collaboratively in small groups, children draw full size outlines of their body shape and draw in the organs they think are most essential for life. This can be done using chalk in the playground, or using large sheets of paper on the floor of the school hall. Take photographs to record their chalk drawings. Children come together to compare their pictures, and explain why the organs they have drawn are essential for life. Probe children's understanding of the digestive system. Focus on their reasons for how they have connected, or not connected, organs together.

Teacher-led discussion

Frankenstein's creature was big and strong. Focus on the size of its skeleton and its muscles. Talk together about the purpose of our skeletons and how our muscles help us move. How do we know when our muscles are working? Ask children to demonstrate the action of their arm muscles.

Scientific enquiry

This enquiry is for children to find out how their muscles work. They will need their PE kit for this activity. Arrange the playground into areas for different events such as high jump, long jump, shot put (use soft ball), sprinting, javelin (foam), hurdles and triple jump (hop, skip and jump). Working together in groups children measure and record their performance for each event. Data for the whole class can be correlated and displayed in suitable tables and bar charts in the classroom.

After each event children record which part of their body they used, and whether they could feel their muscles working. Draw out what they understand about the parts of their bodies which influenced their performance, especially their muscles. Groups work collaboratively to decide on the role skeletons and muscles play in the way they move and lift objects. They then come together to share what they know about the purpose of their skeletons and their muscles.

The enquiry could then be extended to explore how physical factors such as height, arm length, leg length and weight influence the children's performance for each event.

Scientific enquiry

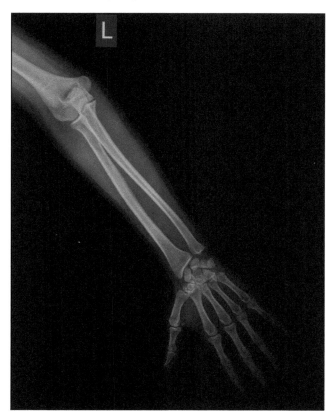

Figure 6.4 **X-ray of arm bones**

Source: iStock

Show children an x-ray picture of the arm. Help them identify the radius, ulna and humerus bones. Working in groups, ask them to imagine how the muscles are attached to the bones to make the arm move. They can examine their own arms to imagine how the muscles are attached. By holding a small weight with their arm out-stretched, children can feel their arm muscles working. They will sense the tension in their arm muscles as they take the strain. When they lift their arms and weight upward they can feel with their other hands the biceps muscles on the top of their arms contract, and the triceps muscles on the back of their arms relax. What happens when they lower the weight? If the movement is repeated a few times children will start to feel the strain in their muscles. They record their results by drawing the bones shown on the x-ray, and then draw in where they think the muscles are attached. Small groups can combine to form bigger groups and compare and share their ideas. Groups continue to combine and share ideas until they agree on a diagram which represents their shared understanding of how the muscles in the arms work.

Modelling

Children can make simple models to show how their muscles move their arms. They use elastic bands to represent the muscles, and thick card to make the bones. Let children design and make their own models. If they need help, instructions for making models can be found on the web. Ask children to demonstrate their models, and use them to explain how their muscles control the movement of their arms.

Formative assessment

Provide opportunities for children to voice what they have learnt in the exploratory stage. Use evidence from their responses to the puzzle and other activities to assess differences between children's ideas and the scientific view. Plan how you will use the re-describing stage to help the children address their *learning needs* (see Chapter 1). You may need to modify the activities depending on the collective and individual needs of your children.

Re-describing stage

Children's talk involves making sense of scientific ideas

Teacher-led discussion

Start by discussing children's drawings and address inaccuracies concerning the organs in the upper part of the body. Use video clips to compare their ideas with the scientific view. Make it clear that all the organs play their role in keeping us alive. Focus on the digestive system. Wear a tabard model of the digestive system and use it to discuss the function of the main organs. The BBC Bitesize clip 'Digestion – how does breakfast affect your day?' demonstrates an entertaining way of modelling digestion. Use the ideas to model digestion for the children. Children can make their own tabard models using card or fabric.

Modelling

Here is another way to model how the digestive works. You will need a large space for this activity. Tell children they are going to role-play the digestive system. Some children will act the role of the mouth, others form a tunnel to represent the oesophagus, others link hands in a ring to form the stomach, and others need to work out how to form the large and small intestines. Use large pieces of foam which can be squashed in different parts of the system to represent the digestive process. Help children narrate the process as the food (foam) is chewed in the mouth, passed along the oesophagus, squashed and broken up in the stomach, then absorbed into the blood stream in the small intestine, and finally as the waste passes in to the large intestine (colon). This activity is fully described in the *Primary Science* article by Dan Davies.

Teacher-led discussion

Again focus discussion on children's drawings, but this time talk about their understanding of the skeleton. Talk about the purposes of the human skeleton and focus on support, protection and movement. Explain how the rib cage protects the heart and lungs from accidental damage, and how the brain is protected by the skull. Discuss the purpose of the joints and the role they play, together with the muscles, in movement. Show children some x-ray photographs of different joints which are available on the web. Use video clips, models and diagrams to support the discussion.

Modelling

Finish this part by revisiting the puzzle. To solve the puzzle the class work together to make a full-size display of human anatomy, focusing on the upper part of the body. The display should include models of key organs, bones and muscles. Make the display interactive by attaching the organs with Velcro. Print descriptions of their functions on the back of the organs, so they are revealed when the organs are removed. Use the activity to address any outstanding *learning needs*.

Design and make

Children can design and make simple jigsaw puzzles based on the Frankenstein theme, which involve assembling Frankenstein's creation using pieces depicting different body parts.

Information and teaching resources

BBC Bitesize:

- How do muscles and bones work? *www.bbc.co.uk/education/clips/ztt4p39*

- Muscles needed for movement. *www.bbc.co.uk/education/clips/zpp6n39*

- Skeletons. *www.bbc.co.uk/education/clips/ztfnvcw*

- An introduction to the main organs of the human body. *www.bbc.co.uk/education/clips/zyqfg82*

- Digestion – how does breakfast affect your day? *www.bbc.co.uk/education/clips/zcsdycw*

ASE Journal:

● Primary Science 127 (March/April 2013) *Taking a giant tour to explore the human body* by Dan Davies.

Exploration stage

Children's talk involves trying out their own ideas

Robotic sea turtles

Figure 6.5 **Bio-hybrid robot**

Source: Robot created by researchers at Case Western Reserve University and imaged by Dr. Andrew Horchler. Webster, V., Chapin, K., Hawley, E., Patel, J., Akkus O., Chiel, H., Quinn, R. '*Aplysia californica* as a Novel Source of Material for Biohybrid Robots and Organic Machines', in *Biomimetic and Biohybrid Systems: Proceedings of Living Machines 2016.* July 18-22, 2016 Edinburgh, Scotland.

Shelley's *Frankenstein* was a story about a scientist who tried to create the perfect human being, but unintentionally created a pitiful creature. Of course, Shelley's story is pure fiction. In real life the idea of creating a human or any other animal from 'spare parts' is absurd, or is it? Researchers in America have combined body parts from a sea slug with flexible 3-D printed components to build 'bio-hybrid' robots that can crawl like sea turtles on the beach. Children can use information sources to find out about the world of robotics, and discover what present-day robots are capable of doing.

Robotic arms

Robotic machines are widely used in industry because of their speed, endurance and precision. Articulated machines such as robotic arms are commonly used for jobs such as painting, welding, precision movement of objects, packaging and making electrical circuit boards. Controllable robotic arm kits are widely available from toy and educational suppliers and can be used to demonstrate the link between science, computing and technology. Are there similarities between the robot arm and a human arm? Children can compare the variety of movement of the robotic arm with the capability of their own arms. Which arm is more versatile and capable of doing a wider range of jobs?

Design a robot

Children imagine they are engineers of the future and have been asked to design a robot which can out-run and out-jump any living thing on earth. They start with research into how animals run and jump. Groups look for patterns which link the structure of an animal's skeleton to its ability to run fast and/or jump high.

The idea is to combine the characteristic body structures of fast and mobile animals into the design of a robot. The children's design drawings do not need to be detailed, but they should be able to explain why the structure of the robot helps it run fast and jump high. Groups make interactive 2D models of their robots to add to the anatomy display. When groups present their designs to the class, they should explain the research on which the design is based, and how they worked together to agree on the final design.

Information and teaching resources

● Researchers build a crawling robot from sea slug parts and a 3-D printed body. *www.sciencedaily.com/releases/2016/07/160718111611.htm*

Topic: Life cycles

Age group: 9–11 years

Introduction

This topic provides opportunities for children to describe and compare the life cycles of a variety of animals, including humans. Activities enable children to examine the reasons why some animals lay eggs, while others give birth to live young. They also explore the stages of development of humans from birth to adulthood. In the application stage children explore the life cycle of the Large White butterfly, and examine the harm it can do to crops. This leads to an evaluation of the advantages and disadvantages of chemical and organic farming, and their effects on life cycles.

Scientific view

All living things follow a life cycle specific to their species which includes birth, growth and reproduction. Because it is a continuous cycle, there is no start and no end to the process. Individual animals die, and their offspring grow up to take their place in the life cycle of the species. Some species produce offspring that are very similar to the adult form, such as most mammals, birds and reptiles. Others produce offspring which undergo a transformation, called metamorphosis, before developing into an adult.

Working scientifically

In these activities children will:

- plan and carry out different types of scientific enquiries;
- record data and results using diagrams and tables;
- report and present findings from enquiries in oral and written forms such as displays and presentations;
- use established scientific knowledge to support or refute ideas and arguments.

Health and safety

Children in step-families and those who are adopted may be sensitive about the subject of heredity, so this must be approached with care. Check on school policy regarding children bringing in and displaying photographs of themselves. Reference should also be made for this topic to the school Sex Education policy. The visit to the allotment needs to follow ASE guidance for hygiene and care for the environment, as well as any sensitivities or allergies.

Exploration stage

Children's talk involves trying out their own ideas

Setting the scene

Figure 6.6 **Pair of barn owls meet and greet in an oak tree**

Source: iStock

Start this topic by showing children pictures of barn owls in an oak tree. Ask them to describe the differences and similarities between an owl and a tree. Ask groups to write on cards three differences and three similarities. Display and discuss the cards. Any statements on which agreement cannot be reached can be listed under the heading 'not sure'.

Talking points: true, false or not sure?

- An owl is living thing, whereas a tree is not.
- Both owls and trees grow old and die.
- Both owls and trees produce babies.
- Trees cannot move, but owls can.
- Both owls and trees lay eggs.
- Both owls and trees are predators.
- Both owls and trees reproduce.
- Both owls and trees produce young which grow into adults.
- Both owls and trees depend on light to survive.

Discuss children's responses to the talking points. Probe their thinking, and find out what children know about the characteristics of living things. Ask children to compare the life cycles of birds and trees.

Story-telling

Children work collaboratively, with the help of information sources, to compare the life cycle of an oak tree with that of a barn owl. A feature of the story is to compare the development of the offspring as they grow to maturity. Children might think that life cycles refer to individual animals, and start with their birth and end when they die. Point out that the cycle of life describes changes that happen in a species, not to individual animals. As the name implies, a life cycle is a continuous process. Use children's stories to stimulate discussion about life cycles of living things. Are the life cycles of all plants the same? Are the life cycles of all animals the same? What are the similarities between the life cycles of plants and animals?

Children extend their story-telling by using information sources to explore and compare the life cycles of a range of woodland mammals and birds. They should focus on the development of the animals from birth to maturity, and discuss the times when the offspring are most vulnerable. Children can tell their stories in the form of a documentary, using IT to present evocative images and video.

Puzzle

Why do owls, and other birds, lay eggs and not give birth to live young? Children can start to resolve the puzzle by listing all the animals they know which lay eggs and those which give birth to live young. Listen to children's initial ideas and display their theories.

Story-telling

This is an opportunity for creative writing. Children are to write an imaginary story entitled *Why elephants do not lay eggs*. It can be written in the style of a traditional folk tale, and told by the children verbally. Their stories can be recorded. When children tell their stories, probe their thinking about the advantages for elephants in giving birth to live young. Focus their attention on the gestation period for an elephant compared to the incubation period for an owl or a chicken. Is it feasible for an elephant to incubate an egg for 20 months? How could an elephant keep an egg warm? How could it store enough food inside the egg to keep the young alive for 20 months? How big would the egg have to be?

Birds often lay multiple eggs. Would this be an advantage for an elephant? Imagine if an elephant were able to lay multiple eggs with an incubation period of about 30 days. The young would be very small, but there would be more of them. Would this be an advantage or a problem for an elephant? Being a mammal, how would an elephant feed such a litter?

Figure 6.7 **Elephant cartoon**

Scientific enquiry

Children use information sources to compare the incubation periods of different birds and the gestation periods of different mammals.

TABLE 6.1 Animal reproduction

Animal	Type of animal	Gestation/ incubation period (days)	Average number of offspring per pregnancy	Average life span of the animal
owl	bird	31–32	5–6	
chicken	bird	21	up to 30 in a clutch	
elephant	mammal	640	1	
domestic cat				
robin				
human				
eagle				
others				

The data could be extended to include reptiles, amphibians and fish, or to look at further stages of each animal's life. What conclusions can children draw from the data?

● Which types of animals have the longest and shortest gestation periods?

● Is there any relationship between the size of the animal and the length of its gestation period?

● Is there any relationship between the size of the animal and the number of offspring per pregnancy?

● Is there any relationship between the average lifespan of an animal and the number of offspring per pregnancy?

● Why do you think some animals give birth to multiple offspring and some only one or two?

● Which of the animals require the longest period of parental support before they leave their parents and begin having babies themselves?

● How do we (humans) compare with other animals? How long do parents look after their children before they 'fly the nest'?

● Humans can continue to care for their offspring long after the children have offspring of their own. Grandparents can play an important part in the upbringing of their grandchildren. Do any other animals act in this way?

Scientific enquiry

Use information sources to compare the development of humans with other mammals. Children could look at the time from birth before they can walk, how long the adults nurse their young and which mammals retain life-long bonds with their parents. For example, orangutans breastfeed, ride on their mother's body and sleep in her nest for seven years. The young stay with their mothers at least until a new baby arrives. How does this compare with other mammals? It would be interesting to compare what different mammals are able to do at the same ages. Children can ask questions and research answers to their own questions.

Formative assessment

Provide opportunities for children to voice what they have learnt in the exploratory stage. Use evidence from their responses to the puzzle, talking points and other activities to assess differences between children's ideas and the scientific view. Plan how you will use the re-describing stage to help the children address their *learning needs* (see Chapter 1). You may need to modify the activities depending on the collective and individual needs of your children.

Information and teaching resources

BBC Bitesize:

- Life cycle of a dandelion. *www.bbc.co.uk/education/clips/zpcg9j6*
- The life cycles of different organisms. *www.bbc.co.uk/education/clips/zwrn2p3*
- Characteristics of living things. *www.bbc.co.uk/education/clips/zy9tfrd*
- Life cycles. *www.bbc.co.uk/education/clips/zp62tfr*
- The life cycle of a plant. *www.bbc.co.uk/education/clips/zc234j6*

Re-describing stage

Children's talk involves making sense of scientific ideas

Teacher-led discussion

Start this part by addressing the puzzle. It is generally thought that birds lay eggs because they would find it difficult to fly with their offspring developing inside their bodies. One of the problems of laying eggs is keeping them safe from predators. Most mammals do not need to fly, and by giving birth to live young they can protect their offspring from predators as they develop inside their bodies. Use video clips to illustrate the concept of a life cycle, and explain how it has no start or end point, because it refers to a species and not an individual animal.

Teacher-led discussion

Ask adults and children, if it is permitted, to bring in photographs of themselves at a range of different ages, starting with when they were a baby. Display the baby pictures, and see if children can identify their classmates. Ask volunteers to talk about their own pictures, focusing on the way they have developed since birth. The stories should include their earliest memories and describe things which they can do now which they could not do as a baby. Discuss when they think they were most vulnerable, and what their parents did to protect them. When do they think they would be ready to look after themselves? Children finish this part by drawing a timeline to indicate stages of growth and development of humans.

Discuss children's timelines and talk about stages of development such as babyhood, childhood, adolescence and adulthood. Which stage do they think they have reached in their development? Ask them to justify their responses.

Scientific enquiry

This activity focuses on the physical differences between babies, children and adults. If possible, arrange for a mother to bring her baby into school. Ask the mother to talk about the needs of her baby. Children ask questions concerning the development of the child. Take photographs to start a display of human development.

Carefully measure different parts of the baby, including the size of its head (chin to the top), the body size (height), length of its arms and legs, and the size of its feet. Children then work out ratios of head to body length, size of feet to body length, arms to body length and legs to body length. More data can be collected using photographs of new born babies or using life-like dolls which are available from educational suppliers.

Working in groups children take the same measurements of their peers, and work out the ratios. Use the data to compare growth patterns for babies and the children in the class. Talk about and explain any differences. Corresponding data can be collected from the youngest children in the school, as well as adults. Children look for patterns in the data and draw conclusions about how humans develop physically.

Children can extend the enquiry by looking for answers to their own questions, and comparing their results with Leonardo da Vinci's *Vitruvian Man*. They can explore Leonardo's work and ideas on human anatomy.

Teacher-led discussion

Explain that when children develop from childhood to adolescence, they change physically as well as emotionally while their bodies prepare to be able to reproduce and have babies. Show children a video clip of the physical changes that occur in puberty and discuss their questions. Talk about puberty and how, as it approaches, people's emotions change. Discuss how they may deal with their feelings towards themselves, their family and others in a positive way. You can find detailed plans for teaching about puberty on the Hamilton Trust Website. Invite a paediatrician or a midwife into school to talk about their work and to answer children's questions. Plan the session in advance with the visitor.

Information and teaching resources

BBC Bitesize:

- Growing up and puberty videos. *www.bbc.co.uk/education/topics/z3xxsbk/videos/1*

- The life cycles of animals. *www.bbc.co.uk/guides/zttckqt*

- What is the life cycle of an animal? *www.bbc.co.uk/education/clips/zt96sg8*

Other websites:

- Life cycles. *www.stem.org.uk/elibrary/resource/36134*

- Vitruvian man. *www.youtube.com/watch?v=IN-q3Bj9a_A*

- Proportion – Da Vinci's *Vitruvian Man*.
  http://math.afterschooltreats.com/wfdata/frame119-1019/pressrel2.asp

Application stage
Children's talk involves trying out scientific ideas

Metamorphosis

Use video clips and photographs to talk about the life cycle of animals which undergo transformations as they develop. For example, frogs, toads, bees and butterflies undergo metamorphosis as they develop from birth to maturity. Children depict these different stages by drawing pictures on long strips of paper which can be formed into a loop, to show that a life cycle is continuous. Use the activity to address outstanding *learning needs*.

The Large White butterfly – A case study

Figure 6.8 **Cabbage White butterfly**

Source: Photo by Anna Loxley

The Large White butterfly, commonly called the *Cabbage White,* is the bane of allotment holders all over the British Isles. The larvae of this species can reach pest proportions, and decimate cabbages to the point that they become mere skeletons of their former selves. The female is distinguished from the male by the presence of two black spots, together with a black dash, on the forewing upper side. The Large White is found in a wide variety of habitats, including gardens, allotments, parks, meadows, open grassland, and hedgerows. The Large White produces two broods a year, one in spring and one in summer. Children can use information sources to trace its life cycle, to identify its habitat and to find out about its vulnerability to the ichneumon wasp. Children can also explore the life cycle of the ichneumon wasp.

Organise a visit to a local allotment or other place where members of the cabbage family are grown. Talk to the owners about pests and how they control them. Ask their permission to look at some of their plants closely. Groups can record the different types of cabbages, the numbers of caterpillars on each, and the number of plants with holes in their leaves. They can take photographs of the damage caused by caterpillars. The Large White is not a species of conservation concern so larvae can be collected and kept in appropriate conditions in the classroom until the adult emerges from the pupal stage. Caterpillars collected from allotments can be fed on the same type of fresh vegetables as those on which they were found. Children can use information sources to design a suitable home for their caterpillars. Release the adult butterflies back into the area in which their larvae were found.

Real-life dilemma

Children use the data collected at the allotment, and the conversations of the owners, to judge what problems Large White butterflies present for vegetable growers. Working in small groups, children discuss methods to limit the damage caused by caterpillars. They can consider the following options commonly used by gardeners:

- Inspect plants regularly and pick off the pale yellow butterfly eggs and caterpillars.
- Grow rows of companion plants such as celeriac or French marigold to mask their smell.
- Grow plants under fine netting or horticultural fleece which prevents butterflies laying their eggs.
- Use a biological control consisting of a mixture of pathogenic nematodes.
- Spray soap and garlic water on the cabbage to mask its smell, to keep butterflies away.
- Spray plants with a pesticide which kills the caterpillar as it crawls over the sprayed leaves.

Groups consider each of the methods, together with their own ideas, and try to decide which they think are the best methods. Groups come together to present their ideas, and the reasons behind their decision making. Pick up on the use of insecticides and explore the advantages and disadvantages.

Organic gardening

Invite a STEM ambassador to school to talk about vegetable farming. Discuss the session with the ambassador in advance, and provide a list of questions prepared by the children. Ask the ambassador to talk about organic farming, and to present both the positive and negative arguments.

Finish this part by debating the virtues of organic and chemical farming. Groups should prepare their arguments from a range of information sources. These should include consideration of the effects farming methods may have on the life cycles of various animals. Children record the outcomes of the debate by producing a display which illustrates the advantages and disadvantages of each method.

Endangered species

When the life cycle is broken, the species becomes extinct. Today there are many species of animal around the world which are in danger of extinction. Children use information sources to discover some of our endangered animals. They may be surprised to discover how many are in danger of extinction.

High on the endangered list is the green turtle. Green turtles are hunted and their eggs are collected by humans, a legal practice in some countries. They are also threatened by destruction of nesting areas and foraging areas in the sea. Sometimes green turtles are accidentally caught in fishing nets, further decreasing their population.

Children find out about the life cycle of the green turtle and what happens to it at each stage of its life. They explore the reasons why it is in danger of extinction, and how many of the problems are caused by human activity. Children can research a wide variety of endangered animals and compile their own *Red List of Endangered Species*. The list should include the life cycles of the animals, the reasons they are endangered and whether human activity has played a part. Children can make recommendations concerning how the animals can be saved.

Information and teaching resources

BBC Bitesize:

- How caterpillars change into butterflies. *www.bbc.co.uk/education/clips/zfqd7ty*

Other websites:

- The life cycle of the Large White butterfly. *www.youtube.com/watch?v=l2SApdV210ky*
- Cabbage White butterfly emerging from its cocoon. *www.youtube.com/watch?v=qXPa9IdleVc*
- Ichneumon wasp. *www.arkive.org/ichneumon-wasp/ophion-luteus/#text=Biology*
- Endangered species. *www.arkive.org/endangered-species/?gclid=CPr8y72skc4CFWsW0wodEcUPrw*
- The IUCN Red List of Threatened Species. *www.iucnredlist.org/details/4615/0*

Chapter 7
Decomposers

If you don't like bacteria, you're on the wrong planet.

Stewart Brand, writer on environment and sustainability (b. 1938)

Decomposers play a crucial role in maintaining ecosystems by recycling nutrients from dead and decaying organisms back into the soil, making them available to growing plants. Detritivores, such as woodlice, also play an important recycling role. In this chapter, young children explore woodlice habitats, both outdoors and more closely in the classroom. Later topics focus on fungi, such as mushrooms and mould, and examine how micro-organisms can be both helpful and harmful.

Topics in this chapter:

- What have woodlice ever done for us?

- What have mushrooms ever done for us?

- What has mould ever done for us?

Subject knowledge to support the teaching of these topics can be found in the core book, Loxley, P., Dawes, D., Nicholls, L. and Dore, B. (2018) *Teaching primary science: Promoting enjoyment and developing understanding*, Abingdon: Routledge, Chapter 13: Interdependence, Chapter 15: Adaptation and evolution and Chapter 16: Health and well-being.

What have decomposers ever done for us?

People hug trees and talk to plants, so why not say thanks to the decomposers for doing all of nature's dirty work? Decomposers are nature's waste management and recycling agents, who are responsible for the decay of dead animals and plants. Decay is an essential life process which returns organic materials used by animals and plants to grow and keep healthy when they were alive, back to the soil after they die. All living things borrow the materials that make up our bodies; on death they need to recycle them back so other plants and animals can use them. Without the decomposers life on this planet as we know it would not exist.

Many of us enjoy eating mushrooms. They contain essential nutrients and are good for our health. I am of course talking about the edible ones! Providing a good meal is not the only thing mushrooms do for us. Mushrooms, along with other types of fungi, are some of nature's chief decomposers. The part we call a mushroom is the fruiting part of the fungus; the equivalent is an apple on a tree. The main part of the fungus lives out of sight, either beneath the soil, or inside wood or any other organic material it feeds on. If a mushroom pops up on your lawn, you can be sure that hidden underground is a mass of very thin thread like structures called hyphae which are responsible for digesting organic material in the soil.

Did you know that the largest organism in the world is a mushroom? Deep in Oregon's Blue Mountains in the USA, there is a fruiting fungus which occupies nearly four square kilometres. Compared to this, the world's largest animal, the blue whale, is a mere dwarf. The fungus is believed to be around 2,400 years old, but could possibly be even older, making it not only the biggest, but also one of the oldest living organisms.

Fungi are aided in their work by some of the soil's smallest creatures, bacteria. Bacteria are single-celled micro-organisms which can only be seen through a microscope. Both bacteria and fungi can be found hard at work in the garden compost. Bacteria dominate the early process in compost and probably will make up 80–90% of compost microbes. A teaspoon of fertile soil can contain anywhere from 100 million to a billion bacteria, and a teaspoon of compost might have ten times that number. Bacteria feed on simple, easy to digest carbon compounds such as fresh young weeds and leaves. Fungi can break down all sorts of organic matter including wood. On walks in the woodland it is not usual to see fungi of various sorts living on fallen logs, or even growing out of the trunks of healthy trees.

If we look beneath the rotting vegetation on the woodland floor we will find all kinds of animals busily helping the fungi and bacteria to break down the detritus and return nutrients to the soil. Woodlice break up rotting wood so the fungi can digest it more quickly. Millipedes, dung flies, maggots, worms and some kinds of beetles all play their roles in helping bacteria and fungi to recycle precious organic material.

As if maintaining the ecosystem is not enough, the decomposers also serve us in many other ways including the food, medicine and agricultural industries. Yeasts have been used in bread making and the production of alcohol since the beginning of civilisation. In modern times penicillin and other fungi-based medicines have been developed to protect us from disease. Today, the use of fungi to produce medicines is a multibillion dollar worldwide industry. Bacteria are also put to good use, especially in the sewage industry, and are used to clean oil spills and break down pesticides, herbicides and other soil pollutants. If we want to know what decomposers have done for us, then we can look in our homes, hospitals, industries and all over the natural world to find them working their socks off to help feed us and keep us safe.

Ideas for practice

Topic: What have woodlice ever done for us?

Age group: 5–7 years

Introduction

This topic provides children with opportunities to study the woodlouse both in its habitat and more closely in the classroom. The purpose is to make the children aware of the important role this tiny animal plays in the world around them, and how its activity supports the lives of a variety of plants and animals in its habitat. In the application stage children help build homes for wildlife in the school grounds, for conservation purposes and also to enable them to study their behaviour.

Scientific view

Habitats are places which provide for the basic needs of the organisms which live there. Basic needs for woodlice include food and shelter from predators. Woodlice eat fallen wood and leaves, and other rotting vegetation. They are one of nature's ways of cleaning up the environment.

Working scientifically

In these activities children will:

- ask questions;
- observe closely using simple equipment;
- identify and classify;
- use observations to answer questions.

Health and safety

This topic involves working outdoors and handling materials such as rotting vegetation, as well as woodlice. Children should wear disposable gloves when working outdoors and wash their hands thoroughly before and after handling any animals. Working surfaces and equipment should be cleaned thoroughly immediately after use, and surplus food for the woodlice should be removed before it begins to decompose. Care should also be taken to protect each mini-beast when handling and to return it to its habitat. Refer to the ASE safety code for keeping and studying animals in the booklet *Be Safe!* (2011) when planning the topic.

Exploration stage

Children's talk involves trying out their own ideas

Setting the scene

Making bug hotels is a popular way of studying invertebrates. Some can be quite substantial structures made from many layers of materials. Those sold commercially can be more like 'luxury apartments' than basic bug accommodation.

Figure 7.1 **Bug hotel**

Source: iStock

Show children a picture of a commercially-made bug hotel. Ask them whether they know what it is, and what it is used for. Can children name any tiny creatures which could live in the bug hotel? Can they explain why they would want to live there?

Story-telling

Provide children with pictures of invertebrates such as bees, wasps, slugs, snails, woodlice, beetles, millipedes or spiders. Ask them what they know about these tiny animals. Where do they think they live, what do they eat and how do they keep safe? Listen to their stories and the language they use when describing the animals. Discover what children know about these common invertebrates. Children can tell their own stories of particular animals in words and pictures.

Scientific enquiry

Using the pictures children sort the animals into three groups depending on the number of legs. Groupings could be based on: animals with no legs, those with six legs and those with more than six legs. Help children distinguish between the insects and the other animals.

Puzzle

Project a large picture of a woodlouse on the IWB. Tell the children that woodlice are very special animals. Without them many other animals and plants would not be able to live. Do the children know where they live and what they do which is so special?

Figure 7.2 **Woodlouse**

Source: iStock

Scientific enquiry

Take the children on a hunt for woodlice in the school grounds. Look under objects on the ground including logs, bricks, stones, dead leaves and so on. Take magnifiers and cameras so children can observe and take photographs of the woodlice in their micro-habitats. Ask children why they think the woodlice live underneath things on the ground. What do they think they eat? What animals may eat them? Use the word 'habitat', as well as 'home', when talking about where the woodlice live. Discuss children's ideas and probe their thinking about how the woodlice survive in their habitat.

Working with adult support, children can collect a small number of woodlice in secure transparent containers to take back to the classroom. In the classroom, they can use magnifiers to closely observe the woodlice. They record their observations through drawings and by creating a fact sheet. Talk about the appearance of a woodlouse including its 14 legs, its outer shell and its antennae. Refer to the woodlice as small animals, and use pictures to compare their appearance to insects and other invertebrates.

Children can observe how the woodlice move when put into a large tray. Do they move in a straight line, or do they zig-zag or keep turning? What happens if a light is shone on them? What happens if one side of the tray is made damp, while the other remains dry? Some woodlice curl up into a ball when threatened. These are called pill woodlice. Do children think curling up into a ball is a good way for the woodlice to protect themselves?

Modelling

In a large space children can mime the movement of woodlice. On occasions freeze-frame the movement and ask them to explain the way they are moving. How does their movement mimic the way woodlice move? How would they react to a predator such as spider? Children can roll up into a ball and try to roll away. Why would curling up into a ball help the woodlice survive?

Scientific enquiry

Ask children to make a home for their woodlice in the classroom. Working in groups children can discuss what the home should be made from.

Talking points: true, false or not sure?

- A log would make a good home.
- A pile of rotting leaves would make woodlice very happy.
- Woodlice prefer to live in a hole under the ground.
- A cardboard box would make a good home.
- An old shoe would make a great home for woodlice.
- Woodlice would love living in a sand castle.
- Woodlice do not need a big home; they would prefer to live under a stone.

Let children discuss the talking points in groups supported by an adult. Remind them of the ground rules for discussing talking points (see Chapter 1). Later the class come together and groups share their ideas, and explain their reasons. Pick up on some of the children's ideas when making a home for a woodlice colony.

One way of making the home requires a large plastic container or tank with steep sides, and a loose-fitting top. Dead leaves and soil from the school grounds can be placed in the bottom, with flat stones, twigs and cardboard tubes from kitchen rolls placed on top. Raw potatoes and vegetables can be used for food. Spray the contents of the container with water, and add the woodlice. Place the container in a large black bin or bag to cut out the light. Twice a week replace mouldy food with fresh, and spray the colony with water. Full details of how to maintain an indoor woodlice colony can be found on the CLEAPSS website.

Children can observe the behaviour of the woodlice over a period of weeks. Where do they prefer to live within the tank? What happens when light is shone into the tank? By looking underneath the stones and other objects you may be able to observe whether any offspring are produced. Set up a display close to the woodlice colony which presents facts and information about woodlice. The display can include the outcomes of the outside enquiry, and what children have learnt from observing the colony in the classroom. Ultimately, return the woodlice to appropriate habitats in the school grounds.

Formative assessment

Provide opportunities for children to voice what they have learnt in the exploratory stage. Use evidence from their responses to the puzzle, talking points and other activities to assess differences between children's ideas and the scientific view. Plan how you will use the re-describing stage to help the children address their *learning needs* (see Chapter 1). You may need to modify the activities depending on the collective and individual needs of your children.

Information and teaching resources

● CLEAPSS – indoor woodlice colony.
 http://science.cleapss.org.uk/Resource-Info/Setting-up-an-indoor-woodlice-colony.aspx

Re-describing stage

Children's talk involves making sense of scientific ideas

Teacher-led discussion

Start by addressing the puzzle. Ask children to draw and describe in words the perfect natural habitat or home for woodlice. How would it differ from the one they created in the classroom? Remind them that 'habitat' is the scientific name for where they live in the outside world. Talk about habitats and how they provide food and shelter for the animals that live there. Encourage children to justify their drawings in terms of where the woodlice would find their food and how they would keep safe. Compare children's ideas with video clips of woodlice habitats. Use the videos to talk about how woodlice eat rotting leaves, and wood such as twigs and logs. Focus on their role as detritivores (decomposers) and show how they feed on and break down rotting wood and leaves. Introduce the term herbivore to describe an animal that eats plants. Woodlice are special herbivores because they eat dead parts of plants. They are very special because they are nature's way of cleaning up all the rotting plants.

Scientific enquiry

To see how special woodlice are, children set up micro-habitats consisting of dead leaves, sticks and small logs in different areas of the school grounds which are free from woodlice. Take photographs to record the occupiers at regular intervals and identify other small animals which share the habitat with the woodlice. Over time, children evaluate whether they created a good place for woodlice to live. Which habitat did they prefer? Display the photographs to show how the woodlice and other animals colonised the different habitats. Talk about the display and what it tells us about the behaviour of woodlice. Encourage questions and address any outstanding *learning needs*.

Modelling

With the support of an adult, children can make 3D woodlice models using plastic cups, drinking straws with a bendy section, sticky tape, sheets of card and other materials. Also make a model of an insect to contrast with the structure of a woodlouse. Make it clear that woodlice are not insects, because all insects have six legs. Compare woodlice to pictures of crabs and lobsters. Point out that woodlice are small relatives of these creatures. Can children see any similarities?

Use the models as part of a display depicting a garden habitat. Include models of other creatures which are commonly found in gardens. Also include at least one predator which is part of the same food chain as a woodlouse.

Information and teaching resources

BBC Bitesize:

- The insects living on a decomposing tree. *www.bbc.co.uk/education/clips/zg9g4wx*
- The life cycle and inhabitants of an oak tree. *www.bbc.co.uk/education/clips/zx3ygk7*

Other websites:

- Common Woodlouse.
  www.arkive.org/common-woodlouse/oniscus-asellus/video-00.html
- Woodlice for kids. *www.youtube.com/watch?v=JjX2pO6irGg*
- Nuffield Foundation – Practical work for learning woodlice.
  www.youtube.com/watch?v=dhSOO5ChIlU
- Making models of woodlice *www.bbsrc.ac.uk/documents/real-bugs-23-43-pdf/*
- Making a maze for woodlice. *www2.schoolcircular.co.uk/lib/attachments/ CLEAPPS_PST_Autumn_2014_Newsletter_60_Weds_8_November_2014.pdf*

Application stage

Children's talk involves trying out scientific ideas

Providing homes for wildlife

There are things which can be done to attract wildlife into the school grounds, and stimulate children's interest in the natural world. For example, providing homes for wildlife not only helps to protect animals from ever diminishing habitats, but also helps connect the children to nature. Having a hand in building and maintaining homes for wildlife in the school grounds can make children aware of the great variety of animals which share their environment and provide the first step towards developing a life-long interest in animals and their welfare. Invite a STEM ambassador or someone from the RSPB into school to talk about how to protect and support wildlife at school and home.

Here are some ideas taken from the RSPB and the British Hedgehog Society websites for turning your school grounds into a haven for wildlife.

1   Make your own 5-star bug hotel (see Figure 7.3)

     A simple way of creating a home for wildlife is to stack a number of builder's pallets on top of each other. Make sure they are secure and fill the spaces with things for invertebrates, small mammals and amphibians to live in.

2   Create an underground den for amphibians in need

     Find a corner of your school grounds where plants struggle to grow and create an underground den where frogs, toads and newts can find safe lodging through the winter's chill. Some frogs may use the mud at the bottom of ponds, but many amphibians spend the winter on land. Give them a helping hand by digging tunnels where they can keep warm and safe throughout the winter.

3   Build a cozy hedgehog home (see Figure 7.5)

     Cozy winter nests are essential if hedgehogs are to survive hibernation. In autumn, hedgehogs begin to build nests from leaves, grass, straw, bracken and reeds. They build nests under hedgerows, fallen logs or piles of brushwood. In gardens they often build their nests under sheds, compost heaps, shrubs and piles of leaves, or behind stacks of logs. Most often the owner of the garden never knows about their winter guest.

     At school you may wish to provide your uninvited, yet welcomed guest, with a more permanent home of its own. Any available timber can be used to create a box without a top, with an opening through which the hedgehog can enter. Place the box near the hedge or a hole in the fence facing south. Use bricks to create an entrance tunnel and use a piece of slate with brick on top to create the roof. Leave straw and leaves outside for your guest to use for bedding. You can cover the box in plastic sheeting, soil and twigs to camouflage it and make it really cozy inside. Check whether your guest uses the materials provided, but do not be tempted to open the nest to look inside, and keep the entrance clear. In spring the nest can be opened and cleaned for when your guest returns in autumn.

Figure 7.3 Bug hotel made from builder's pallets

Source: iStock

Figure 7.4 **Hedgehog in need of a home**

Source: Photo by Anna Loxley

Figure 7.5 **Cozy 'hog' home**

Source: Alamy

If you do not want to build a permanent home, you can use a large plastic storage box with a hole cut in it, or even a large terracotta plant pot placed on its side and all but the entrance covered in soil and twigs.

4   Accommodation for solitary bees

Solitary bees are not like honeybees that live in hives. As their name suggests, they make their nests on their own and lay their eggs in tunnels, such as in dead wood or hard soil. Tunnels to attract solitary bees can be made by bundling some bamboo canes together. They can be fixed inside a structure, or just securely tied together and placed in a part of the school grounds least affected by wind. A small shallow dish of water nearby would be appreciated by the bees.

5   Build a nesting box for birds

Nesting boxes provide ideal homes for some of the regular visitors to our gardens. Over 60 species of birds are known to have used nest boxes, including blue, great and coal tits, nuthatches, house and tree sparrows, starlings, spotted and pied flycatchers, robins, house martins, kestrels and tawny owls. Much depends on the type of the box, where it is located and its surroundings. There is a wide range of information on the web to help you build nest boxes in the school grounds. Together with bird feeders and water baths, nest boxes can attract a wide variety of birds for children to study.

Information and teaching resources

● Build a bug hotel. *ww2.rspb.org.uk/makeahomeforwildlife/givenatureahome inyourgarden/gardenactivities/build-a-bug-hotel/*

● RSPB – Giving nature a home. *www.rspb.org.uk*

● Hedgehog homes. *www.britishhedgehogs.org.uk/leaflets/L5-Hedgehog-Homes.pdf*

● Nest boxes for small birds. *https://rspb.org.uk/makeahomeforwildlife/advice/helpingbirds/nestboxes/smallbirds/ index.aspx*

● How to get hands-on with wildlife. *www.bbc.co.uk/nature/22720319*

Topic: What have mushrooms ever done for us?

Age group: 7–9 years

Introduction

In this topic children are provided with a new way of thinking about mushrooms. It is likely children think of them as plants which they eat at home. In this topic they are depicted as nature's recyclers which help clean up the environment and also provide nutrients for new plants to grow. In the application stage children use mushrooms as a food source, and also look at how other types of fungi are used.

Scientific view

Decomposers such as mushrooms play a crucial role in ecosystems by providing nutrients for plants to grow. Mushrooms are types of fungi which are nature's recyclers. They decay organic materials such as leaves and wood and return their nutrients to the soil. Ecosystems as we know them could not exist without decomposers.

Working scientifically

In these activities children will:

- ask questions and use scientific enquiry to answer them;
- make careful observations;
- record and report findings using photographs and displays;
- use results to draw conclusions;
- use established scientific knowledge to answer questions.

Health and safety

This topic involves an autumn visit to a parkland or woodland to photograph mushrooms. Make sure children's clothing is appropriate. Children need to be well supervised and told not to touch, pick or taste any mushrooms because they may be poisonous. Also some children may be allergic to the spores that mushrooms produce. It is advisable that children wear disposable gloves when looking through leaf litter, and you may want them to wear face masks. They need to wash their hands with gels or wipes before eating or drinking anything. The application stage involves the preparation of food. Ensure high standards of hygiene and the safe use of equipment. Refer to guidance in the ASE publication *Be Safe!* (2011) when planning these activities.

Exploration stage

Children's talk involves trying out their own ideas

Setting the scene

Get started by showing children a picture of mushrooms growing in the wild. Ask them what they know about mushrooms. How many types can they name? Where can they be found? At what time of the year to do they grow? Do they eat them at home? Can they tell the difference between a toadstool and a mushroom? Should they eat wild mushrooms?

Figure 7.6 **Mushrooms found in local woodland**

Source: Photos by Anna Loxley

Puzzle

Some children may think that a mushroom is a weird plant. Or could it be some other kind of organism? In groups children provide arguments for whether a mushroom is a plant or a different type of organism. Remind them to listen to each other, and to justify their ideas with evidence and reasoning.

Scientific enquiry

For this enquiry you will need a range of types of edible mushrooms, and a variety of known plants which can be dissected. Working in groups, children compare the structure of the mushrooms and the plants. They make detailed observational drawings of a plant and a mushroom and compare the main parts. Can they find evidence for why a mushroom is a plant? If not, what sort of organism is it? Groups present their evidence and share their reasoning with the class.

Having discussed the talking points in groups children share their ideas and try to come to a common view on the puzzle. Probe their thinking and challenge their reasoning.

Talking points: true, false or not sure?

- Mushrooms are plants because they grow in the ground.
- Mushrooms are not plants because they have no leaves.
- All plants have leaves.
- The top of the mushroom is its flower.
- Mushrooms do not have roots.
- Mushrooms grow in the dark.
- Plants need light to grow.

Story-telling

Children use information sources to explore the wide variety of mushrooms which exist in the wild. Groups tell stories about different types of mushrooms and their habitats around the world. They can use your school's preferred presentational app to present pictures, videos and text which show the wonderful range of mushrooms that exist in different parts of the world. Mushrooms are fascinating because they are just the fruit of the body of the fungus (mycelium) which grows beneath the soil. In fact, the largest organism in the world is a honey fungus which has grown to 3.8km or 2.4 miles across.

Scientific enquiry

Children can hunt for mushrooms as part of an autumn walk to the local park or woodland. Do not collect any mushrooms. Take cameras or tablets to record the diversity of mushrooms in their habitats. Use a fungi identification app on the iPhone, iPad or Android device for information and to help you talk about the mushrooms which you observe. Scientifically there is no difference between mushrooms and toadstools; often people think of toadstools as poisonous mushrooms.

Children identify and record all the places mushrooms like to grow: for example, on trees, in the ground and on rotting logs. What is the most unusual place for mushrooms to grow? Point out that the mushroom is the fruit of a larger plant that lives beneath the soil, inside rotting wood or another food source. Encourage the children to look out for invertebrates which share the mushroom's habitat, especially worms and woodlice.

Back in school create a display of the mushroom photographs to illustrate where different types were found. Which are most abundant? Children use information sources to explore the structure of mushrooms to find out how they feed on rotting organic materials. Keys can be created to identify common mushrooms and added to the display. Children can also identify animals in the woodland which feed on mushrooms, and also the plants they feed on and their predators. Use the information to create food chains for the habitat.

Figure 7.7 **Growing White Cap or Button mushrooms**

Source: iStock

Scientific enquiry

White Cap mushrooms, which are commonly sold in supermarkets, can be grown from spawn bought from a local garden supplier or from the web. With the help of adults, children can explore different ways of growing mushrooms either in the school grounds or in a shed or garden frame. White Caps can also be grown in lawns.

Mushrooms require damp conditions and rich organic compost to grow. Children can investigate the effects of growing mushrooms in different types of composts, and in different conditions. There is information on the web about how to grow mushrooms.

Formative assessment

Provide opportunities for children to voice what they have learnt in the exploratory stage. Use evidence from their responses to the puzzle, talking points and other activities to assess differences between children's ideas and the scientific view. Plan how you will use the re-describing stage to help the children address their *learning needs* (see Chapter 1). You may need to modify the activities depending on the collective and individual needs of your children.

Information and teaching resources

- How to grow mushrooms. *www.thompson-morgan.com/how-to-grow-mushrooms*
- Mushrooms and toadstools. *www.woodlands.co.uk/blog/flora-and-fauna/the-national-trust-mushrooms-and-toadstools/*

Re-describing stage

Children's talk involves making sense of scientific ideas

Teacher-led discussion

Return to the puzzle, review children's ideas and establish that a mushroom is not a plant. Compare pictures of a mushroom and a plant. Point out that mushrooms do not have the same parts as plants, the most obvious difference being that mushrooms have no leaves. Talk about children's stories in the exploration stage and what they found out about mushrooms. Confirm that mushrooms are types of fungi which feed on decaying vegetation such as dead plants, leaves, twigs and logs. Mushrooms are decomposers because they help to break down and recycle dead plant material so that it can be used by growing plants. Use video clips to show how mushrooms are one of nature's recyclers.

Story-telling

Children use pictures and words to tell the story of a woodland ecosystem which includes decomposers, producers and both primary and secondary consumers. Children tell the story of how each organism depends on the others for the energy it needs to survive.

Scientific enquiry

Provide children with breadsticks, melt-in-the-mouth shortbread biscuits or a mint which dissolves in the mouth. Before they put anything in their mouths remind the children that there are chemicals in their saliva which help break down (digest) their food. Children are not to chew the food with their teeth; they should let it break down naturally until they can swallow it.

Ask the children to describe what happened to the biscuit while it was in their mouths. Mushrooms digest their food in similar ways by using chemicals to break it down. The chemicals they use are so strong that they can digest wood. Children use information sources to find out how mushrooms feed on rotting vegetation, how they grow and reproduce. Probe children's thinking as they work and address any outstanding *learning needs*.

Information and teaching resources

BBC Bitesize:

- How fallen leaves are broken down by worms, fungi and slime mould. *www.bbc.co.uk/education/clips/z2tnr82*

Other websites:

- Producers, consumers and decomposers. *www.youtube.com/watch?v=MPZI2M1fDi8*

- The dirt on decomposers: Crash course kids. *www.youtube.com/watch?v=uB61rfeeAsM*

- Fruit and vegetable decomposition time lapse. *www.youtube.com/watch?v=c0En-_BVbGc*

Application stage

Children's talk involves trying out scientific ideas

Design and make a mushroom salad

Mushrooms are a nutritious food; they are low in fat and high in vitamins and minerals. Combined with sources of carbohydrates and proteins they can form part of a balanced diet. Mushrooms we get from the supermarket can be eaten raw, and are therefore ideal for salads.

Salads are not always children's favourite meal, so this is a chance for them to design their own using ingredients they prefer. The only rules are that the salad must include mushrooms and be balanced.

Making bread

It would be fun for children to bake their own bread rolls or pizzas to eat with their salad. There are a wide range of recipes on the web. A key ingredient is yeast. Explain that yeast is a type of fungus, but much smaller than mushrooms. It is so small, in fact, that it can only be seen under a microscope. Set up a yeast slide for the electronic microscope and let children see the yeast cells projected onto the IWB. Show magnified images from the web and explain how quickly they reproduce.

Children can investigate the conditions in which yeast thrives by adding it to bottles of sugary water with deflated balloons fixed to the tops. Using controlled experiments, they could find the temperature at which yeast cells are most active. As with all living things, carbon dioxide is a by-product of respiration. In the case of the yeast experiment, the carbon dioxide collects in the balloons. The more inflated the balloon, the more active the yeast. For reasons of health and safety, because yeast releases spores to which some children may be allergic, do not leave the bottles open to the air with active yeast in them. Put plugs of cotton wool in the tops. If necessary children can wear face masks when working close to the active yeast.

As a follow-up to the meal children can produce illustrated scientific articles which analyse the nutritional value of the ingredients in the salad and the bread, and explain the role played by the yeast in the bread-making. They will need access to information sources.

Information and teaching resources

BBC Bitesize:

- Use of microbes in the food and drink industry. *www.bbc.co.uk/education/clips/z73vr82*
- Microbes. *v/www.bbc.co.uk/education/clips/zbbygk7*

Topic: What has mould ever done for us?

Age group: 9–11 years

Introduction

This topic develops children's understanding of micro-organisms that can be both helpful and harmful. It provides opportunities for children to explore the best conditions for growing mould. Activities relate to work carried out into the development of new medicines in the biotechnology industry. In the application stage children explore developments in the treatment of diseases since the middle of the eighteenth century. The *ideas for practice* in this topic are informed and supported by resources produced by the Chemical Industry Education Centre.

Scientific view

Moulds, like mushrooms, are types of fungi and are an important part of the ecosystem. They are decomposers and in the right conditions are capable of decaying (digesting) organic materials so the nutrients can be returned to the soil. Conditions which affect mould growth are temperature, moisture and oxygen.

Working scientifically

In these activities children will:

- plan enquiries to answer questions including recognising and controlling variables;
- record data and results using tables and suitable graphs;
- draw conclusions and present findings from the enquiry;
- use established scientific knowledge to support findings and help answer questions.

Health and safety

The activities include growing mould. When growing mould, all containers should be securely closed but not sealed. Containers should never be opened when inspecting the mould and should eventually be disposed of as part of kitchen waste and placed unopened in the dustbin normally used for the school refuse. Label all cultures and promptly dispose of anything that begins to smell unpleasant. When planning this topic refer to the guidance provided in the ASE publication *Be Safe!* (2011).

Exploration stage

Children's talk involves trying out their own ideas

Setting the scene

About two weeks before you teach this topic prepare a mould garden. Use foods such as bread, different types of fruit, vegetables, cheese, bread or cake. Do not use meat or fish. Cut the food up into smallish pieces about the size of a grape. After dipping the food in water, place the pieces next to each other inside a largish see-through plastic jar which is resting on its side. Do not stack the food. Close the container with a secure lid, and never open it. Leave the container in a dark, warm place until mould starts to appear.

Begin the topic by showing children your mould garden. Tell them how you made it, and ask them what they think the mould is and where it came from. Do they think the mould is harmful? Listen to what children know about mould. Prompt them to supply reasons and evidence from their experience to support their ideas.

> ### Talking points: true, false or not sure?
>
> - Mould is everywhere.
> - Mould is the dead parts of the food.
> - Mould is a micro-organism.
> - Mould is a type of poison.
> - Mould is good for you.
> - Shops sell mouldy cheese.
> - Mould is caused by rotten food.
> - Mould only grows on food.
> - Mould cannot grow without water.
> - Keeping food in the fridge stops mould growing on it.

Working in groups, children share their ideas in response to the talking points. Probe their thinking to discover what they know about the nature of mould. Do they see it as a living thing, or something else? Are they aware it is a micro-organism? Do they think it is harmful?

Scientific enquiry

Take photographs of the mould inside the container and record which types of food are most affected. Continue observing and taking photographs each day until the mould is well established. Display the photographs to show how the mould developed.

Story-telling

Talk about the work of Alexander Fleming and how he discovered a bacteria-destroying mould called penicillin. Discuss what children know about penicillin and whether they have been prescribed it by their doctor. Children use information sources to explore the life and work of Fleming, and find out how he accidentally discovered penicillin.

The discovery of the antibiotic penicillin by Fleming made a big impact on the fight against disease, and led to improvements in the health of people around the world. Not only did it lead to a cure for bacterial infections that were once deadly, but it also began a big interest in finding new antibiotics. Today many different types of antibiotics are available, and the biotechnology industry is constantly working to develop others. Many of today's antibiotics are produced from moulds, and creating the best conditions for growing them is an important part of the process.

Puzzle

What are the best types of conditions to grow mould? Children can discuss the puzzle and hypothesise about the solution. Probe children's reasons for their responses.

Scientific enquiry

Children can try to find the best conditions for mould growth on bread by setting up tests in which they control the variables temperature, light and water. Children will need transparent freezer bags and slices of bread, plus other general equipment such as sticky tape, water droppers, scissors and labels.

Before they start children will need to decide where they will put their samples so that they can control the variables, and how they will set up their experiments to make sure their comparisons are fair. Also they have to think carefully about how to record their results. They need to be able to measure and compare the mould growth on each sample. This is not easy. Here are some ideas to consider:

1   Children can inspect the samples and use terms such as 'a bit mouldy,' 'fairly mouldy' or 'very mouldy'.

2   They can draw the slices of bread and colour the mouldy areas.

3   They can use a scale from 0–10 to compare the amount of mould on the samples, where 10 represents a sample which is fully covered in mould.

4   Use a grid marked out on a transparent sheet of plastic which can be placed over the bread on the outside of the freezer bag. The squares which contain mould can be counted each day to provide a measure of the rate at which it develops.

Children discuss the options and decide which would provide them with the most accurate results, which could be plotted on a graph. Of course children can record their results in more than one way.

When setting up their samples children should make sure that they use the same amount of bread and equal amounts of water. Once set up, the freezer bags should be sealed and never opened. Children wash their hands before and after setting up the samples, and also any time after they touch them.

Data can be collected each day for two or three weeks and recorded in drawings, tables and graphs. Children use the results to draw conclusions about the best way to grow mould. They can write formal reports explaining their methods and results to the biotechnology industry, using spreadsheet software to present their data.

Formative assessment

Provide opportunities for children to voice what they have learnt in the exploratory stage. Use evidence from their responses to the puzzle, talking points and scientific enquiry to assess differences between children's ideas and the scientific view. Plan how you will use the re-describing stage to help the children address their *learning needs* (see Chapter 1). You may need to modify the activities depending on the collective and individual needs of your children.

Information and teaching resources

Websites:

- Chemical Industry Education Centre. *www.ciec.org.uk/primary.html*
- Medicines from microbes. *www.ciec.org.uk/pdfs/resources/medicines-from-microbes.pdf*
- Grow your own mould. *www.youtube.com/watch?v=LUBXUgoGM98*
- *e-Bug. www.e-bug.eu*

ASE Journal:

- Primary Science 136 (Jan/Feb 2015) *Children's ideas about microbes* by Michael Allen, Georgina Bridle and Elizabeth Briten.

Re-describing stage

Children's talk involves making sense of scientific ideas

Teacher-led discussion

Start by discussing the puzzle and the outcomes of the children's enquires. Establish that temperature, moisture and food are important for growing mould. Mould prefers warm, moist conditions to grow. Also establish that mould is a living thing and it needs oxygen, as we do, to grow. Compare fungi with ourselves, and how our bodies require the right temperature, water, food and oxygen to survive.

Discuss how mould is a type of fungus. Show children some magnified images and point out how the spores of some moulds can resemble tiny mushrooms. Show a time lapse video of decaying food and talk about how the fungus (mould) feeds on the food and breaks it down. Reinforce the role moulds play in nature to recycle vital nutrients for plant growth. Make the point that all living things rot (decay) when they die and provide nutrients that other animals and plants need to survive.

Story-telling

In the form of a cartoon, children tell a story of nature's way of recycling a windfall apple. From the time it grew on the tree until its nutrients were released back into the ground through the action of fungi and other decomposers. Children should use information sources to help them describe in detail the process of decay. Listen to children's stories and address any outstanding *learning needs*.

Link to design and technology

Children use their understanding of decay to suggest ways different foods can be preserved. They then use information sources to explore how foods are traditionally and commercially preserved. These may include freezing, canning, drying, salting, pickling and adding sugar. Encourage children to find out why these processes prevent food decaying. As part of their D&T work, children can preserve a variety of vegetables and fruit using these methods. There is a wide range of information on the web which clearly explains the processes. Refer to the ASE publication *Be Safe!* (2011) when planning these activities.

Information and teaching resources

BBC Bitesize:

- Time-lapse photography of decaying fruit. *www.bbc.co.uk/education/clips/zwx76sg*
- Understanding the size of bacteria. *www.bbc.co.uk/education/clips/zkptsbk*
- Micro-organisms. *www.bbc.co.uk/education/clips/zggvr82*
- Micro-organisms at work in the sewage farm. *www.bbc.co.uk/education/clips/zrr3cdm*
- Seeing the bacteria carried on hands. *www.bbc.co.uk/education/clips/z34rkqt*

Application stage

Children's talk involves trying out scientific ideas

Science's fight against disease

Although much progress was made in science and medicine during the Renaissance, doctors could not cure diseases such as smallpox and bubonic plague which killed millions of people around the world. It was not until the mid-eighteenth century that scientists began to find ways to beat diseases caused by viruses and bacteria.

Using information sources children can tell the story of *Science's fight against disease*. They start by describing how doctors treated diseases such as smallpox and bubonic plague prior to the discovery of the smallpox vaccination by Edward Jenner in 1796. From this point in time, they can trace developments in our understanding and treatment of these types of diseases up to the present day. Children should compare scientific methods used in the eighteenth and nineteenth centuries with the methods scientists use today to develop new medicines. They can also focus on improvements in hygiene and how the development of antiseptics helped save lives.

Children conclude with an overview of the biotechnology industry and the challenges we face today in our continuing fight against diseases. They can include the race to discover new antibiotics to replace those we have over-used or which are no longer effective. Invite a STEM ambassador into school from the biotech industry to talk about his/her work.

Know your microbes

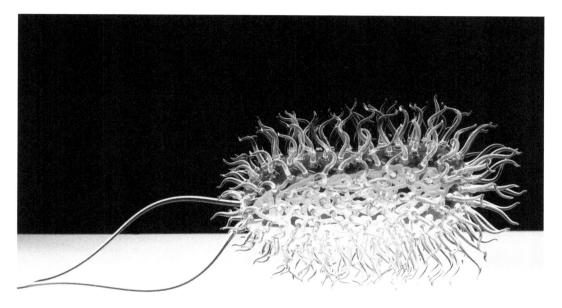

Figure 7.8   **E.coli, Glass Microbiology artwork by Luke Jerram**

Microbes are found everywhere, in the air we breathe, on the food we eat, all over our skin, in our mouth, nose and stomach. There are three main types of microbes known as bacteria, viruses and fungi. How do we know which microbes are useful and/or harmless, and which can damage our health?

There are many examples of how bacteria and fungi usefully serve nature and ourselves, but what about viruses, are they all pathogenic? Ask children to use information sources to deliver a formal lecture on microbes in the form of a multimedia presentation. This should explain the differences between the three main types of microbes, and shed light on the causes of some common ailments such as chicken pox, the common cold, influenza, measles, mumps and rubella.

Information and teaching resources

BBC Bitesize:

- Edward Jenner – the discovery of the smallpox vaccine.
  www.bbc.co.uk/education/clips/zgj8q6f

- Sir Alexander Fleming – the discovery of penicillin.
  www.bbc.co.uk/education/clips/zwm76sg

- The bacteria that lives on the skin. *www.bbc.co.uk/education/clips/ztvfb9q*

- The importance of handwashing in food hygiene.
  www.bbc.co.uk/education/clips/zr7jmp3

- What germs can be found on your hands? *www.bbc.co.uk/education/clips/zmcg9j6*

- Defending against infection. *www.bbc.co.uk/schools/gcsebitesize/science/
  edexcel_pre_2011/health/defendingagainstinfectionrev1.shtml*

- Infectious diseases – diseases. www.abpischools.org.uk/page/modules/diseases/
  diseases1.cfm?coSiteNavigation_allTopic=1

Other websites:

- BBSRC. *www.bbsrc.ac.uk*

- Teaching resources from *e-Bug. www.e-bug.eu/lang_eng/primary_pack/downloads/
  UK%20Junior%20Pack%20Complete.pdf*

ASE Journal:

- Primary Science 136 (Jan/Feb 2015) *Children's ideas about microbes* by Michael Allan,
  Georgina Bridle and Elizabeth Briten.

Chapter 8

Nutrition

We have these weapons of mass destruction on every street corner, and they're called donuts, cheeseburgers, French fries, potato chips, junk food. Our kids are living on a junk food diet.

Joel Fuhrman, US scientist (b. 1953)

Good nutrition means avoiding junk food, and eating healthy foods in the right combinations. To make healthy choices, children need to identify foods which are good for them, and know how to combine them to make nutritionally balanced meals. In the first topic, young children are encouraged to reflect on their eating habits, and are introduced to the importance of fruit and vegetables. The second topic examines the problems of consuming too much sugar, and promotes the benefits of a balanced diet. Older children explore the effects of exercise, and discover how their circulatory system works to transport food to parts of their bodies.

Topics in this chapter:

- Five a day

- Eating the right kinds of foods

- The circulatory system

Subject knowledge to support the teaching of these topics can be found in the core book, Loxley, P., Dawes, D., Nicholls, L. and Dore, B. (2018) *Teaching primary science: Promoting enjoyment and developing understanding*, Abingdon: Routledge, Chapter 16: Health and well-being.

Keeping healthy

Obesity is a common problem, estimated to affect around one in every four adults and about one in every five children aged 10 to 11 in the UK. People who are obese are clinically overweight, and this can cause health problems such as diabetes, heart disease, breast cancer, bowel cancer and stroke. Obesity can also affect a person's quality of life leading to mental health problems such as low self-esteem and depression. The best way to avoid obesity is to eat a balanced diet and take regular exercise.

When planning a balanced diet, we should first attend to foods which will provide the energy we need to keep mentally and physically active. The Sun is the primary source of energy in our world, and plants use its energy to produce food through photosynthesis. Food produced by plants is a way of storing the Sun's energy in the form of carbohydrates such as starches or sugars. By eating food produced by plants we are able to obtain the energy our bodies need to function.

The human body uses carbohydrates as a source of energy for growth, movement and repair. We eat carbohydrates in the form of sugars or starch (found in grains such as rice and wheat). These are broken down through the process of digestion and transported in our blood to various parts of the body by our circulatory system. Our bodies cannot store excess carbohydrate; so if more sugar and starch is eaten than the body can use, it is stored as fat. Proteins, from either meat or pulses, yield a range of chemicals that are used to replace and repair damaged tissue. Within a balanced diet we also need to consume foods rich in vitamins to help control reactions within the body, and in minerals, such as calcium, to support the building of bones and maintain nerve function. Living tissue is made up mostly of water, so we need to replace water lost through urination, sweating and exhalation. Finally, although we cannot digest cellulose (fibre found in vegetables, fruits, whole grains), it still forms an essential part of our daily diet as our bodies need it to speed up the passage of food through the gut. This fibre is also known as roughage.

As part of a balanced diet it is recommended that we eat five portions of fruit and vegetables each day. Fruit and vegetables are a good source of vitamins and minerals. They are also an excellent source of dietary fibre, and can reduce the risk of heart disease, stroke and some cancers. Fruit and vegetables are also usually low in fat, and eating them can help maintain a healthy weight.

In addition to a balanced diet we also need to exercise to keep healthy. It is recommended that children aged 5 to 11 should do at least 60 minutes of activity a day which gets the heart beating faster. Moderate exercise raises the heart rate and breaks a sweat. Vigorous exercise increases breathing to heavy and fast, and also increases heart rates appreciably. As part of their daily exercise children should also do activities which strengthen their muscles.

In developed countries, the abundance and relative cheapness of foodstuffs have led to a growing concern about rising levels of obesity. Many foods are highly processed and contain high levels of sugars, fats and salt. Maintaining a healthy lifestyle requires good nutrition and exercise, and children need to be encouraged to recognise the link between the two.

Topic: Five a day

Age group: 5–7 years

Introduction

The purpose of this topic is to introduce children to the importance of eating fruit and vegetables as part of their daily diet. Opportunities are provided for children to reflect on their eating habits and decide whether they could make healthier choices. In the application stage children prepare their own balanced meals.

Scientific view

We obtain the things our bodies need to work and play, and to grow and to keep healthy, from the foods we eat. To keep healthy, we need to exercise and consume a balanced diet which includes fruit and vegetables.

Working scientifically

In these activities children will:

- ask and find answers to questions;
- perform simple tests and comparisons;
- identify and classify;
- use their observations and ideas to suggest answers to questions.

Health and safety

This is a good opportunity to reinforce hygiene rules. Teach children to wash their hands before and after handling food. When foods are used for investigations, ensure all surfaces and utensils are clean and that children do not share spoons or cups. Be aware of any medical, cultural or religious reason why children should not handle or eat certain foods.

Exploration stage

Children's talk involves trying out their own ideas

Setting the scene

Start by reading to the children the book or showing them the video on the internet of *I will not ever never eat a tomato* by Lauren Child. This is about Lola, who is persuaded to eat a range of healthy foods when her brother Charlie re-brands them, and discovers she loves them. Encourage the children to talk about the foods which they like and dislike. Ask them to imagine what would happen to them if they didn't eat any food at all? Can they live without food? Encourage children to provide reasons for their responses.

Talking points: true, false or not sure?

- The food I eat keeps me healthy.
- Eating too much food could make me fat.
- I like chips, but I don't like vegetables.
- I think eating vegetables is a waste of time.
- I would rather eat tomatoes than eat burgers.
- I like all types of vegetables.
- I prefer fruit to vegetables.
- Eating sweet foods makes me happy.

Talk together about their responses. Prompt children to provide reasons and examples of the types of vegetables or fruits they like or dislike. Establish which their favourite meals are, and whether they include vegetables or fruit.

Puzzle

Jamie Oliver found that, shockingly, most children in a class of six-year-olds could not recognise common types of fruit and vegetables (a link to the video is given on page 160). How many types of fruit and vegetables can your children recognise? Can they tell the difference between fruit and vegetables?

For this activity you will need to display a wide range of fruit and vegetables, and cards with the names of the different foods printed on them. The game is for each group in turn to pick a card and to match it to a piece of fruit or vegetable in the display. Before they label the food, groups should explain what they know about it, where they have seen it before and whether they have ever eaten it.

Scientific enquiry

Find out whether children can distinguish between fruits and vegetables by asking them to sort apples, bananas, oranges, potatoes, cabbage, carrots and tomatoes in as many ways as they can. Prompt them to justify their groupings. Then focus the discussion on groups who have divided their foods into fruits and vegetables. Ask them to justify their choices and share their ideas with the class. Can they think of any reasons why their choices may or may not be correct?

Discuss what children know about fruit and vegetables. Use questions to promote recall, and then prompt children to justify their answers to help create discussion.

- How do fruits taste different from vegetables?
- Which fruits taste the sweetest?
- Do we normally cook fruits before we eat them?
- What types of vegetables do we normally cook?
- Do you eat fruit and vegetables every day?
- Are fruit and vegetables good for you?

Scientific enquiry

Figure 8.1 *Tomatoes, or Love-Apples.* **Illustration from Ernst Benary's 'Album Benary' – Tab. XXIV, 1876–82**

Source: © The Trustees of the Royal Botanic Gardens, Kew

Although Lola doesn't like tomatoes, they are the world's most popular fruit. Tomatoes were first cultivated in BCE 700 by Aztecs and Incas. Explorers returning from Mexico introduced the tomato into Europe, where it was first mentioned in 1556 CE. The French called it the 'apple of love,' the Germans the 'apple of paradise'. Lola calls them 'moon-squirters'.

Working in groups children can use their senses to test different types of tomatoes and decide what they like and don't like about them. Talk about hygiene, and remind children to wash their hands before they touch any food.

1   Children discuss colour, size, smell and taste of the tomatoes. They can group them according to sweetness. Help them choose words other than nice or horrible to describe the tomatoes. Use words such sweet, sugary, sour, bitter, not so sweet, tasteless, and watery and so on. Children use their comparisons to justify their choice of the best tasting tomato.

2   In this activity children try to identify different types of fruits using their senses. Remind them that tomatoes are fruits like apples, pears, grapes, oranges and bananas. Talk to the children about their favourite fruits and whether they think they can identify them by their taste. Show the children the fruits you want them to test with the skins still on and see if they can name them. Provide samples of the fruits cut into bite size pieces and place them in numbered dishes. This can be a group or class activity. Closing their eyes or using blindfolds children describe and identify the fruits by tasting them.

    Children compare the taste of the fruits with the tomatoes. Focus discussion on the words they use. Which were the sweetest? Which of the fruits do they think Lola may have liked. Discuss reasons. Can they think of names for the fruits which would trick Lola into eating them?

Formative assessment

Provide opportunities for children to voice what they have learnt in the exploratory stage. Use evidence from their responses to the puzzle, talking points and other activities to assess differences between children's ideas and the scientific view. Plan how you will use the re-describing stage to help the children address their *learning needs* (see Chapter 1). You may need to modify the activities depending on the collective and individual needs of your children.

Information and teaching resources

Useful websites:

● Children fail to recognise vegetables. *www.takepart.com/video/2015/06/24/ watch-group-first-graders-not-know-what-vegetables-names-are*

● Charlie and Lola: I will not ever never eat a tomato. *www.youtube.com/watch?v=0Vd-0pFOFs0*

● Jamie's Kitchen Garden. *www.jamieskitchengarden.org*

Book:

● Child, Lauren (2000) *I will not ever never eat a tomato*, Orchard Books.

Re-describing stage

Children's talk involves making sense of scientific ideas

Teacher-led discussion

Start by reviewing the different types of fruit and vegetables in the display, so children become familiar with their names. Point out that we are advised to eat five portions of fruit and vegetables each day to keep healthy. We do not have to eat them all at once. We can have some with our breakfast, as a snack, with our lunch or as part of our evening meal. Working in groups, children can decide which five fruit and vegetables they would choose, and when during the day they would prefer to eat them. Use video clips to explain how fruits and vegetables help us keep healthy. Focus on how they help keep us well, provide us with energy to work and play, and help us grow.

Story-telling

Figure 8.2 **Gorillas stick to a mainly vegetarian diet**

Source: iStock

Use BBC Bitesize video clips to talk about why animals also need a healthy diet. Focus on gorillas. Point out that gorillas eat fruits and vegetables to keep fit and strong. What do children think would happen to the gorillas if they ate things like chips, crisps, pizzas, cakes and cola all day long? Using words and pictures children can tell the story of a young gorilla who refused to eat fruit and vegetables, and instead ate chips, cakes and chocolate bars which it got from a young boy who visited the forest. Discuss children's stories and talk about why these and other foods high in fat and added sugar are not healthy for gorillas and humans. Measure out the number of spoons of sugar contained in some cakes and popular chocolate bars. Often, sugar makes up half the ingredients in a chocolate bar.

Talking points: true, false or not sure?

Should children be made to eat five portions of fruit and vegetables every day? Should they not have a say in what they eat? Provide several talking points for children to debate and express their opinions about healthy eating. For example:

- Children should eat vegetables even if they dislike them.
- Children should always eat their vegetables, because they are good for them.
- If children eat their vegetables, they should be rewarded with sweets.
- Children should choose which foods they eat.

Add to or modify the points to suit your children. Listen to children's responses, and encourage them to justify their ideas in terms of the consequences regarding their health. Identify and address outstanding *learning needs*.

Scientific enquiry

Use multimedia resources to show children how vegetables and fruits are the parts of plants that we eat. Emphasise that these are all natural foods which are good for us. This topic can be linked to work done on growing plants. Grow vegetables and fruits in pots or grow-bags. Tomatoes are easy to grow, and they taste much better than the ones in the supermarket. Children living in urban environments would benefit from a visit to a farm to see how crops, which eventually end up on the shelves in their local supermarket, are grown.

Information and teaching resources

BBC Bitesize:

- What do humans need to stay healthy? *www.bbc.co.uk/guides/zxvkd2p*
- Why do we need to eat fruit and vegetables? *www.bbc.co.uk/education/clips/z3ptsbk*
- Keeping healthy. *www.bbc.co.uk/education/clips/z84g9j6*

- Five types of food. *www.bbc.co.uk/education/clips/zcmqxnb*

- Eating a varied diet. *www.bbc.co.uk/education/clips/zy9rkqt*

- Why animals need a healthy diet. *www.bbc.co.uk/education/clips/zf2qxnb*

Application stage

Children's talk involves trying out scientific ideas

Two-course lunch

Children design a healthy two-course cold lunch including a tomato salad and a fruit cocktail. Talk about hygiene and demonstrate how to cut the fruit and other ingredients safely. Children need to be closely supervised when using kitchen equipment, especially knives. Like Charlie and Lola, they may wish to 're-brand' their ingredients on a menu card.

Tomato salad

Provide children with a choice of ready-cooked, protein-rich food to go with their tomato salad. These could be sliced chicken or ham, or tinned tuna. Children prepare their own tomato salad. This is a good opportunity to introduce children to herbs and explain why they are also natural foods. Explore what the children already know and which herbs they can recognise. Provide a choice of herbs which are growing in pots so children can see they are types of plants.

Idea for a tasty tomato salad:

- vine ripened tomatoes

- pinch of sea salt

- basil leaves, rolled and thinly sliced

- small amounts of balsamic vinegar

- small amounts of extra virgin olive oil

Fruit cocktail

Children choose their favourite fruits and prepare them for the salad. Working in groups they will need to agree on tasks, and which fruits to include. Remind groups that everyone should be included in the discussion and decision making. They should seek agreement before they start making the salad.

Smoothie alternative

Rather than make a fruit cocktail, children could use their fruits to make a smoothie. As the name implies smoothies require a smooth, creamy texture which usually requires bananas to be added to the fruits which give it its taste. Children can experiment with different combinations of fruits to achieve the required consistency and taste. An adult should operate the blender.

After they have finished their lunch and washed up, talk about what the children enjoyed about their meal. Reinforce the value of eating fruit. Talk about the other ingredients, how the meat or fish will help them to grow, and how the herbs will help keep them healthy.

Topic: Eating the right kinds of food

Age group: 7–9 years

Introduction

This topic starts by putting cola on trial for being a danger to children's health. Throughout the topic children reflect on the value of good nutrition, and explore the food groups which combine to create a balanced diet. The focus shifts to the dietary needs of Olympic gymnasts in the application stage, where children take on the role of nutritionists.

Scientific view

We need a balanced diet for our bodies to work properly. Good health involves drinking enough water and eating the right types and amounts of food. Our diets need to contain a balance of carbohydrates, proteins, fats, vitamins and minerals. Eating too much sugar and fat can damage our health.

Working scientifically

In these activities children will:

- ask questions and use scientific enquiry to answer them;
- set up practical enquiries and comparative tests;
- gather and present data in ways which will help answer questions;
- report findings from enquiries using posters and presentations;
- use their results to draw conclusions.

Health and safety

When using equipment such as toothbrushes and mugs, these should not be shared.

Exploration stage

Children's talk involves trying out their own ideas

Setting the scene

Cola on trial. Set up the classroom to resemble a courtroom. In the area reserved for the defendant (the dock) place a large bottle of any cola. Tell the children that you are going to put cola on trial for damaging the health of children all over the world. If it is found guilty the cola will be poured down the sink, and any of its kind will never be allowed in the classroom again.

Figure 8.3 **Cola is accused of damaging children's health**

Scientific enquiry

To prepare for the trial children use information sources to research the nutritional value of different types of food, and identify foods which they should eat to keep healthy.

TABLE 8.1 What happens when we eat…

If we eat…	What is going to happen?
… vegetables	
… fruit	
… meat	
… cakes	
… pasta	
… crisps	
… sugary drinks like cola	
… other foods	

Using a table like this one, encourage children to discover the effects different food have on their health. Children can add their favourite foods to the list.

Scientific enquiry

So that cola can get a fair trial, it important that you establish exactly how much sugar it contains. Investigate the amount of sugar in a can of cola by slowly heating it in a saucepan until all the liquid has evaporated. For health and safety reasons, the teacher should demonstrate this enquiry.

There are about 35 grams of sugar (the equivalent of seven teaspoons) in a 330 ml can. This is more than the amount of added sugar that a child should consume in a day. When the added sugar in biscuits, sweets and cakes is taken into account, it becomes clear how easy it is for children to eat too much sugar.

Story-telling: The trial

Choose three judges and twelve jury members. The rest of the class can be divided into groups representing advocates for the prosecution, advocates for the defence and expert witnesses.

In turn advocates for the prosecution and defence bring forward expert witnesses to support their cases. When all the evidence has been presented, the cases for the prosecution and defence should be summed up by the advocates. It is the judges' job to sum up all the evidence and to challenge any claims they feel are inaccurate or not relevant. After time for discussion the jury can give their verdict, clearly stating the evidence on which their decision is based. The judges have the final say by commenting on the fairness of the verdict and handing down the punishment.

Formative assessment

Provide opportunities for children to voice what they have learnt in the exploratory stage. Use evidence from their responses to the activities to assess differences between children's ideas and the scientific view. Plan how you will use the re-describing stage to help the children address their *learning needs* (see Chapter 1). You may need to modify the activities depending on the collective and individual needs of your children.

Re-describing stage

Children's talk involves making sense of scientific ideas

Teacher-led discussion

Discuss the problems with cola from a scientific point of view. Foods like cola contain added sugars that are high in energy but have few other nutrients. We all need energy to live, but generally we can get what we need from foods with their own natural sugars such as fruit and vegetables which also have other benefits for our health. Make the point that eating too much sugar can damage our health, leading to weight gain, obesity, tooth decay and other problems. Talk to the children about obesity and what it means.

Modelling

Talk about the role the teeth play in the digestive system. Does all the sugary food pass into their stomachs? What happens to the food that sticks to their teeth? Place sticks of chalk in sugary drinks, including cola, and observe what happens to them over the next few days. Discuss whether this is a good model for what could happen to our teeth if we do not clean them. Use video clips to show what can happen to our teeth if we do not look after them.

Scientific enquiry

Start by showing the BBC Bitesize video clip entitled *Developing a new toothpaste*. Children can plan their own tests to compare different toothpastes. Children will not be testing the toothpastes on their own teeth. Groups start by agreeing criteria for comparing different toothpastes, for example:

- whether it has a good taste;
- whether the texture is right – not too thick and not too runny;
- whether it has a pleasing colour;
- whether it has a pleasing smell;
- whether it is good for cleaning.

Children discuss how to make each of their tests fair. The big challenge is to think of ways of comparing the cleaning ability of the toothpastes. Since they cannot do this using their own teeth, they could use tarnished metal objects, cups with tea or coffee stains or crayon marks on a painted surface instead. Children present their results as part of an advertising campaign for a particular toothpaste, using comparisons as evidence for their claims. Think of a slogan which will help sell the toothpaste, and design some new packaging.

Scientific enquiry

For this enquiry you will need to collect a range of breakfast cereals. Start the enquiry by looking at the BBC Bitesize video entitled *Does eating breakfast affect concentration?* Talk together about the video. Ask children whether they think breakfast is important, and what types of food provide the nutrition they need. Be sensitive to the fact that children may not have breakfast provided at home, or may attend the school's breakfast club.

In groups, children compare the nutritional information from their breakfast products and use it to work out the nutritional value of the portions they might eat. To do this, children pour out and measure their normal servings, and use the nutritional information on the box to work out and record its nutritional content. The nutritional data in Table 8.2 has been taken from a box of a well known brand of cornflakes.

TABLE 8.2 Cornflake cereal nutrition data

Nutrition	Per 100g	Per 30g serving
energy	1604 kJ	481 kJ
fat	9g	0.3g
carbohydrates	84g (sugar 8g)	25g (sugar 2.4g)
fibre	3g	0.9g
protein	7g	2.1g
salt	1.13g	0.34g
minerals (iron)	8.0 mg	2.4mg
vitamins (various)	83% of NRV	25% of NRV

Explain to the children what the symbols 'kJ' and 'mg' mean. NRV (Nutrient Reference Value) is the recommended daily intake of the vitamins listed on the package.

Children use information sources to compare the energy from their cereal with the amount of energy they are likely to use during the day. Children aged 7–9 years need approximately 7,000kJ per day. More detailed information can be found on the web. How much of the energy they need to keep mentally and physically active during the day can they get from their cereal? A 30g serving of cornflakes provides approximate 7% of a child's energy needs. Children compare their data, especially the amount of sugar in their cereal. Some cereals contain over 30% added sugar. Remind children that foods with a lot of added sugar are not good for them. It would be better to eat cereals with a lower sugar content and add some fruit which is a natural energy food.

Teacher-led discussion

Use video clips such as BBC Bitesize *Five types of food* to illustrate what is meant by a balanced diet. Make the point that their diet needs to supply them with more than just the energy to get through the day, as they also need nutrients to help them grow, and keep them fit and healthy. Explain how a balanced diet can provide all the nutrients they need. Introduce children to the idea that a balanced diet each day should contain:

- fruit and vegetables;
- meat, fish or alternatives;
- milk and dairy products;
- bread, other cereals and potatoes;
- not too much fat and sugars;
- water.

Working in groups, children can choose different food groups to research. They start by working together to think of three things they would like to know about their food groups, and write them down as questions. Groups then use information sources to find answers to their questions, and present their findings to the class. After their presentation groups take questions from the class. Questions which need further research can be written down, with groups reporting back to the class after they have found the answers.

Information and teaching resources

BBC Bitesize:

- An introduction to the main organs of the human body. *www.bbc.co.uk/education/clips/zyqfg82*

- Digestion – how does breakfast affect your day? *www.bbc.co.uk/education/clips/zcsdycw*

- The effects of different drinks on teeth. *www.bbc.co.uk/education/clips/zscg9j6*

- Developing a new tooth paste. *www.bbc.co.uk/education/clips/zycb4wx*

- Does eating breakfast affect concentration? *www.bbc.co.uk/education/clips/zwtmhyc*

- Five types of food. www.bbc.co.uk/education/clips/z4x76sg

Other websites:

- How many calories does a child of 7–10 need? *www.nhs.uk/chq/Pages/how-many-calories-do-children-need.aspx?CategoryID=51*

- Sweet breakfast cereals 'too sugary' for kids. *www.nhs.uk/news/2012/02February/Pages/breakfast-cereals-still-too-high-in-sugar.aspx*

Application stage

Children's talk involves trying out scientific ideas

Nutritionists use their knowledge of the science of food to help individuals and groups make the right choices about what they eat. In the following activities children take on the role of nutritionists to plan a diet for a young gymnast training for the Olympic Games.

Children can start by exploring websites to find out how high level gymnasts train for events such as the Olympic Games. They have to be fit and strong to perform their disciplines.

The diet should include breakfast, lunch, evening meal and snacks. It should also include all their drinks. Children may not envisage sugary drinks as food, and not normally think of them as equivalent to snacking on biscuits or cakes.

They can start by working out the types of foods gymnasts should eat based on what they need to be able to do. Do they need high energy foods? What foods will help build up their strength?

Groups work collaboratively to reach agreement on the types of foods the gymnast should eat and then plan a daily diet. Groups present their diets to the class and justify their choice of foods. Bar charts can be used to compare the relative amounts of the different foods the gymnast should consume in a day. Produce displays featuring prominent Olympic gymnasts and the diets recommended by the class nutritionists.

Children can use information sources to find out about the work of nutritionists and food scientists. Invite a STEM ambassador to talk about nutrition and the work of nutritionists. Children help manage the session by providing topics and questions in advance for the STEM ambassador to answer.

Information and teaching resources

ASE Journals:

- Primary Science 133 (May/June 2014) *'Vegecating' children* by Katherine Bagshaw, Hannah Barham, Rebecca Betts, Amie Felton and Joshua Knatt.

- Primary Science 128 (May/June 2013) *A child-centred approach to learning about healthy eating* by Francesca Telford.

Topic: The circulatory system

Age group: 9–11 years

Introduction

This topic provides opportunities for children to examine the history and nature of science, as well as discover how the human circulatory system works. Activities also enable children to recognise the impact of diet and exercise on the way their bodies function. In the application stage children apply their knowledge to planning the menu for a healthy eating restaurant, and to addressing issues which connect achievement in school to diet and exercise.

Scientific view

Our bodies need food to function. We get the energy we need from the food we digest, and the oxygen we breathe. High energy foods such as pasta, vegetables and fruit are called carbohydrates. Digested food and oxygen are transported by our circulatory system to all the organs in our body where they combine in the cells to release energy. The process by which energy stored in our food is released in our cells is called respiration.

Working scientifically

In these activities children will:

- plan scientific enquiries to answer questions;
- take measurements using scientific instruments;
- record data using tables and graphs;
- report and present findings from enquiries;
- use established scientific knowledge to challenge or support ideas and arguments.

Health and safety

Take care that children with medical problems are not put at risk. Avoid situations that can lead to emotional stress: investigations can sometimes change to competitions and some children may feel they are being identified as 'abnormal'. When investigating pulse rate, keep exercises to the same level as is normal in PE.

Exploration stage

Children's talk involves trying out their own ideas

Setting the scene

Figure 8.4 **Galen**

Source: Alamy

This topic provides an opportunity to link science and history. Because of their practice of embalming the dead, the Ancient Egyptians were well aware of the different organs inside our bodies. Talk about the practice of embalming and ask the children to draw a picture of the inside of a human body showing all the organs that the Ancient Egyptians would have removed and stored. Children work in groups and come together as a class to share their ideas. Encourage children to politely challenge each other's ideas when they hold alternative views. Prompt children to use talk tools such 'I agree because …' and 'I disagree because …'.

Story-telling

Groups work collaboratively to research and tell stories from antiquity about the human body. Each group researches a specific culture and presents its story hand written, with hand-drawn illustrations in the style of an ancient text. The stories can be published together to create a book about ancient medicine.

Groups could choose from one of the following, or any other ancient medicine they might find interesting:

- Egyptian medicine
- Indian medicine
- Chinese medicine
- Greek medicine
- Roman medicine.

Ask groups to talk about what they have learnt, and to summarise in no more than 100 words. Groups then share their summaries with the class. Discuss whether any of the ancient ideas about the human body still apply today, and whether ancient medicine has had any influence on what we know today.

Teacher-led discussion

The most influential physician from ancient times was Galen. He was a Roman doctor who treated wounded soldiers and gladiators. His ideas about human anatomy dominated European thinking well into the sixteenth century. Groups which researched Roman medicine would have discovered insights into the life and work of Galen. Discuss his beliefs about blood flow in the body, and provide a list of his key ideas.

Galen believed that:

- blood was only sent to organs that needed it;
- blood produced in the liver and veins was consumed (used up) in the body's organs and limbs;
- veins carrying blood to the heart were on the right side of the body;
- arteries carrying blood from the heart were on the left side of the body;
- blood passed from one side of the heart to the other through lots of tiny holes;

● the heart pumped blood through the arteries with something called 'pneuma' obtained from the lungs when air was breathed in.

Much of Galen's research was done on animals such as apes and pigs, so it would not be surprising to find he got some things wrong. Are any of Galen's ideas still valid today? How do they compare with our modern ideas?

With the help of information sources, children identify up-to-date scientific knowledge which can be used to refute or support his ideas. Groups work collaboratively, providing alternative explanations where necessary, and create a list of modern day ideas about how the circulatory system works. Groups come together to share and compare their ideas. Encourage children to elaborate in order to clarify ideas where necessary. From the discussion produce a list of ideas which represent modern-day thinking.

Puzzle

When we exercise our hearts beat faster and we breathe more heavily. Does this happen because we are not fit, or is there another reason? Discuss children's responses to the puzzle, and ask them to plan an enquiry to determine how exercise affects their heart rate and breathing.

Scientific enquiry

1   Make their own stethoscope

    Stethoscopes are useful instruments for listening to our heartbeat and our breathing. Children can make their own listening devices using funnels and plastic tubing. Alternatively, they can use plastic or polystyrene cups with a hole cut in the bottom. Let children investigate how to make their stethoscope.

2   Measuring heartbeat and breathing rates

    Children should practise taking each other's pulses, and establish what their normal heart rates are when resting. Working in small groups they do some moderate exercise like brisk walking or skipping for about 30 seconds and then check their heart rates, and describe the effects on their breathing. They should rest until their heart rates are back to their rest level. They then do the same exercise for say 60 seconds, check pulse and rest. They should keep increasing the exercise time until they have four results to plot on a line graph. They can then repeat the process involving more demanding exercise such as sprinting.

TABLE 8.3 Exercise rates

Type exercise	Length of exercise	Heartbeat	Breathing
resting	–		
	30		
	60		
	90		
	120		

Having recording the data they compare their heart rates and breathing when they are at rest, when doing moderate and more demanding exercise. Ask the children to interpret the results in terms of how exercise influences their heartbeat and breathing.

Talking points: true, false or not sure?

- My heart beats faster when I run because it pumps more blood around my body.
- My heart beats slower when I rest because it is tired.
- My heart beats faster when my body needs more energy.
- My heart beats faster when my body needs more food.
- I breathe more heavily when I am tired.
- My circulatory system only supplies energy to my legs when I run.
- When I am asleep my heart stops beating because I am resting.
- I breathe heavily when I run because I am excited.

Children discuss talking points in groups and then come together to share and compare their responses. Encourage them to negotiate to develop shared understanding. Probe the reasons behind their responses.

Formative assessment

Provide opportunities for children to voice what they have learnt in the exploratory stage. Use evidence from their responses to the puzzle, talking points and other activities to assess differences between children's ideas and the scientific view. Plan how you will use the re-describing stage to help the children address their *learning needs* (see Chapter 1). You may need to modify the activities depending on the collective and individual needs of your children.

Re-describing stage

Children's talk involves making sense of scientific ideas

Teacher-led discussion

Children may be aware that they use their muscles when they exercise, but not know that muscles need a supply of food and oxygen to function. Use a simple model of the circulatory system to explain how the heart pumps both oxygenated and deoxygenated blood around the body. In effect the heart is two pumps in one, pumping blood around two separate systems. One system flows through the lungs and back to the heart. The other flows around the body delivering food and oxygen to the organs. Interactive models can be found on the web.

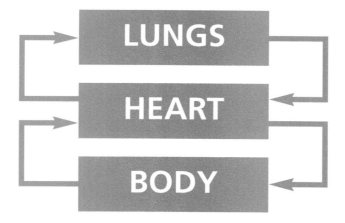

Figure 8.5 **Model of circulatory system showing double circulation**

Modelling

The children can think of ways of role-playing the circulatory system. One idea is for children to take on the role of the blood. In the school playground a giant model of the circulatory system can be marked out in different coloured chalk. One colour can be used for the arteries taking blood from the heart, and another for the veins returning blood to it. Children acting as the blood move around the two systems. They are pumped by the heart to the lungs to collect oxygen and travel back to the heart. They are then pumped by the heart to the body where they give up their oxygen, before returning to the heart. Children can think of ways of adding the digestive system to the model.

Another way of modelling is to create their own animations using stop-motion filming techniques, and their imaginations. They will need a digital camcorder with animation software, plus materials for their models.

Teacher-led discussion

Encourage children to use the scientific model of the circulatory system to explain why exercise increases their breathing and heart rate. Address any outstanding *learning needs*. Reinforce the idea that the food we eat contains the nutrients our bodies need to function and stay healthy. Foods which are high in carbohydrates provide the energy we need to keep warm, and to keep physically and mentally active. Our bodies require more food and oxygen when we exercise, therefore the heart beats faster and increases the flow of blood to our organs. If appropriate, introduce the concept of respiration and explain how oxygen and digested food carried by the blood combine together in our muscles (and other organs) to provide the energy we need.

Puzzle

Which are the best ten foods to give you energy?

Working in groups children discuss the puzzle, and compile a list of what they think are the best energy foods. They write the names of the foods on cards and display these in the class. The class come together and, through negotiation, agree on the top ten. To extend this activity, they negotiate sorting them into categories such as natural foods, processed foods and not sure. Encourage children to develop arguments for and against choosing particular foods. Children use information sources to help challenge each other's ideas. Having researched the different foods, children can design their own energy-rich snacks to get them through a hard day at school!

Information and teaching resources

BBC Bitesize:

● Digestion – How does breakfast affect your day?
www.bbc.co.uk/education/clips/zcsdycw

● An introduction to the main organs of the body *www.bbc.co.uk/education/clips/zyqfg82*

● How our circulatory system keeps us alive. *www.bbc.co.uk/education/clips/z92chv4*

● Respiration – How is oxygen transported round the body?
www.bbc.co.uk/education/clips/zy8sj6f

● Lungs and keeping them healthy. *www.bbc.co.uk/education/clips/zcr3cdm*

● The heart and how it works. *www.bbc.co.uk/education/clips/zncg9j6*

Other websites:

● Heart and circulation.
www.abpischools.org.uk/page/modules/heartandcirculation/heart3.cfm?coSite Navigation_allTopic=1

ASE Journals:

● Primary Science 136 (Jan/Feb 2015) *Playground science* by Alan Cross and Jon Board.

● Primary Science 123 (May/June 2012) *Using models to promote children's scientific understanding* by Jane Maloney and Sheila Curtis.

Application stage

Children's talk involves trying out scientific ideas

The nature of science

Talk about the nature of science and how it proceeds by challenging and modifying existing beliefs in light of new evidence. In this case, Galen's beliefs about the human body were accepted for over 500 years until Andreas Vesalius (1514–1564) and then William Harvey (1578–1657) challenged them. It is from this era in history that our present understanding of the circulatory system has developed. Children research how our understanding of the circulatory system has developed since the sixteenth century, and tell the story in the form of an audio book.

Healthy eating restaurant

Role-play scenario: children have just bought a restaurant and they need to plan the lunch menu for the opening day. The restaurant is situated in an urban shopping centre and there is a lot of competition for lunch time customers from a range of other restaurants including a number of fast food outlets. The customers they want to target are those who are health-conscious, yet do not have a lot of money to spend.

The task includes choosing a name for their restaurant which will attract their target customers and to produce an advertising leaflet that can be distributed round the shopping centre. They also need to produce a fixed-price lunch menu with three choices for starters, mains and sweets. The cost of producing the meals on the menu should be carefully calculated to ensure there is a profit in the fixed price. All ingredients for the meals should be chosen to ensure customers are provided with a healthy and balanced diet. Children justify their menus in terms of health benefits, cost and appeal.

If your school has the facilities children can produce a selection of actual meals from their menu. Refer to the ASE publication *Be Safe!* (2011) when planning the activities.

'Fitter kids are better at mathematics' say researchers in the USA

Researchers at the University of Illinois in the USA found that children aged between 9 and 10 years old who were physically fitter were better at mathematics than their less fit peers. The full report can be found in *Science Daily* published online on the 15th August 2015.[1]

Share the above headlines with the children and ask for their comments. Do they think being good at a subject like mathematics has anything to do with fitness? Can they think of any reasons why being fit and healthy may help their school work?

1   Discussion: If I am fit I will be able to concentrate more on my school work.

    Children discuss whether or not they agree with the talking point. Remind them that persuasive arguments require reasons and evidence to support their views. Extend the discussion to include tiredness. Is this just a result of lack of sleep or can it be connected to poor physical health. Do children sleep better when they have been active during the day? Does a good night's sleep help children keep fit?

2   Discussion: How do I know whether I am fit?

    Ask the children to discuss whether they think they are fit and to justify their responses. How much exercise to they do each day? What types of physical activity do they do?

    Provide children with the following questions which are based on an online NHS fitness self-assessment tool.

- Children of your age should be active for 60 minutes every day. On an average day, how close are you to achieving this?

- On average, how many days a week do you do activities that strengthen your muscles?

- If you're not doing enough physical activity, can you explain why not?

- Describe how you feel after climbing a flight of stairs. Do you get out of breath when walking up a hill?

The Department of Health recommends that people under the age of 18 should be doing an hour of physical activity each day including activities which help strengthen their muscles. Discuss whether the children are doing enough.

Working collaboratively children plan a sensible fitness regime for their age group, especially for children not involved in sport. Using information sources, they can find out about suitable aerobic activities which could be done each day, and muscle strengthening activities which they could do at school. Stress that agreement should be sought, and unresolved disagreements should be recorded. Each group should present and justify their regimes to the whole class with the aim of producing a common programme for their age group. Some of the agreed activities could be included in PE lessons.

3   Discussion: What else can I do to keep fit?

Use the opportunity to revisit and develop children's understanding of the importance of a healthy diet. You may also want to explore with them the dangers to their health of smoking, drinking alcohol and using other drugs. Children can use information sources to help produce warning posters about smoking and the use of drugs.

4   Discussion: What can I do to improve my school work?

Children address this talking point individually and decide what changes they can make to their lifestyle which may improve their performance at school.

Information and teaching resources

- NHS website. *www.nhs.uk/Tools/Pages/Fitness.aspx.*

- Science Daily. *www.sciencedaily.com*

Note

1   *Science Daily* (2015) 'Cardiorespiratory fitness linked to thinner gray matter and better math skills in kids,' www.sciencedaily.com/releases/2015/08/150812151229.htm

Chapter 9
The material world

We humans have become addicted to plastic for a range of uses, from packaging to products.
Reducing our use of plastic bags is an easy place to start getting our addiction under control.

David Suzuki, scientist (b. 1936)

This chapter presents ideas for practice to guide the way children explore aspects of the material world. Learning starts with younger children exploring the names, properties and uses of common materials. In the next topic children further develop their knowledge of materials by enquiring into the properties and uses of textiles. The third topic focuses on the use of plastics and real-world issues associated with their use.

Topics in the chapter:

- Everyday materials
- Fabrics
- Plastic waste

Subject knowledge to support the teaching of these topics can be found in the core book, Loxley, P., Dawes, D., Nicholls, L. and Dore, B. (2018) *Teaching primary science: Promoting enjoyment and developing understanding*, Abingdon: Routledge, Chapter 17: The particle nature of materials.

Woolly saucepan

Could I have
a woolly saucepan
a metal jumper
a glass chair
and a wooden window-pane please?

Er – sorry – I mean
a woolly chair
a glass jumper
a wooden saucepan
and a metal window-pane please?

Er – sorry – I mean
Oh – blow it!
You know what I mean, don't you?

Woolly saucepan *by Michael Rosen*

In his poem 'Woolly saucepan' Michael Rosen teases the reader by describing objects in very odd ways. In the first verse he asks for a woolly saucepan, a metal jumper, a glass chair and a wooden window-pane. Materials are used for different jobs on the basis of their properties. Wool may be a good material for a jumper, but it would be a very poor material for a saucepan – unless of course some very clever person invented a new way of heating liquids!

We know that inventors invent clever and complex things. The television, the telephone and the motor car are complicated machines which are important parts of our modern lives. But what about more basic devices? Inventions do not have to be complicated to be useful and to influence the way we live. Think of the ballpoint pen as a device that changed people's lives. Love them or hate them, it can be argued ballpoint pens radically improved education by enabling writing in the classroom to be far easier and quicker.

Another simple invention we rarely think about is the paper bag. The flat-bottomed paper bag was an idea thought up by a factory worker called Margaret Knight towards the end of the nineteenth century. When working in a paper bag factory Margaret realised that the bags would be easier to pack if they had flat bottoms. Her idea inspired her to invent a machine which could make flat-bottom paper bags, which are still used today.

As well as paper, bags are made from a wide range of materials which include cotton, wool, leather and plastic. Cotton, wool and leather are natural materials, whereas paper and plastic are man-made. Although they are both man-made, plastic and paper are very different. Paper is made from trees. The wood is turned into pulp and then compressed to make paper. This means the raw material is just converted into another form. Essentially paper is just another form of wood. The same cannot be said for plastics. Plastics are manufactured from a combination of materials including oil, which are changed chemically to make new products. Plastics are perhaps the most versatile group of materials; they are cheap to manufacture and can be used to make almost anything. The problem is, whereas paper decays within months, plastics could take over 500 years to rot away. It is easy to make plastics, but getting rid of the waste is a huge environmental problem.

We may not have invented a woolly saucepan as yet, but we can already buy plastic saucepans, plastic jumpers, plastic chairs, plastic window-panes and plastic nearly everything else!

Reference

- Rosen, M. (2000) 'Woolly Saucepan' in *Centrally heated knickers,* London: Puffin Poetry.

Information sources

- About ballpoint pens. *http://blogs.ubc.ca/etec540sept12/2012/10/28/the-invention-of-the-ballpoint-pen-and-its-effects-on-literacy/*
- Famous women inventors. *www.women-inventors.com/Margaret-Knight.asp*

Ideas for practice

Topic: Everyday materials

Age group: 5–7 years

Introduction

The purpose of this topic is to enable children to describe and explore the properties of familiar materials. The activities provide opportunities for children to talk about a range of materials and their uses, and practise using scientific language. Enquiries include testing different types of paper for making bags, and other materials to make a tent for teddy.

Scientific view

Objects in the world are made from materials such as paper, plastic, glass, rubber, wood and metal. Materials have their own properties. For example, materials may be soft or hard, stretchy or stiff, rough or smooth, absorbent or not absorbent and so on. The material from which an object is made depends on its purpose. A bouncy ball can be made from rubber but not from metal. Rubber is squashy and bouncy, and good for making a ball, whereas metal is strong, hard and not very bouncy. Metal is often used for making things which need to be solid and strong such as hammers, nails, knives, pans and many other things we use in our homes.

Working scientifically

In these activities children will:

- ask questions, recognising they can be answered in different ways;
- use simple equipment;
- perform simple tests;
- identify and classify materials;
- use their observations to answer questions.

Health and safety

Choose appropriate materials, tools and glues for making and testing activities. Support and supervise activities following the ASE guidelines in *Be Safe!* (2011). Make sure all electrical equipment is PAT tested and used under close supervision.

Exploration stage

Children's talk involves trying out their own ideas

Setting the scene

Start by reading Michael Rosen's poem 'Woolly saucepan'. Discuss the poem with the children. What do they think about the idea of having a woolly saucepan? What would happen to it if it were put on the stove? How would they like to wear a metal jumper, sit on a glass chair or live in a house with wooden window-panes? Together, re-write the poem so that it makes more sense. Children should justify the changes. For example, they should give reasons why metal is a better material for a saucepan than wool and so on. Use the terms 'material' and 'properties' in discussion.

Modelling

Prepare large lucky dip boxes for each group with lots of different objects. These should include things made from plastic and paper such as a plastic bottle of water, bag of crisps, plastic toy, plastic cup, paper bag, a piece of writing paper, small cardboard box and small book, as well as objects made from other materials.

Start by sitting children in a circle with a lucky dip box in the middle. Put your hand in the box without looking, choose an object and describe how it feels. Model the scientific words which you want the children to use such as soft, squashy, stretchy, stiff, bendy, hard, brittle, rough, smooth and so. Use words which will be familiar to them. Encourage them to ask questions which could help identify the object. Reveal the object and talk about the material it is made from and its uses. Can children say why the material is suitable? Ask for a volunteer to choose an object and repeat the game.

Scientific enquiry

In groups children play the lucky dip game. Once they have identified an object they should name the material it is made from. Focus on children's use of scientific language. Model the use of the words 'materials' and 'properties' when discussing the objects. They can draw a picture of the object and record its properties. Children finish the game by sorting the objects into groups with similar materials. Discuss what the word 'material' means to the children. Do they understand that objects are made from materials?

Evaluating products

Figure 9.1 **Desk tidy**

Source: iStock

Create a display of different types of desk tidies or organisers. Children will probably be familiar with their use. Discuss what children know about them. Talk about their purpose. Provide each group with a different tidy, and ask them to decide if it would be suitable for them to use. What would they keep in it? Using items which they normally use on their tables, children can test whether they think their tidy is the right design for them. Groups present their ideas, and demonstrate the use of their tidy. Focus discussion on the types of materials, and their properties. Do children think the materials are suitable? Explore their reasons. Can they think of any other materials which could be used for a desk tidy? If they made their own desk tidy, which materials would they use?

Puzzle

Tell children that they can make their own desk tidy, but first they need to decide what it would look like and what materials they would use to make it.

Design and make

Provide children with a range of materials and items to choose from including small cardboard boxes, cardboard tubes, plastic cups, paper cups, polystyrene cups, corrugated plastic sheets, a range of sheet cardboard and any other useful materials. Groups can sort the items and materials according to whether they think they are useful for making a desk tidy. Groups should justify their choices. They then discuss how they will use the items and materials, and agree on a design for their desk tidy. Children can sketch and discuss a range of designs, before agreeing on a final one. They present their final design drawings to the class, and justify their product with regard to what they intend to put in it. They should also explain why the properties of the materials are appropriate.

Provide appropriate tools, supervision and support for making the product. Children evaluate their desk tidy by demonstrating its use to the class.

Formative assessment

Provide opportunities for children to voice what they have learnt in the exploratory stage. Use evidence from their responses to the puzzle and other activities to assess differences between children's ideas and the scientific view. Plan how you will use the re-describing stage to help the children address their *learning needs* (see Chapter 1). You may need to modify the activities depending on the collective and individual needs of your children.

Information and teaching resources

BBC Bitesize:

- Sorting and using materials.
  www.bbc.co.uk/schools/scienceclips/ages/5_6/sorting_using_mate.shtml

Re-describing stage

Children's talk involves making sense of scientific ideas

Teacher-led discussion

Referring to substances such as metal, rubber, plastic and wood as materials can be confusing. When children hear the word 'material' they often equate it with the word fabric or cloth. Review children's understanding of the word by creating a display of products made from plastic, metal, wood, glass, rubber, paper and fabric. Ask children to identify the materials. Pick up on misconceptions about the meaning of the word. Point out that 'material' is a scientific word and refers to what anything is made from, not only fabric or cloth. Focus on developing scientific language. Use BBC and BPES video clips to extend the discussion to everyday objects and materials found outside the classroom.

Model 'silly materials' statements and let children make up their own.

- A cotton sink is silly because …. A sink can made from ….
- A paper house is silly because … A house can be made from ….
- A glass bag is silly because …. A bag can be made from ….

Story-telling

Figure 9.2 **The flat-bottomed paper bag was invented by Margaret Knight**

Source: iStock

Tell children the story of Margaret Knight and how she was the first person to invent the flat-bottomed paper bag. Tell them about how someone else tried to claim the credit. There is extensive information about her on the web.

Puzzle

Show children examples of different types of paper bags and discuss their uses. Is paper a good material to make a bag? What other materials could be used? Discuss children's responses and encourage them to provide reasons for their ideas.

Scientific enquiry

Ask children how they could find out which type of paper is best for making a shopping bag. What properties does the paper need? Does it need to be strong, stretchy, hard, bendy, flexible, waterproof, brittle or stiff? Model words for children to consider. Together, decide on the properties required and draw out the idea that the paper needs to be strong and flexible.

Provide different types of paper for children to test, some of which are clearly not appropriate for the job. For example, include things like tissue and poor quality kitchen paper, as well as card which is clearly not flexible enough. Help groups devise simple tests to sort the materials according to whether they are strong and flexible enough to make a shopping bag.

Design and make

Before finally deciding which paper to use groups need to consider the design of the bag. Remind them of its purpose and model some possible designs. Are they going to make a flat-bottomed bag? Children draw pictures of what their bag will look like. Remind them to consider how they will carry it. Children present and justify their designs.

Provide appropriate tools, supervision and support for making the product. Children evaluate their shopping bag by demonstrating its use to the class.

Modelling

Modelling ideas through mime is a fun and effective way for children to convey their thinking. Contexts for mime need to be familiar and meaningful for the children. For example, ask children to mime climbing a metal ladder. Then swap the metal ladder for one made from a different material such as jelly or paper, and ask them to continue their mime. Stop them during their mime to explain their actions. For this topic, possible mimes could be:

- Washing in a metal bath, then swapping to one made of cardboard, chocolate or ice.
- Riding a metal bicycle, then swapping to one made from paper, rubber or glass.
- Rowing a wooden boat, then swapping to one made from stone, sponge or wool.

Ideas about 'dramatic science' can be found in the *Primary Science* article listed below.

Story-telling

Children think of their favourite three objects at home, draw pictures and talk about how they use them and the materials from which they are made.

> **Talking points: true, false or not sure?**
>
> - It is better to make bottles out of plastic than paper.
> - It is better to make a bouncy ball out of stone rather than rubber.
> - It is better to make a hat out of glass than wool.
> - It is better to make a window-pane out of glass rather than metal.
> - It is better to make a knife out of paper than metal.

Discuss children's reasons for their responses to the talking points. Probe their ideas and identify any outstanding *learning needs*.

Information and teaching resources

BBC Bitesize:

- What are objects made from? *www.bbc.co.uk/education/clips/zf7jmp3*

- Materials and their uses. *www.bbc.co.uk/education/clips/zm2jmp3*

- Materials and their properties: *www.bbc.co.uk/education/clips/z7qd7ty*

- Which material do we use? *www.bbc.co.uk/guides/z9pgcdm*

Other websites:

- BP Educational Services – Introducing materials. *http://bpes.bp.com/primary-resources/science/ages-4-to-7/uses-of-everyday-materials/introducing-materials/*

- BP Educational Services – Testing the strength of paper. *http://bpes.bp.com/primary-resources/geography/ages-7-to-11/geography/measuring-strength-of-materials-experiment-activity/*

- Famous women inventors. *www.women-inventors.com/Margaret-Knight.asp*

ASE Journals:

- Primary Science 123 (May/June 2012) *Dramatic science at key stage 1: Modelling ideas within an Olympic theme* by Deb McGregor and Wendy Precious.

Application stage

Children's talk involves trying out scientific ideas

Design and make a tent for teddy

Erect a simple tent in the school grounds and put a teddy inside. Start your lesson in the classroom by showing children a picture of people camping. If you have been camping show them some of your photographs. Ask the children whether they have ever been camping and listen to their stories. Encourage them to describe their family tents. Talk about the purpose of their tent? What do they think it is made from?

Take the children outside to see the tent. Compare it with tents the children have used. Describe what it is made from and how it is erected. Focus on the canvas and talk about its properties. Draw out that it needs to be strong to protect from the wind and waterproof to keep out the rain.

Let children look inside and find teddy. Tell them teddy is having a camping holiday, but he is not happy. The tent is too big. He would like his own tent. Do they think they could make a teddy-size tent to make him happy?

Back in the classroom talk about suitable materials to make teddy's tent. Remind them that the material should be strong and waterproof. Provide a range of sheet materials for children to test such as paper, cotton, nylon, polythene and wool. Include some which are clearly

Figure 9.3 **Make a tent for teddy**

Source: iStock

not suitable for making a tent. Groups can test small pieces of the materials to find those which have the right properties. Guide the planning of their tests and ask them to sort the materials into ones which are suitable and those which are not. Discuss the reasons for their choices.

Groups can make a simple tent for teddy using construction kits for the frame, covered with a sheet of their chosen material. Alternatively, they can use lengths of dowel stuck in Plasticine to make a frame. Groups will need to measure teddy to make sure their tent is big enough for him. Test the tents using a small watering can to see if they are waterproof, and use a hairdryer or fan (supervised by an adult) to test whether they are windproof. Challenge children to think of ways to improve the design of their tents. Extend the project by designing and making a camp bed for teddy to sleep on, and suitable camping clothing and other equipment he may need.

Information and teaching resources

BBC Bitesize:

● What materials are waterproof. *www.bbc.co.uk/education/clips/z26mbk7*

Other websites:

● BPES – Introducing materials. *http://bpes.bp.com/primary-resources/science/ages-4-to-7/uses-of-everyday-materials/introducing-materials/*

● Duct tape teddy bear tent. www.youtube.com/watch?v=py-EN3Z3G3Q

Topic: Fabrics

Age group: 7–9 years

Introduction

The purpose of this topic is to build on children's understanding of properties of materials and their uses. In the exploration stage children enquire into the thermal properties and structure of textiles and examine their uses. They also try their hand at simple weaving techniques. In the application stage children apply their knowledge to solve a problem which involves making thermal insoles for their shoes.

Scientific view

Clothes are mainly made from materials called textiles, often also called fabrics. Textiles are made from natural materials such as cotton and wool, or man-made materials such as nylon and polyester. Different types of fabrics have their own properties. Woollen fabrics tend to be stretchy, warm, fluffy and soft, and are often used for winter coats, jumpers and hats because they are good thermal insulators. Cotton fabrics are generally thinner, less stretchy and not as warm as woollen materials. Cotton fabrics are worn all the year around, but are generally cooler and more comfortable to wear than wool in summer.

Working scientifically

In these activities children will:

- ask questions and use scientific enquiries to answer them;
- set up simple practical enquiries, and comparative and fair tests;
- make systematic observations and measurements using standard units;
- record findings using scientific language, drawings, tables and charts;
- report findings orally and through displays and presentations;
- use results to draw conclusions.

Health and safety

It is not recommended to use mercury-filled thermometers in primary classrooms. Use the correct tools for textiles. Choose cutting and making tools appropriate to the age and capability of the children. Supervise all making activities following ASE guidance in *Be Safe!* (2011).

Exploration stage

Children's talk involves trying out their own ideas

Setting the scene

Start with a hot-seating activity. The child in the hot-seat is given a card with the name of a material on it. He/she then has to mime an object made from the material and the class have to guess what that object is. Volunteers can mime other objects made from the same material for the class to guess. After modelling the activity, the class can divide into groups, each receiving a card with a different material named on it. Children take turns miming objects made of that material for their partners to guess. Each group can choose its favourite mime and perform it for the class to guess both the object and the material. Children must explain why the properties of the material are appropriate for the object.

Puzzle

Link to the last activity by asking children to mime things made from ice and snow. Have fun miming melting snow. Show them a video clip of *The snowman* by Raymond Briggs. Ask children how they could stop the snowman melting. Discuss their ideas.

Figure 9.4 **How can we stop a snowman melting?**

Source: iStock

Talking points: true, false or not sure?

- His hat will help stop his head from melting.
- His hat will make his head melt faster.
- His hat will make his head warm.
- His hat will keep his head cold.

Groups discuss the talking points and develop a view about the effect the hat will have on the snowman. Groups come together to share their ideas. They explain their thinking, and try to arrive at a common view.

Scientific enquiry

In groups children review their responses to the puzzle and decide how to test whether their ideas are valid. Have ready woollen fabric, small ice balloons, thermometers/data recorders, stopwatches and other equipment children may need to test their ideas. The ice balloons can be used to represent the snowman's head. Children take appropriate temperature measurements and record their data. Talk to children as they are working and probe the reasons for their response to the talking points, and their approaches to the enquiry. Children present their results by drawing their own cartoon with captions explaining what they have found out. Conclude the best way to help prevent a snowman melting.

Story-telling

Bring your favourite winter hat into school. Tell children the story of why and when you bought it. Talk about what it is made from and how it keeps your head warm. Discuss other types of clothes you wear in winter to keep warm. Listen to children's stories about their hats and the warm clothing which they wear in winter. Try to arrive at some consensus about the types of materials which best keep us warm.

Scientific enquiry

Provide groups with samples of different fabrics including natural and man-made materials, and make available equipment to test their thermal insulation properties. Help children plan tests to compare the thermal properties of the fabrics and find the ones most suitable for winter clothing such as hats or gloves. Children create annotated pictures of the type of clothing which could be made from each of the fabrics. Make a display of their pictures together with samples of the fabrics and their thermal properties. Assess whether their scientific language is appropriate when children are talking about the outcomes of the enquiry.

Scientific enquiry

Display a range of hats made from different materials. Ask children to predict which hat would best prevent the snowman's head melting. To test their predictions, place each hat on a similar sized ice balloon (the snowman's head) and observe what happens over a period of time. Start the experiment at the beginning of the day, and take photographs at regular intervals until the results are clear. Which hat had the best insulation properties? Was it made from a man-made or natural material? Display the photographs.

Story-telling

Children use information sources to research the clothes worn by people who live in very cold climates. They can tell the story of the lives of people such as the Inuit. Their narrative should try to explain how their clothes keep them warm. Do they keep the warmth in, or do their clothes keep the cold out?

Formative assessment

Provide opportunities for children to voice what they have learnt in the exploratory stage. Use evidence from their responses to the puzzle, talking points and other activities to assess differences between children's ideas and the scientific view. Plan how you will use the re-describing stage to help the children address their *learning needs* (see Chapter 1). You may need to modify the activities depending on the collective and individual needs of your children.

Information and teaching resources

BBC Bitesize:

- Making sculptures out of snow and ice. *www.bbc.co.uk/education/clips/zw7w2hv*

- Product testing. *www.bbc.co.uk/education/clips/zvhqxnb*

- Testing materials. *www.bbc.co.uk/education/clips/zgsmhyc*

Other websites:

- Resources from the RSC. *www.primaryresources.co.uk/science/pdfs/rsc_tc_nc1.pdf*

- Miming activity. *http://bpes.bp.com/media/2844/Material%20Mime.pdf*

- BPES classifying materials. *http://bpes.bp.com/primary-resources/science/ages-7-to-9/materials/classifying-materials-online-experiment/*

- The Snowman. *www.youtube.com/watch?v=HHCZhUZXhZU*

- Walking in the air (The Snowman). *www.youtube.com/watch?v=ubeVUnGQOIk*

ASE Journal:

- Primary Science 130 (Nov/Dec 2013) *Getting third graders to put on their science 'thinking caps'* by Sonali Raje and Elizabeth Bartleson.

Re-describing stage

Children's talk involves making sense of scientific ideas

Teacher-led discussion

Use video clips to talk about how wool and cotton fabrics are produced. Compare their properties. Discuss examples of the raw materials and trace them back to sheep and cotton plants. Discuss how wool is a form of hair which sheep grow all over their bodies to keep them warm and dry in winter.

Scientific enquiry

Children use magnifiers to explore the structure of wool and cotton fabrics. Use electronic microscopes and upload images directly onto the smart board. Children can make drawings of what they observe and compare them with magnified pictures of the fabrics from the web. Point out how air is trapped between the fibres, especially in woollen material, giving it its insulating properties.

Demonstrate how to use a simple card loom to weave a woollen textile. A range of video clips on the web demonstrate how it is done (refer to the websites listed below). Once children have developed the skill they can design and make their own multi-coloured sampler.

Story-telling

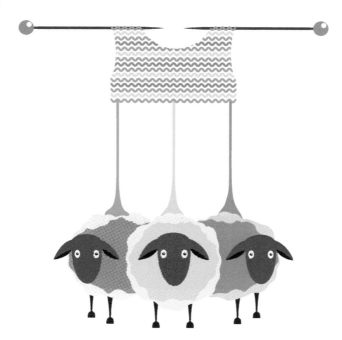

Figure 9.5 **From sheep to woolly jumper**

Source: iStock

Children use information sources to tell the stories of cotton and wool starting with the raw materials at the farm and ending up as products in the shops. Children contrast how their stories begin in different parts of the world yet can end up as products in the same shop not far from their homes. Children present their story in the form of a blog entry.

Information and teaching resources

BBC Bitesize:

- Making cotton fabric. *www.bbc.co.uk/education/clips/ztfpyrd*
- How wool is made. *www.bbc.co.uk/education/clips/zbspyrd*

Other websites:

- BPSE – Thermal insulators and conductors. *http://bpes.bp.com/primary-resources/science/ages-7-to-9/materials/thermal-conductors-and-insulators-online-experiment/*
- Kids video show – how does wool become a sweater. *www.youtube.com/watch?v=8v9ej4ulR98*
- Weaving activity. *www.youtube.com/watch?v=-ByYj5G4-Hc*
- Weaving activity. *www.youtube.com/watch?v=LbtKnvc_9No*
- Weaving with paper. *www.youtube.com/watch?v=QL6QTVvDTgc*
- STEM Centre – simple weaving. *www.stem.org.uk/system/files/elibrary-resources/legacy_files_migrated/2921-loomfish-2696.pdf*

Application stage

Children's talk involves trying out scientific ideas

Problem-solving in Greenland

Arrange the chairs in the classroom as if they were seats on an aeroplane. Tell children you are the pilot and you are going to take them on a trip to Greenland. What do they expect Greenland will be like?

Ask children how they would prepare for the trip. What questions would they ask a travel agent to help them prepare? In groups children can make a list of questions to ask about Greenland. They then research the answers on the web. Children make a list of the clothes they need to take with them. Each group should justify the types of clothes they have chosen.

Back on the plane children talk about what they would like to do when they get there. Would they like a dog sled tour to see the icebergs and spend a night inside an ice cave? Unfortunately, after they land their bags go missing with all their warm clothing, and the trip to see the icebergs is the very next day. Warm coats can be found for them but there are no warm shoes which will fit them. What are they going to do? Having cold feet in Greenland is not exactly fun. Perhaps they can design and make insoles for the shoes in which they travelled which will protect them against the cold?

The challenge is to choose appropriate materials, and then design and make a shoe insole to keep their feet warm. Make available a range of common of materials such as paper, card and different types of fabric.

The requirements for the design of the insole are:

1   The insole should be built from a maximum of two kinds of insulating materials.

2   The insole should be a maximum of 2cm thick.

3   The insole should be comfortable to wear inside the shoe.

Working in groups, children plan and carry out tests to find a combination of materials with the best thermal properties. They then make design drawings, take careful measurements and make patterns before making the product. Comfort is an important test of any footwear, so children should test whether their insoles are comfortable and warm. Test results should be presented so that the thermal properties of their insoles can be compared to other groups. From the comparisons the insoles can be put on a scale of very good, good and not good. Use the presentations to probe and assess children's ideas and identify any outstanding *learning needs*.

This project, called Cosy Toes, is taken from the STEM Centre website where you can find further details and resources.

Information and teaching resources

BBC Bitesize:

● Designing and making shoes. *www.bbc.co.uk/education/clips/zkj8q6f*

● Building sculptures out of snow. *www.bbc.co.uk/education/clips/zqmqxnb*

Other websites:

● STEM Centre – Cosy Toes project. *www.stem.org.uk/elibrary/resource/35618/cosy-toes-winter-proof-a-pair-of-shoes*

Topic: Plastic waste

Age group: 9–11 years

Introduction

What to do with the vast amount of waste produced by the developed and developing world is a major challenge for governments around the world. The purpose of this topic is to make children aware of the problem and to encourage them to look at waste plastics as a possible resource using inspirational ideas from the developing world.

Scientific view

Waste is a problem for all of us, especially plastics which take a long time to decompose. Plastic is a synthetic material, meaning it has been made by chemically changing another substance, in this case oil. The manufacture of plastics needs a lot of energy. For example, 9 supermarket carrier bags require the equivalent energy to driving a car a distance of 1km. Before supermarkets charged for supplying bags, the UK used up to 20 billion plastic bags every year. Let the children do the maths to find the equivalent in car miles. That's a lot of energy and a lot of waste. Plastic bags are strong and last hundreds of years so why waste them by sending them to landfill.

Working scientifically

In these activities children will:

- plan scientific enquiries to answer questions including controlling variables where necessary;
- take measurements using scientific equipment;
- record data and compare results;
- report and present findings from enquiries in appropriate ways;
- use scientific information to inform and evaluate their enquiries.

Health and safety

Ensure any plastics for enquiries are safe and clean. Use protective gloves where necessary. Follow ASE guidance in *Be Safe!* (2011) for organising and supervising making activities. Risk assess a visit to a recycling plant in accordance with your school policy.

Exploration stage

Children's talk involves trying out their own ideas

Setting the scene

Show children a picture of a landfill site. What comes into the children's minds? Do they know what types of materials are put in landfill? In groups children discuss materials which they think are put into landfill and those which are recycled. Here are some facts about landfill to share with the children.

- On average every person in the UK throws away their own body weight in rubbish every 7 weeks. In less than 2 hours the UK could fill the Albert Hall with its waste.
- 8 million nappies are thrown away every day.
- 7 million trees are cut down each year to make disposable nappies.

● It is estimated that as much as 80% of the contents of our general waste wheelie bin could have been recycled or composted.

● Each year in the UK, we dispose of enough electrical and electronic waste to equal the weight of 1,000,000 cars or 150,000 double decker buses.

Children talk about the things which they put in their bins at home, and what they think happens to them. Probe their understanding of the problems with landfill and the reasons for recycling.

Figure 9.6 **Landfill site**

Source: iStock

Scientific enquiry

Groups use information sources to research what happens to the waste we produce in our homes and explore the environmental and resource problems our rubbish represents. From the research, groups create information posters designed to make children of their age aware of the need to dispose of waste responsibly.

Puzzle

Focus children's attention on the use of plastics. Most plastics are non-biodegradable and cause problems in waste incineration since many of them give off poisonous gases when burned. They can persist in the environment for hundreds of years, in our soils, seas, rivers and lakes where they are a danger to wildlife. 75% of domestic plastic waste ends up in landfill sites where it will pollute the earth for hundreds of years to come. The puzzle is, what can be done to alleviate the problem?

Scientific enquiry

To reduce plastic waste, shops and supermarkets now charge for supplying plastic shopping bags to their customers. It is thought this will considerably reduce the amount of plastic bags which end up in landfill. However, plastic bags are not only used for shopping. They have a wide variety of uses both in the home and at work. Children can investigate the uses of plastic bags at home and at school. They can also explore the use of plastic packaging in supermarkets and other shops. They present the outcomes of their enquiries in a display which features the wide range of plastic materials which are destined to end up in landfill.

Based on their enquiry children suggest ways of reducing the use of plastic bags at home and plastic packaging in supermarkets. Would selling more fresh food, rather than packaged ready-made meals make a significant difference? Are paper bags more environmentally friendly than plastic? Children can look at a range of options and make recommendations which can be added to the display.

Scientific enquiry

Recycling plastics reduces the amount that end up in landfill. Plastics are not all the same and the first process in recycling is to sort into similar types. For this enquiry children bring a range of clean waste plastic items into school until there is enough to fill a big black plastic bin bag for each group. Try to use degradable bin bags.

Provide each group with a bag of waste plastic items. They should first sort them according to their uses. They then test the items to see if those with common uses have similar properties. The following are common tests used to identify plastics.

1 Translucency – light test.

2 Hardness – scratch test – use end of scissors.

3 Flexibility – stiff or easy to bend without stressing.

4 Buoyancy – float or sink.

5 Stress marks – white marks on edges when cut.

6 Density – mass (grams) per unit volume (cubic centimetres).

Children use appropriate tables to record the results of their tests and use the outcomes to sort the plastics by their properties. They can then use symbols on the items and information sources to identify the different types of plastics. Some plastics are harder to recycle than others. Children can find out which of their items are destined to be recycled, and which are likely to end up in landfill.

TABLE 9.1 Possible table for results

Samples taken from:	Translucency	Hardness	Flexibility	Buoyancy	Stress marks	Density
cola bottle						
water bottle						
sauce bottle						
packaging for vegetables						
bags						
other products						

WHAT DO RECYCLING SYMBOLS ON PLASTICS MEAN?

PET, PETE
(Polyethylene Terephthalate)
- Soft drink; water and salad dressing bottles; peanut butter and jam jars…
- Suitable to store cold or warm drinks. Bad idea for hot drinks.

PP
(Polyethylene)
- Reusable microwaveable ware; kitchenware; yogurt containers; microwaveable disposable take-away containers; disposable cups; plates…

HDPE
(High-density Polyethylene)
- Water pipes; milk; juice and water bottles; grocery bags; some shampoo / toiletry bottles…

PS
(Polystyrene)
- Egg cartons; packing peanuts; disposable cups; plates; trays and cutlery; disposable take-away containers… **Avoid for food storage**

PVC
(Polyvinyl Chloride)
- Not used for food packaging.
- Pipes; cables; furniture; clothes, toys…

Other
(often Polycarbonate or ABS)
- Beverage bottles; baby milk bottles; compact discs; 'unbreakable' glazing; lenses including sunglasses, prescription glasses, automotive headlamps, riot shields, instrument panels…

LDPE
(Low-density Polyethylene)
- Frozen food bags; squeezable bottles; e.g. honey; mustard; cling films; flexible container lids…

Figure 9.7 **Symbols on plastic products**

Story-telling

Children use information sources to help tell the story of a plastic bottle from the time it is dropped in their recycling bin at home to the time they pick up a product from a supermarket made from recycled plastic of a similar type. Children share their stories with their family at home so they all know what happens to their waste plastic bottles.

Visit a recycling plant

Organise a visit to a recycling plant to see how the waste plastic products are sorted, and treated. If this is not possible, contact your local council to organise a visit to the school from an environmental education officer. In each case, plan the visit in advance with the children so they can prepare probing questions.

Formative assessment

Provide opportunities for children to voice what they have learnt in the exploratory stage. Use evidence from their responses to the puzzle and other activities to assess differences between children's ideas and the scientific view. Plan how you will use the re-describing stage to help the children address their *learning needs* (see Chapter 1). You may need to modify the activities depending on the collective and individual needs of your children.

Information and teaching resources

BBC Bitesize:

- Plastics. *www.bbc.co.uk/bitesize/ks2/science/materials/material_properties/read/4/*

- How paper is made. *www.bbc.co.uk/education/clips/z89g9j6*

- Production and use of plastics. *www.bbc.co.uk/education/clips/z3rb4wx*

Other websites:

- Facts about waste and recycling. *www.recyclingbins.co.uk/recycling-facts/*

- Facts and quiz about waste and recycling. *www.cbenvironmental.co.uk/docs/Recycling%20Activity%20Pack%20v2%20.pdf*

- How plastic bottles are recycled. *https://vimeo.com/7217407*

- Recycling plastic bottles in football jerseys. *http://604now.com/2013/05/03/video-nike-recycles-plastic-water-bottles-into-football-jerseys/*

- How paper is made. *www.youtube.com/watch?v=7IP0Ch1Va44*

- How plastic is made. *www.youtube.com/watch?v=6eCt0VDg-Kc*

Re-describing stage

Children's talk involves making sense of scientific ideas

Teacher-led discussion

This is an opportunity to review the things children learnt in the exploration stage. Start with video clips showing how waste is sorted for recycling. Focus on plastic and use information sources and video clips from the web to discuss how it is recycled. Point out that not all plastic is recycled. Most plastic bags are not recycled and end up in landfill sites. Talk about the energy wasted and the problems associated with landfill.

Discuss the types of items which are not recycled. Brainstorm all the items children can come up with. Remind them that 80% of items which we put in our general waste bins could be recycled. For example, waste food products such as tea bags, banana, apple, and orange and potato peel, apple cores and other vegetable matter could be composted. Mountains of discarded clothing and other textiles which end up in landfill could be recycled. Challenge children to work out what else could be recycled from the general waste.

Proposing solutions to the puzzle

Groups debate the problems an ever-increasing consumer population presents for waste management and what can be done about it. Ask them to identify the problems and suggest some solutions. Each group presents a set of proposals to be negotiated. Groups present arguments for their proposals to be accepted by the class.

Here are some ideas from the 'Young People's Trust for the Environment' to help reduce the amount of rubbish which ends up in landfill. Compare their ideas with the children's and find out which of these things they do at home.

● Don't mix up your rubbish. Separate glass, paper, metal and organic waste.

● Buy and use recycled paper products wherever possible. A list of stockists is available from Friends of the Earth.

● Use your own shopping bag.

● Refuse to buy over-packaged goods. Buy fresh unpackaged food whenever possible.

● When shopping look out for goods in recyclable containers.

● Contact your local authority and ask about their waste disposal and recycling policies.

● Contact Oxfam and other charities to find out what they are collecting. Items might include aluminium foil, cans, clothing and newspapers.

Children complete this activity by researching the work done by designers, scientists and engineers who are developing more sustainable solutions to oil-based plastics.

Information and teaching resources

BBC Bitesize:

● How long does it take rubbish to rot? *www.bbc.co.uk/education/clips/z268p39*

● What is the best way to sort waste? *www.bbc.co.uk/education/clips/z7x2tfr*

● Sorting materials to be recycled. *www.bbc.co.uk/education/clips/z373qty*

- What should I do with my rubbish? *www.bbc.co.uk/education/clips/zwywmnb*

Other websites:

- Measuring biodegradability. *http://sciencelearn.org.nz/Contexts/Enviro-imprints/Looking-Closer/Measuring-biodegradability*

- Recycling plastic waste. *https://vimeo.com/1910107*

- A view on biodegradable plastics. *http://testtube.com/dnews/the-shocking-truth-about-biodegradable-plastics*

- Young People's Trust for the Environment. *http://ypte.org.uk/factsheets/recycling/rubbish#section*

- Recycling egg shells. *https://student.societyforscience.org/article/eggshells-help-hatch-new-idea-packaging*

- Friends of the Earth. *www.foe.co.uk*

Application stage

Children's talk involves trying out scientific ideas

Recycling plastic products

Figure 9.8 **Child looking for materials to recycle**

Source: Practical Action

Show children the picture from the Practical Action website featuring a child in Nepal sorting through a rubbish tip. What comes into the children's minds when they see the picture? In groups children discuss their responses to the picture. Groups come together to discuss moral and social issues, as well as scientific ones. Children can visit the Practical Action website to find out how the charity makes use of technology to help the poor in developing countries.

The child is looking for plastic to recycle. For poor people who live in the developing world, waste plastic can be a valuable material from which they can make products to use and sell. *Plastics Challenge* is a project produced by Practical Action designed to help children explore how waste plastic is put into use. The full project can be found on the STEM Centre website.

The project focuses on the work of people in Nepal who use plastic bags to make household items like bowls, coasters, purses and bracelets.

Figure 9.9 **Basket made from plastic bags**

Source: Practical Action Nepal

Children may not be able to make anything as demanding as the above bowl, but they can explore the use of waste plastic for making simple products. Here are some ideas:

1 Cut plastic bags into strips and stretch the strips to make 'plarn' (plastic yarn). Investigate which type of plastic makes the best plarn. The plarn can be used to crochet simple coasters and bracelets, or anything else the children may want to make. Video clips showing ways of crocheting, weaving or knitting waste plastic can be found on the web. Refer to the websites listed below.

2   An interesting challenge is to design and make a vase using a plastic bottle. To have appeal a vase must have both function and style. Children should start by deciding what part the bottle will play in the design. They should decide who their product is aimed at, and work out how the bottle can be incorporated into a design which will appeal to the target market.

3   Plastic bottles can be made into interesting toys. Groups can design toys which appeal to younger children in the school. Form, performance and safety should be top of the design criteria. Groups start by canvassing the young children's ideas and then design toys to fit their expectations. Products should be tested and evaluated by the young children in a safe environment supervised by adults.

Information and teaching resources

● Practical Action website. *http://practicalaction.org/*

● STEM Centre Plastic Challenge. *www.stem.org.uk/elibrary/resource/35961/plastics-challenge*

● Weaving plastic bags. *www.youtube.com/watch?v=E_r96mDkSY0*

● Weaving plastic bags. *www.youtube.com/watch?v=cngkx8moTuE*

● Weaving plastic bags. *www.youtube.com/watch?v=clweSfS-PqQ*

● Making a flower from plastic bags. *www.youtube.com/watch?v=IuTUXWiryTc*

● Ways of re-using plastic bottles. *www.designrulz.com/product-design/2012/11/45-ideas-of-how-to-recycle-plastic-bottles/*

● Making a vase. *www.youtube.com/watch?v=MZrUW4DAfvw*

● Making a purse. *www.youtube.com/watch?v=bu7b0BTaZ94*

● Making a coaster. *www.youtube.com/watch?v=tPWUR4swQTE*

Chapter 10
Changing materials

I think it is a sad reflection on our civilization that while we can and do measure the temperature in the atmosphere of Venus, we do not know what goes on inside our soufflés.

Nicholas Kurti, physicist and chef (1908–1998)

Water features prominently in this chapter. In the first topic, young children learn to make homemade fruit juice, and then freeze the juice to make fruity ice cubes. The key ideas are melting and freezing. The next topic focuses on evaporation and condensation, and applies the ideas to explaining the water cycle. This topic also examines problems faced by people in developing countries in gaining access to clean water. The third topic starts by looking at milk as an example of a suspension which children experience every day. As the topic develops children explore different types of suspensions, which they compare with solutions. The final part of this topic focuses on irreversible changes, with children making plastic from milk and vinegar.

Topics in this chapter:

- In the kitchen
- The water cycle
- Solutions and suspensions

Subject knowledge to support the teaching of these topics can be found in the core book, Loxley, P., Dawes, D., Nicholls, L. and Dore, B. (2018) *Teaching primary science: Promoting enjoyment and developing understanding*, Abingdon: Routledge, Chapter 17: The particle nature of materials and Chapter 18: Changing materials.

Water, water, everywhere

In Coleridge's *Rime of the Ancient Mariner*[1], the sailor uses these words when describing his time stranded at sea:

> Water, water, everywhere,
> Nor any drop to drink.

Although Coleridge's poem relates to the experiences of a sailor who has returned from a long and dangerous sea voyage, the lines could just as easily apply to many people around the world who find it difficult to access clean drinking water.

There are over one billion people in the world who do not have access to clean water, and over two million die from waterborne diseases annually. Obtaining clean water in Africa and Asia often requires people, mainly women, to walk on average about 4km. In many developing countries time lost gathering water, and illness caused by water-borne diseases, limits people's lives to merely trying to survive. Lack of clean water is devastating for the lives of children. Education is lost to sickness and time spent searching for water, and as a result they are unable to escape the poverty in which they are trapped.

Water is the foundation of life. Most of the water on Earth resides in the oceans. If it remained there, life could not exist on the land. Fortunately, water readily evaporates and condenses. This means that when the sun shines on the oceans, water evaporates and rises in the air to form clouds. As the clouds rise and cool, they start to condense and droplets of water are formed. As the droplets become larger they also become heavier, and eventually gravity pulls them back down to earth. Where they end up depends on the movement of the clouds. If the clouds have moved away from the ocean, the rain could fall on the land, providing much needed water for animals, plants and other living things. Some of this water will find its way into rivers and underground channels, and eventually flow back to the ocean. This is the water cycle.

Unfortunately, nature does not distribute the rain evenly around the world. Some areas suffer drought, while others experience devastating floods. In many countries, low temperatures in winter turn rain to snow and ice, creating dangerous travelling conditions. Temperatures in some countries can drop below −40°C. The lowest natural temperature ever recorded at ground level is −89.2°C, which was at the Soviet Vostok Station in Antarctica. Pure water only exists as a liquid between the temperatures of 0° and 100° Centigrade. Water freezes at 0°C and turns into solid water, which we call ice. This process can be reversed by heating the ice until it returns to 0°C. Adding substances to water can reduce the temperature at which it freezes. For example, adding salt to water can reduce its freezing temperature to as low as −20°C.

When salt and water are mixed, the salt dissolves to form a solution. This means its structure breaks down into tiny particles which are not visible even with a microscope. To reverse the process, the water needs to be evaporated off and condensed leaving the salt behind. Not all substances mix with water to form solutions. For example, sand and oil do not dissolve in water and their large particles can easily be seen. A mixture which does not dissolve is called a suspension. Milk is a good example of a natural suspension in which the white fatty nutrients can be seen suspended in the liquid. Suspensions can be separated by physical processes such as standing, shaking, sieving and filtering.

Aid programmes in the developing world are producing inexpensive ways of filtering and purifying unclean water to help the people improve their lives. There is a lot of information and ideas to talk about in school available on the web.

Topic: In the kitchen

Age group: 5–7 years

Introduction

This topic provides children with opportunities to develop their understanding of freezing and melting in a range of familiar, everyday contexts. In the application stage children are introduced to the idea of irreversible change when making their own pizzas.

Scientific view

When water and other materials are cold enough they change from a liquid into a solid. When the solid is heated and becomes warm enough, it can change back to a liquid. Changing from a liquid to a solid is called freezing, and changing from a solid to a liquid is called melting.

Working scientifically

In these activities children will:

● ask questions and seek answers through enquiry methods;

● perform tests, observe their effects and collect data;

● use their observations and data to suggest answers to questions.

Health and safety

In this topic children work with different foods and hence ensuring high standards of hygiene is important. Before working with food children should tie back long hair, wash their hands and cover any cuts and scratches on their hands with waterproof dressings. Encourage children to wear aprons. Check children rewash their hands after breaks and visits to the toilet. Make sure all working surfaces and equipment are thoroughly cleaned before and after use. When planning this topic refer to the ASE publication *Be Safe!* (2011) for up-to-date health and safety guidance.

Exploration stage

Children's talk involves trying out their own ideas

Setting the scene

Start this topic with an adult making a simple fruit drink. Typically you will need about 450g of fruit such as blackberries and 500ml of water. Clean the fruit and remove all stalks. Add all the ingredients to a saucepan and simmer gently for ten minutes. Let the mixture cool and add to a clean glass container so children can see all the bits of fruit inside. Discuss what the bits are and whether the children know how to remove them. Listen to their ideas and pick up on ones which involve using a sieve.

Scientific enquiry

Using part of the juice, children explore ways to separate out the bits of fruit. Provide a range of different sieves, one of which is fine enough to trap the bits. Can they explain how the sieve works and why not every sieve managed to separate out the fruit?

Demonstrate how to use a fine sieve to remove bits of fruit from the juice and talk about how it works. Using clear plastic cups children taste the undiluted juice and then dilute it with water to taste. Add sugar to taste. Children compare the colour, taste and smell of the diluted and undiluted juice. Why does it taste so sweet? Can they see the sugar? Encourage children to speculate about what has happened to the sugar which was added to the pan. They might think it has disappeared. Pick up on their ideas and reinforce the idea that the sugar is there in the cordial but it is too small to be seen. If appropriate for your class, introduce them to the concept of dissolving.

Ask the children whether they like fruit lollies or ices. How could they turn fruit juice into ice? Provide suitable moulds and make ice lollies or blocks in the freezer. At suitable intervals children observe how their juice turns to ice.

Provide small ice cubes. Working in groups children use their senses to compare the properties of ice with water at room temperature. Encourage the children to find as many words as they can to describe them. How can they turn ice into water? One way is to put ice cubes in polythene bags, place the bags in warm tap water and watch the ice melt. Can they explain why it melts?

In groups, children talk about what they have learnt from the scientific enquiry. Bring the class back together, and ask each group to describe two things which they have learnt.

Puzzle

Show children the BBC Bitesize video *How to lift an ice cube with a piece of cotton*. Help groups to perform the same trick. Can they explain why it works? Probe their understanding of freezing and melting.

Scientific enquiry

Ask children whether they know any other things that melt. Can they name three things that would melt in their hand? Demonstrate how chocolate, butter and ice cream melt easily in the hand.

Which sweets melt in the hand? Which melt quickest: chocolate drops, smarties or jelly beans? Discuss children's ideas, explore their thinking and encourage them to make predictions. Help them plan tests to find which sweets melt quickest. Does the type of chocolate or colour of the sweet make a difference? Use simple digital timers or perhaps egg timers as ways to compare times. Children record their results using simple annotated drawings. Challenge children to explain their results. Why do some sweets melt in their hands? How can they make them solid again?

(Food used in such enquiries should always be disposed of, not consumed.)

Modelling

Set up a bowl of hot water with a metal saucer over it. Make sure children observe from a safe distance. In turn, add the different sweets to the saucer and time how long they take to melt. Ask children to describe what caused the chocolate to melt. Focus on the relationship between heating and melting. What words would they use to describe the chocolate before and after it melted?

Scientific enquiry

Finish this section by making chocolate chip cookies. Many easy recipes can be found on the web. Working with the help of adults, groups can measure out and combine the ingredients. The focus of the science is to observe and record all changes that take place, firstly after the ingredients are mixed, and then after they are baked in the oven. Children can talk and write about the changes, and their causes.

Formative assessment

Provide opportunities for children to voice what they have learnt in the exploratory stage. Use evidence from their responses to the puzzle and other activities to assess differences between children's ideas and the scientific view. Plan how you will use the re-describing stage to help the children address their *learning needs* (see Chapter 1). You may need to modify the activities depending on the collective and individual needs of your children.

Information and teaching resources

BBC Bitesize:

- Which materials dissolve in water? *www.bbc.co.uk/guides/zpd6hyc*
- Separating solids and liquids. www.bbc.co.uk/education/clips/zr89wmn
- How to lift an ice cube with a piece of cotton. *www.bbc.co.uk/education/clips/zjtkxnb*

Re-describing stage

Children's talk involves making sense of scientific ideas

Teacher-led discussion

Recap on what children learnt in the exploratory stage. Show children the video clip *Snow, ice and water* and discuss why the ice and snow are melting. Ask children to describe what ice feels like as it melts in their hands. How can they make the water into ice again? Talk together about the difference between a solid and a liquid, and the difference between freezing and melting. Help them elaborate on their ideas.

Scientific enquiry

Figure 10.1 **Icy roads in winter**

Source: iStock

Show children pictures of traffic chaos caused by icy roads. Ask them whether they know what is put on the roads in winter to melt the ice to prevent accidents. Talk about how salt is used. Have they ever seen big trucks spraying salt on the roads? Listen to children's stories and find out what they know.

Tell children they are going to do their own experiments to find out which materials can be used to melt ice. Help children plan tests to discover how quickly sprinkling salt over ice makes it melt. Compare tests with and without salt. Is salt the best material to use? Groups can test other household materials such as flour, baking powder, vinegar, sugar and safe sand. Use suitable timers to collect data. Children record data and draw their own conclusions.

What do their parents do in winter to melt ice on the windscreen of their car? Listen to children's stories and pick up on the use of de-icer sprays. In a well-ventilated area, demonstrate the use of a commercial de-icer. Do not allow children close to the ice when you are applying the spray. Compare how quickly equal amounts of crushed ice melt with and without the de-icer being applied. Does the de-icer work better than the materials they tested? Encourage children to use evidence to justify their views.

Finally, return to the puzzle. Can groups explain the trick? Probe their understanding of freezing and melting and address any outstanding *learning needs*.

Information and teaching resources

BBC Bitesize:

- Heating and cooling materials. *www.bbc.co.uk/guides/z2cq2hv*

- Snow, ice and water. *www.bbc.co.uk/education/clips/zpvfb9q*

- Changes in the state of materials. *www.bbc.co.uk/education/clips/zrkc87h*

- Building sculptures out of snow and ice. *www.bbc.co.uk/education/clips/zj2jmp3*

- Solids and liquids. *www.bbc.co.uk/education/clips/zfg3cdm*

Application stage
Children's talk involves trying out scientific ideas

Design and make a pizza

Children can make pizzas, naan or other types of bread. Below is a recipe for Pizza Margherita in 4 easy steps. Adult help and supervision will be needed at each stage. Be aware of medical, religious or cultural reasons for children being unable to handle or eat certain foods.

1   Children make the base by mixing flour, yeast and salt in a large bowl and adding 200ml of warm water and a tablespoon of olive oil. Mix well, and knead on a floured surface until the mixture is smooth.

2   Roll out the dough thinly so the pizza will cook quickly. Cut out mini pizzas from the dough, in whatever shapes the children like.

3   Use tomato paste for the base topping, and add healthy toppings chosen by the children. Grated cheese, cherry tomatoes and basil leaves would be my choice.

4   Bake in the oven at 240°C for about 10 minutes until crisp.

Show children the BBC Bitesize clip below and compare with how the children made their pizzas. Talk together about whether it would be possible to separate their ingredients by sieving or any other method after they are mixed together and after they are baked. Discuss how baking the mixture of materials in the oven has created something new called bread.

Information and teaching resources

BBC Bitesize:

● How ingredients mix together to create new materials.
  www.bbc.co.uk/education/clips/z92jfrd

Other websites:

● *BBC Good Food Show. www.bbcgoodfood.com/recipes/4683/pizza-margherita-in-4-easy-steps*

Topic: The water cycle

Age group: 7–9 years

Introduction

This topic provides opportunities for children to develop their understanding of evaporation and condensation, and then to apply their knowledge when explaining the water cycle. To provide a context for the work, children examine wet and dry climates around the world, and in the application stage explore how vital it is for people to have access to clean drinking water.

Scientific view

About 71% of the Earth's surface is covered in water, the vast majority of it being in the oceans. When the Sun shines on the water, some of it evaporates and rises. As the water vapour rises, it cools and condenses to form clouds made up of water droplets. As the clouds are blown over land by the wind, the water droplets can become bigger and heavier, and eventually fall to the ground as rain. This precipitation finds its way back into lakes, rivers and ultimately back into the seas and oceans, maintaining the water cycle.

Working scientifically

In these activities children will:

- ask questions and answer them in different ways;
- set up practical enquiries which include fair tests;
- take measurements using appropriate equipment;
- record findings in tables, charts and drawings;
- report findings orally, through displays and presentations;
- use results to draw conclusions and as evidence to support their arguments.

Health and safety

Choose appropriate sources of heat for the activities and have adult supervision at all times.

Exploration stage

Children's talk involves trying out their own ideas

Setting the scene

Figure 10.2 **Wettest place on Earth**

Source: Alamy

Start by asking children whether they know where the wettest place on Earth is. According to the *Guinness Book of Records*, the wettest place on Earth is Mawsynram in India which has an astonishing average annual rainfall of about 12 metres. Ask children to imagine what 12 metres of water would be like if it all fell at once. To get an idea, they can measure the height of the classroom and use the data to approximate the height of different types of buildings. What would be the effect of 12 metres of rain on the school buildings? Would they all be submerged in the flood? How would their homes fare?

Story-telling

Which are the rainiest and the driest parts of the world? Children use information sources to contrast the rainfall in some of the wettest and driest parts of the world. They should describe the times of the year when it rains most, and how the climate in these areas influences the way the people live. Are there any advantages to living in these areas? What are the disadvantages? Groups produce their own documentaries on the subject, using case studies to contrast how wet and dry climates affect people's lives. After the presentations ask children to talk about how they collaborated and whether they benefited from working together, rather than working on their own. Prompt them to provide examples.

Teacher-led discussion

Based on children's presentations, talk together about whether it rains more in places with hot climates, or whether being close to the sea influences rainfall. Does being close to mountains or hills affect annual rainfall? Use their stories and further research to create a display of areas around the world which are prone to flooding.

Puzzle

On average, areas near the sea receive more rainfall than inland regions. Ask the children to explain why.

Talking points: true, false or not sure?

- Sea water and rain are the same thing.
- Rain cannot be sea water otherwise it would taste salty.
- Clouds make rain; rain does not make clouds.
- Rain creates rivers and lakes.
- The Sun makes rain.
- Without rain, there would be no seas.
- Without seas, there would be no rain.

Groups of children discuss the talking points, and try to reach agreement on their responses. Then they come together and share their ideas. Probe their thinking and encourage them to elaborate in order to provide full explanations. Assess their understanding of the causes of rain.

Scientific enquiry

To help children understand the causes of rain they need to investigate the factors which influence evaporation and condensation.

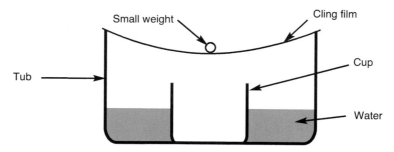

Small weight

Cling film

Cup

Tub

Water

Figure 10.3 **Model of water cycle**

Provide each group with equipment to make a model of the water cycle. Children can plan their own tests firstly to find out how the temperature of water affects the rate of evaporation, and then how the temperature of the cling film influences the amount of condensation. Only allow them to use hand-hot water from the classroom sink. They can change the temperature of the cling film by replacing the weight with ice cubes. Challenge groups to use their enquiry to hypothesise about how rain is produced.

Formative assessment

Provide opportunities for children to voice what they have learnt in the exploratory stage. Use evidence from their responses to the puzzle, talking points and other activities to assess differences between children's ideas and the scientific view. Plan how you will use the re-describing stage to help the children address their *learning needs* (see Chapter 1). You may need to modify the activities depending on the collective and individual needs of your children.

Information and teaching resources

BBC Bitesize:

- Rainfall and flooding around the world. *www.bbc.co.uk/education/clips/zkwxn39*

- The causes and effects of river flooding in Britain. *www.bbc.co.uk/education/clips/zfnb9j6*

- The wet season in Bangladesh. *www.bbc.co.uk/education/clips/zqxsb9q*

- Water and flooding in Bangladesh. *www.bbc.co.uk/education/clips/ztfcd2p*

Re-describing stage

Children's talk involves making sense of scientific ideas

Teacher-led discussion

Start by discussing the outcomes of children's enquiries and how they think rain may be formed. Use their model to explain how rain is produced. Develop the ideas using video clips and describe the water cycle. Use words such as evaporation, condensation and precipitation.

Modelling

Children will need space to role-play evaporation. Use the school hall or playground. To model a puddle of water children can huddle together in a group with each one representing a tiny particle of the liquid. Like all liquids water is fluid, meaning that the particles must be free to move within the body of the water. Children can model the fluid nature of the water by moving around within the group. Evaporation is modelled when particles near the edge of the puddle break away from the main group and move off into the air. Discuss what would happen if the puddle was heated by energy from the Sun. Particles would become more energetic, they would move around more vigorously, bumping into each other. The ones moving fastest would fly out of the liquid into the air. The hotter the water became the more vigorous the movement, resulting in higher rates of evaporation.

Scientific enquiry

In the exploratory stage children looked at how temperature influences rates of evaporation. They can now extend their enquiry to look at the effects of surface area and wind factors. Help them plan their tests. One way to test surface area is to use dishes with different diameters, using the same amount of water at the same temperature. For wind factor, they will need to work out ways of controlling the flow of air. Children record their results appropriately and draw conclusions about how different conditions affect rates of evaporation. Challenge children to explain their results by reasoning from the evaporation model described above.

Puzzle

Provide groups with a container of ice which has been kept in the freezer. They should only touch it with gloves on. Ask them to observe what happens to the outside of the container for five or more minutes. Where has all the water come from? Groups discuss and draw annotated pictures to explain. Probe their thinking and address any outstanding *learning needs.*

Story-telling

Finish this section by exploring mythical stories from around the world about the origins of rain. Children can use information sources to explore some of these traditional stories and invent their own myths about the origins of rain. Compare some of the myths with the scientific view. Discuss the difference between a scientific point of view, and a myth, legend, fable or a traditional tale.

Information and teaching resources

BBC Bitesize:

- The water cycle. *www.bbc.co.uk/education/clips/zh4rkqt*
- The water cycle. *www.bbc.co.uk/education/clips/zd7hyrd*

Other websites:

- The water cycle online experiment. *http://bpes.bp.com/primary-resources/science/ages-7-to-9/states-of-matter/the-water-cycle-online-experiment/*
- Myths and legends. *http://myths.e2bn.org/mythsandlegends/userstory14104-how-rain-came-to-man.html*

ASE Journals:

- Primary Science 138 (May/June 2015) *Adventure on the Thames* by Sarah Parker.
- Primary Science 126 (Sept/Oct 2013) *Now here's the weather forecast …* by Mathew Richardson.
- Primary Science 132 (March/April 2014) *Learning about the weather through an integrated STEM approach* by Gokhan Serin.

Application stage

Children's talk involves trying out scientific ideas

The projects in this section examine something that is essential to all life anywhere in the world – water. In particular, clean, drinkable water. Ideas in the projects are complementary and activities could be combined to produce rich, real-life learning opportunities for the children.

Water! Water!

This project has been produced by the charity Practical Action and is suitable for children of ages 7–11 years. It asks children to consider where their water comes from and what life would be like if it were not so readily available. It also examines the importance of the water we use being clean, and the consequences of drinking unclean water. Pupils investigate simple ways of making dirty water clean and improving sanitation. Full details of the project, including activity sheets, can be found on the Practical Action website.

Water for the world

This project was produced jointly by the charities Engineers without Borders and Practical Action. It is suitable for children of ages 7–11 years. The topic explores the problems faced by people in developing countries in gaining access to clean water. The main activity explores ways to make water clean and safe, and involves planning, designing, costing and making a water filter. Full details for the project, including a video clip, PowerPoint presentation and teacher guidance can be found on the STEM Centre website.

Figure 10.4 **Women collecting water in Africa**

Source: iStock

Children could mount an exhibition of their work in their classroom. They could lead an assembly to raise awareness in their school of the important roles water and hygiene play in our lives.

Information and teaching resources

Useful websites:

- Water! Water! *http://practicalaction.org/mtl-water-water*
- Water for the world. *http://practicalaction.org/water-for-the-world*
- Water for the world project details. *www.stem.org.uk/elibrary/collection/3972*
- It starts with water. *www.youtube.com/watch?v=mVTahkpVabw*

ASE Journal:

- Primary Science 129 (Sept/Oct 2013) *How do we clean our water and how clean does it need to be?* By Niki Whitburn.

Topic: Solutions and suspensions

Age group: 9–11 years

Introduction

This topic provides opportunities for children to develop their understanding of mixtures. The activities mainly focus on the structure of milk/cream, and how it can be used to make butter and ice cream. In the application stage milk is used to create a new type of material, which is a form of plastic.

Scientific view

A mixture is a combination of two or more substances which are not chemically combined. Sand and gravel, oil and vinegar, dust in air and salt in water are examples of mixtures. Milk or cream is a mixture of tiny globules of fat suspended in water. Suspensions can be separated by physical processes such as standing, shaking, sieving and filtering. Salt dissolved in water is not a suspension because its structure has broken down at an atomic level. It is a solution. A common way of separating solutions is by distillation involving evaporation.

Working scientifically

In these activities children will:

- plan scientific enquiries to answer questions;
- record data and classify using diagrams and drawings;
- use findings to make predictions and provide answers to questions;
- report and present findings in oral and written forms;
- use established scientific knowledge to further develop their ideas.

Health and safety

Remember to follow the hygiene and supervision rules for the preparation of food. Any equipment used in food-related activities should not be used for other purposes and should be stored in secure, clean conditions. If you do not have a dedicated sink, a washing-up bowl should be reserved exclusively for food. Children should be taught to wash their hands before and after handling any materials or food. All ingredients here are low-hazard, but may still be harmful if taken in sufficient quantity. Remember to check for allergies or cultural objections children may have relating to handling and eating some foods.

Exploration stage

Children's talk involves trying out their own ideas

Setting the scene

Start the lesson by providing each child with a serving of plain ice cream. Before they eat it ask them to describe its properties. Discuss whether its properties provide a clue to how it is made.

> ## Talking points: true, false or not sure?
>
> ● Ice cream comes from a cow.
>
> ● Ice cream is a mixture of fat and water.
>
> ● Ice cream is just ice, sugar and water.
>
> ● Ice cream is made from mashed potatoes.
>
> ● Ice cream is made from ice and cream.
>
> ● Ice cream is sweet because it contains lots of sugar.

Discuss children's responses to the talking points. Draw out that ice cream is indeed made from cream which comes from the milk of a cow. Children can look at a small amount of cream in petri-dishes with a hand magnifier and describe what they can see. Does this help them decide what cream is made from?

Puzzle

What is cream made from? Is it a mixture of things? If so, is it a solution, a suspension or some other type of mixture? Discuss children's ideas. How could they prove it is a mixture?

Scientific enquiry

Children plan their own enquiries to try to separate the materials which make up cream. Make sure their ideas are safe before they try them out. Have ready a range of equipment for sieving and filtering. Activities involving heating the cream should be closely supervised. Maintain hygiene throughout, and make sure the equipment is thoroughly cleaned after use. Do not allow the children to taste the cream at this stage.

One way to find out whether cream is a mixture is by shaking it. Groups will need small plastic jars with firmly fitting lids and lots of cream. Make sure the jars have been well cleaned. Children half-fill the jars with cream, secure the tops and shake them until the cream turns to butter. They can then pour the contents into a clean bowl and discuss what they have produced. Can they explain what has happened to the cream to produce the butter? Ask them to describe the taste of the butter and compare it to the cream. What is the liquid surrounding the butter? Discuss these questions with the children. Establish that due to the shaking, the fat in the cream has separated from the water to form butter. The watery milky by-product is called buttermilk. Children draw pictures to predict what cream might look like when seen through a powerful microscope. Ask them to explain their reasoning based on their enquiry. Display their pictures and encourage other groups to discuss and annotate them in order to challenge or add to the ideas.

Story-telling

Groups use information sources to find out how butter is produced from cow's milk. Their stories should include a comparison between the structure of milk, cream and butter. Groups present their stories using a multimedia format with links to video clips, and magnified images showing the differences between milk, cream and butter. Encourage questions at the end of each presentation. Talk about whether milk and cream are solutions or suspensions. Can they explain the difference?

Formative assessment

Provide opportunities for children to voice what they have learnt in the exploratory stage. Use evidence from their responses to the puzzle, talking points and other activities to assess differences between children's ideas and the scientific view. Plan how you will use the re-describing stage to help the children address their *learning needs* (see Chapter 1). You may need to modify the activities depending on the collective and individual needs of your children.

Re-describing stage

Children's talk involves making sense of scientific ideas

Teacher-led discussion

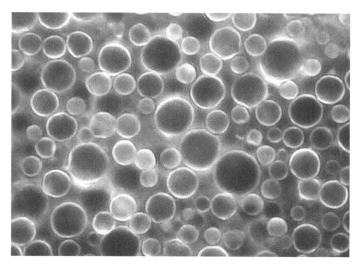

Figure 10.5 **Raw milk magnified 4,200 times**

Source: Beverly Rubik (2012) 'Microphotography of raw and processed milk: a pilot study,' *Wise Traditions in Food, Farming, and the Healing Arts*, Summer 2012, pp. 40–44

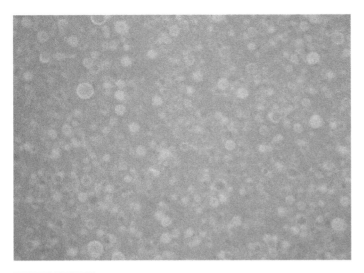

Figure 10.6 **Pasteurised milk magnified 4,200 times**

Source: Beverly Rubik (2012) 'Microphotography of raw and processed milk: a pilot study,' *Wise Traditions in Food, Farming, and the Healing Arts*, Summer 2012, pp. 40–44

Use magnified pictures of raw milk published on the web to show children that it is a mixture of water and particles of fat. Point out how the fat globules are suspended in the water. Compare the structure of raw milk with milk which has been pasteurised. Discuss the process of pasteurisation and point out how it changes the structure of the milk, and hence its taste.

Compare the magnified pictures from the web with the pictures drawn by children in the exploratory stage. Find images of other suspensions and compare them.

Scientific enquiry

Provide groups with a range of substances to make various combinations of mixtures. Sand, salt, sugar, vinegar, water, oil, gravel, paint powder, talcum powder and flour are the obvious ones. Provide magnifying lenses and microscopes so children observe the mixtures up close and record their structures through drawings. Talk about how particles in a suspension are relatively large. They are visible under a microscope and can often be seen with the naked eye.

When observing the solutions, children might think that the solute has simply disappeared, or turned into water. Some may also talk about the sugar or salt melting, rather than dissolving. Discuss how the particles in a solution are so small that they cannot be seen. Encourage children to weigh the water before and after sugar has been added. Using electronic scales, the extra weight of the sugar can be measured. Introduce children to the terms solute, solvent and dissolving when discussing solutions. Children classify their mixtures as either suspensions or solutions.

Each group should separate one suspension and one solution. Refer to *Be Safe!* (2011) when planning suitable sources of heat. Using diagrams children explain why some suspensions can be separated by filtering, but solutions cannot.

Modelling

Based on what they have learnt from the enquiry children should role-play being a suspension and a solution. Two-thirds of the group can represent the liquid particles, and the rest model the suspended or dissolved particles. Children should explain and compare their models. The main thing to talk about is the relative sizes of the particles. The size of the suspended particles should be large compared to the size of the liquid particles. For example, if each child represents a liquid particle, then four children holding hands can represent a suspended particle. For a solution the solute particles and the solvent particles can be a similar size. Discuss children's thinking behind the models, and use suitable video clips to help address any outstanding *learning needs*. Children can use role-play to illustrate the difference between dissolving and melting.

Information and teaching resources

BBC Bitesize:

- Separating mixtures of materials. *www.bbc.co.uk/education/clips/zb9c87h*

- Soluble and insoluble materials. *www.bbc.co.uk/education/clips/zx7w2hv*

- The behaviour of particles in solids, liquids and gases.
  www.bbc.co.uk/education/clips/zpbvr82

- The mineral content of water. *www.bbc.co.uk/education/clips/zfk4d2p*

Other websites:

- Raw milk magnified. *www.westonaprice.org/health-topics/microphotography-of-raw-and-processed-milk/*

ASE Journal:

- Primary Science 140 (Nov/Dec 2015) *Reflections on the use of tablet technology* by Nicki Wise, Deb McGregor and James Bird.

Application stage

Children's talk involves trying out scientific ideas

Design and make ice cream

Children can design and make their own ice cream. Use information sources and video clips to research recipes and instructions for making the ice cream. Children create their own video entitled 'The science of ice cream', which shows how to make ice cream and also explains the changes to the materials at each stage of making.

Making plastic

Traditional plastics are made from crude oil, which is a non-renewable resource. As well as being unsustainable in the future, waste products made from traditional plastics are difficult to dispose of because they take a long time to decay and create dangerous pollutants when incinerated.

Although recycling traditional plastics reduces some of the problems, scientists are looking for alternative raw materials for making new kind of plastics. Children can use information sources to explore the work done by scientists around the world in their search for new types of plastic.

Children may be surprised to find that milk can be used to make a special type of plastic, called casein plastic which is easy to make in the classroom. All they need is a pint of whole milk, 20ml of white vinegar, water, protective gloves and a fine sieve or cotton cloth. Detailed instructions about how to make the plastic can be found on the web. Basically, it involves warming the milk in a saucepan and stirring in the vinegar. The mixture is then separated using a sieve and the white plastic collected and used to make a small artefact. There are opportunities for children to experiment with different types of milk, and different types of vinegar or other mildly acidic liquids. They can also explore using additives to colour the plastic. Activities need to be well supervised. Refer to *Be Safe!* (2011) for H&S guidance.

Discuss the science behind the plastic. The change from milk to plastic is irreversible because the plastic is a new material with a different chemical structure. Be warned, the plastic will go 'off' after a while and will begin to smell. Point out to the children, that casein plastic is just a first step in our search for a new type of sustainable plastic. The Royal Academy of Engineering provides details of a STEM project for making plastic from milk, entitled *Milking it*.

Information and teaching resources

BBC Bitesize:

● How to make ice cream – turning a liquid into a solid.
www.bbc.co.uk/education/clips/z2qdnbk

Other websites:

● How to make plastic from milk and vinegar. *www.youtube.com/watch?v=akhs3wcSDGA*

● Homemade ice cream. *www.youtube.com/watch?v=j70yTq2ysLQ*

● Milking it. *www.raeng.org.uk/RAE/media/Publications/Activity%20Resources/milking-it.pdf*

Note

1   Samuel Taylor Coleridge (Text of 1834) *The Rime of the Ancient Mariner*, www.poetryfoundation.org/poems-and-poets/poems/detail/43997

Chapter 11
Earth and space

The scientific theory I like best is that the rings of Saturn are composed entirely of lost luggage!

Mark Russell (b. 1932)

Over the last few decades NASA has launched many missions out into the Solar System to discover its secrets. Space probes have sent back pictures and made discoveries which have enabled us to understand the structure of our Solar System in great detail. An exciting feature of space exploration is the search for extra-terrestrial life within our Solar System, and the discovery of *Goldilocks Planets* out in deep space with potential to support life.

Topics in this chapter:

- Journey to the Moon
- Mission to Mars
- In search of Goldilocks Planets

Subject knowledge to support the teaching of these topics can be found in the core book, Loxley, P., Dawes, D., Nicholls, L. and Dore, B. (2018) *Teaching primary science: Promoting enjoyment and developing understanding*, Abingdon: Routledge, Chapter 11: The Earth and beyond.

Exploring the Solar System and beyond

How wonderful it be would be to travel to far distant alien worlds. We can only fantasise about space travel as depicted in science fiction stories, but with today's space telescopes we are able to explore the depths of our Galaxy in search of extra-terrestrial life without our feet leaving the ground.

The telescope was first used by Galileo Galilei in the seventeenth century. When he turned his telescope to the heavens he was able to observe things that were impossible to see with the naked eye. For example, he saw that Jupiter had its own moons which orbited the planet. This was a revolutionary discovery, because at the time it was generally believed that everything in the universe went around the Earth.

Galileo was an arrogant man and not well liked by his peers. Many fellow academics refused to look through his telescope. They preferred to stick to their ancient books as the only true sources of information; they had no interest in modern gadgets like Galileo's telescope. With contempt for their ignorance Galileo wrote a scathing letter to Johannes Kepler[1], a fellow believer in a Sun-centred universe.

> *I wish, my dear Kepler, that we could have a good laugh together at the extraordinary stupidity of the mob. What do you think of the foremost philosophers of this University? In spite of my oft-repeated efforts and invitations, they have refused, with the obstinacy of a glutted adder, to look at the planets or Moon or my telescope.*

Isaac Newton was born in the same year Galileo died, and by this time the telescope had helped transform our understanding of the Solar System. In Newton's time there were only five known planets other than Earth, which were Mercury, Venus, Mars, Jupiter and Saturn. Uranus, Neptune, and the dwarf planet Pluto were discovered later as new more powerful telescopes were produced. It is thought that Galileo may have seen Neptune through his telescope but did not recognise it as a planet.

Galileo, Newton, Herschel and other pioneering astronomers would not recognise today's high-tech telescopes, although they would be very impressed by how far they can see into space. Modern telescopes are so powerful that they can see objects out in space more than 13.4 billion light years from Earth, which is like seeing into someone's house in Perth, Australia, from your home in London.

The *Kepler Space Telescope* orbits the Earth above the atmosphere searching our Galaxy for the possibility of alien life. *Kepler* is looking for potentially habitable planets on which we may find extra-terrestrial life-forms. Never accuse scientists of not having a sense of humour; they have coined the name 'Goldilocks Planets' to describe the alien worlds they are looking for, because they are neither too hot, nor too cold, but just right to support alien life.

Ideas for practice

Topic: Journey to the Moon

Age group: 5–7 years

Introduction

This topic provides opportunities for children to find out what our nearest neighbour in space looks like up close, and to hear real-life stories about the people who have travelled there. The *application stage* suggests a range of model-making activities associated with space travel such as making a space rocket, designing a meal in space, and designing their own space suits.

Scientific view

The Moon is our nearest neighbour in space. It is 384,400km away and travelling by car it would take about 20 weeks to get there. Apollo 11 took about three days, but today a spacecraft could make it in a few hours. The Moon is a big rock like the Earth but it does not have an atmosphere and the surface is barren. There are no oceans or rivers, and as far as we know there is no life. The surface is covered with dead volcanoes, impact craters, and lava flows.

Working scientifically

In these activities children will:

- observe using binoculars and telescopes;
- use observations and ideas to suggest answers to questions;
- gather and record information to help answer questions.

Health and safety

When making models using mouldable materials, follow ASE guidelines in their publication *Be Safe!* (2011).

Exploration stage

Children's talk involves trying out their own ideas

Setting the scene

Read Oliver Jeffers' book *The way back home* with the children. Use the book to set the scene for an imaginary trip to the Moon. If children wanted to go to the Moon, how would they get there?

Puzzle

How can we get to the Moon?

Figure 11.1 **How can we get to the Moon?**

Explore children's reasons for their responses to the cartoon. Discuss the best way to travel to the Moon.

Story-telling

1   Children's story

Children draw pictures depicting how they would travel to the Moon. They talk and write about their journey and describe what they think the surface of the Moon would look like.

2   Teacher's story

Tell children that you know a story about a journey to the Moon called *The Eagle has landed!* It is a true story about three spacemen who flew in a space rocket all the way to the Moon. Show the children a picture of Neil Armstrong, Buzz Aldrin and Michael Collins. Share some of the excitement of the mission and talk about the challenges they faced. There is a wide range of information available in books and on the web.

Figure 11.2   **The three astronauts from the Apollo 11 mission**

Source: NASA

Talk about the Apollo 11 mission to the Moon using video clips and images from the web. There are images of Neil Armstrong and Buzz Aldrin walking on the Moon. Why are they wearing space suits? Why are there no trees or plants? Are there any animals on the Moon? Encourage children to ask questions about the mission. Ask children to compare the surface of the Moon to the surface of the Earth. Can they say two things that are similar, and two things which are different?

Children's drawings

Children imagine what it would be like to walk on the Moon. What would they see? Do they think they would be able to see the Earth while standing on the Moon? Ask children to draw what they imagine the Earth to look like viewed from the Moon. Compare their pictures with images of the Earth taken from space. Create a display of children's pictures, together with images taken from the web.

Formative assessment

Provide opportunities for children to voice what they have learnt in the exploratory stage. Use evidence from their responses to the puzzle, talking points and other activities to assess differences between children's ideas and the scientific view. Plan how you will use the re-describing stage to help the children address their *learning needs* (see Chapter 1). You may need to modify the activities depending on the collective and individual needs of your children.

Information and teaching resources

BBC Bitesize:

● Earth, Sun and Moon. *www.bbc.co.uk/education/clips/zscb4wx*

Other websites:

● Apollo 11 introduction. *www.youtube.com/watch?v=8il6rx-9a3c*
● July 20, 1969: One giant leap for mankind.
  www.nasa.gov/mission_pages/apollo/apollo11.html
● Raising the American flag. *www.youtube.com/watch?v=1J9H3niSXj8*
● Buzz Aldrin sets foot on the Moon. *www.youtube.com/watch?v=FepUv3vmIM8*
● Astronauts leaping on the Moon. *www.stem.org.uk/elibrary/resource/26369*

Book:

● Jeffers, O. (2015) *The way back home*, London: HarperCollins.

Re-describing stage
Children's talk involves making sense of scientific ideas

Teacher-led discussion

Show images of the Moon's surface and talk about what it would be like to live there. There is no air to breathe, nor running water to drink, and there are no plants or animals to eat. Interpret the images, pointing out the features. Show archive footage of NASA astronauts walking on the Moon and talk about how their spacesuits keep them safe.

Figure 11.3 **Astronaut walking on the surface of the Moon (Apollo 17 mission)**

Source: NASA

Modelling

1 Children imagine walking on the Moon in their space suits. They would weigh less on the Moon so they would feel lighter and could jump higher. Let children invent their own 'spacewalk' and perform it to music.

2 Make models of the lunar surface using trays of silver sand. Children drop different objects in the sand to make craters and mountains. This links to the activity on Moon craters in the core book (Loxley *et al.*, 2017).

Story-telling

Ask children to re-think their story about an imaginary trip to the Moon. Do they think their story was realistic now they know more about travelling to the Moon? What do they think they should change to make it more accurate? What else would they like to know about the Moon? With support, children use appropriate information sources to discover more about the Moon. Talk together about the scientific ideas, assess their progress and address any outstanding *learning needs*.

Scientific enquiry

Figure 11.4 **Harvest Moon**

Source: iStock

The time of the Harvest Moon in September is a good time for children to view the Moon. You will need to arrange for children to return to school in the evening with their parents. No matter where you are, you will see a full moon ascend over the eastern horizon around the time of Sunset. Organise telescopes and binoculars so children get a good view of the Moon. Invite a local astronomer or STEM ambassador to help out and take photographs.

Back in the classroom, model the size of the Moon compared to the Earth. Use models and animations to show how the Moon travels around the Earth.

Information and teaching resources

BBC Bitesize:

- The Moon. *www.bbc.co.uk/education/clips/zy89wmn*
- What does the Moon look like and why? *www.bbc.co.uk/education/clips/zj3ygk7*

Other websites:

- Breathtaking new images of the Moon. *www.youtube.com/watch?v=sjkPeexEdyI*
- The Moon. *www.nasa.gov/moon*

Application stage

Children's talk involves trying out scientific ideas

Design and make activities

There is a wide range of possible design and make activities which relate to this topic. Here are a few ideas.

- Design and make a model of a Moon rocket.
- Plan a meal to eat on a journey to the Moon.
- Design their own space suits.
- Make papier mâché models of the Moon's surface, which could include a model of the Eagle Landing Module.
- Design and make a Moon buggy.

Topic: Mission to Mars

Age group: 7–9 years

Introduction

In this topic children plan a mission to Mars, following in the footsteps of NASA's space exploration programmes. The context is provided by NASA's robotic rover *Curiosity* which landed on Mars on the 6th of August 2012. Children are challenged in the application stage to design a space station which would enable people to live on Mars.

Scientific view

Mars is the fourth planet from the Sun. Named after the Roman god of war, and often described as the 'Red Planet' due to its reddish appearance, Mars has a thin atmosphere composed primarily of carbon dioxide. Martian gravity is only 37% of the Earth's (meaning you could leap nearly three times higher on Mars). The surface temperatures vary from lows of about −143°C at the winter polar caps to highs of up to 35°C on other parts of the planet. Mars is 1.52 times as far from the Sun as Earth, resulting in it receiving just 43% of the amount of sunlight. Mars also has large dust storms, which can sometimes cover the entire planet.

The jury is still out on whether life has existed on Mars. NASA believe they have found traces of water, which is a good sign. Whatever they find, they do not expect to discover complex organisms such as flowering plants or reptiles. They are looking for microbes and traces of past life.

Working scientifically

In these activities children will:

- use a range of information sources;
- set up simple practical enquiries to test their ideas;
- gather and record data to answer a question;
- use established scientific ideas to support their findings;
- report outcomes as video presentation.

Health and safety

When dropping objects from a height use PE equipment rather than classroom furniture and consider risk from bouncing. For design and make activities follow the ASE guidance in *Be Safe!* (2011).

Exploration stage

Children's talk involves trying out their own ideas

Setting the scene

Start by showing children video footage of NASA's mission to Mars and the landing of the robotic rover *Curiosity*. There is a range of footage on YouTube and the NASA website. *Curiosity* is looking for microscopic signs that life could have once existed on the planet. Find out what the children know about Mars and NASA's mission.

> ## Talking points: true, false or not sure?
>
> ● Mars is a gas planet.
>
> ● Life cannot exist on Mars because it is too hot.
>
> ● Mars is like a desert and only insects, snakes and lizards live there.
>
> ● Life cannot live in Martian seas because they are too salty.
>
> ● Scientists have not found any life on Mars.
>
> ● The atmosphere on Mars is just like our own.
>
> ● It never rains on Mars because there is no water.
>
> ● There was once water on Mars.

Groups can use information sources to help them with the talking points and find out as much as they can about conditions on Mars. Groups come together to present and share their ideas.

Puzzle

Landing *Curiosity* safely on the surface of Mars was one of the most difficult parts of the mission. One of the lead engineers described the difficulties faced in the manoeuvre, saying: 'We are landing a ton of vehicle on the surface of another planet, hundreds of millions of miles away. That is a really hard thing.'

Groups use information sources to examine the way NASA chose to land the rover, and develop arguments about whether there were alternative ways to land *Curiosity* safely. Groups come together to present their ideas along with their reasoning.

Scientific enquiry

Children explore different ways NASA could have chosen to land *Curiosity*. Using an egg to represent the rover children explore ways of landing it safely on a hard surface when dropped from a height of about two metres. Compare different methods with using a parachute. Can children improve on NASA's design?

Figure 11.5 **Artist's image of *Curiosity* landing on Mars**

Source: NASA

Modelling

Once the rover landed it began hunting for evidence of microbes and collecting a host of data and images from the Red Planet. The robot is the size of a car, and can move slowly across uneven ground. Children use information sources to find out what *Curiosity* looks like, how it is powered and how it collects its samples. They can then design and make a model of their own robotic rover suitable for use on Mars. Along with their model children should provide a leaflet which explains how the rover would work and a rationale for its design features.

Story-telling

Children imagine they are NASA scientists in charge of an unmanned mission to Mars. The mission has gone well and now they want to tell the world all about it. Each group produces a video presentation of the mission using pictures and models to show how it was carried out. Crucially they should show how they intended to search for evidence of life. In their video they can use a model car to represent *Curiosity*, and use their own method of landing it on Mars.

Formative assessment

Provide opportunities for children to voice what they have learnt in the exploratory stage. Use evidence from their responses to the puzzle, talking points and other activities to assess differences between children's ideas and the scientific view. Plan how you will use the re-describing stage to help the children address their *learning needs* (see Chapter 1). You may need to modify the activities depending on the collective and individual needs of your children.

Figure 11.6 *Curiosity* on the surface of Mars

Source: NASA

Information and teaching resources

- How do I land on Mars?
  http://mars.jpl.nasa.gov/multimedia/interactives/edlcuriosity/index-2.html

- Mars science laboratory – Curiosity rover. *http://mars.nasa.gov/msl/*

- Mars videos and animations.
  http://mars.nasa.gov/multimedia/videos/?SearchTerm=Mission%3AMSL

Re-describing stage

Children's talk involves making sense of scientific ideas

Teacher-led discussion

Use video clips and images to talk about the structure of Mars. Compare it to the Earth and discuss the problems living things would have to survive on its surface. Talk together about the types of life-forms which could possibly live or may have lived there.

Story-telling

Children explore NASA websites to find up-to-date information about missions to Mars and what has been discovered. Each group can write a newspaper article which comments on the experiments carried out by *Curiosity*, and also describes what new things NASA has discovered on Mars.

Information and teaching resources

BBC Bitesize:

- The planet Mars. *www.bbc.co.uk/education/clips/z96mhyc*

Other websites:

- Mars for kids. *http://mars.nasa.gov/participate/funzone/*
- NASA Space Place. *http://spaceplace.nasa.gov/*
- UK space education office. *www.stem.org.uk/esero*
- NASA homepage. www.nasa.gov

Application stage

Children's talk involves trying out scientific ideas

Space station on Mars

By the time today's children grow up, NASA could have established a space station on Mars. A space station would enable scientists to live on the Red Planet and carry out experiments which robots cannot do on their own. The challenge for the children is to imagine they are space scientists and engineers who have been asked to design a Space Station in which astronauts could live.

There is information on NASA websites which include a site called *Mars for kids*. Children can also explore life aboard the International Space Station which is designed to prepare for a manned expedition to Mars. By finding out how astronauts live on the station as it orbits the Earth, children will be able to get ideas for their Mars design. As a result of their research children can produce plans and models of a Martian Space Station. It is important to provide time and resources for children to research the project, so that their models have some real-life validity.

Information and teaching resources

BBC Bitesize:

- Sleeping in space. *www.bbc.co.uk/education/clips/z2g9xsg*
- Building the International Space Station. *www.bbc.co.uk/education/clips/zd4g9j6*
- The International Space Station. *www.bbc.co.uk/education/clips/zcxpcwx*
- Training to be an astronaut. *www.bbc.co.uk/education/clips/zyw8q6f*

Other websites:

- Living in space. *www.esa.int/esaKIDSen/Livinginspace.html*
- Living in space. *www.nasa.gov/topics/technology/living-in-space/index.html*

Topic: In search of Goldilocks Planets

Age group: 9–11 years

Introduction

We all enjoy a good science fiction story; programmes like *Star Trek* have taken on cult status. We enjoy these shows because they excite our imaginations, and make us question the possibility that life could exist elsewhere in the universe. This topic provides children with an opportunity to 'boldly go where no man has gone before' in search of extra-terrestrial life-forms.

Scientific view

The Solar System was created about 4.6 billion years ago from the debris of an exploded star. The Sun was formed from the lighter materials such as hydrogen and helium, and the planets from a combination of gases and particles of rock, metal and ice. There is evidence that life has existed on Earth for 3.5 billion years, although it is not known how it started. There are a number of theories including that life may have arrived on the back of a comet. Life has not been found anywhere else in the Solar System, although scientists are optimistic that simple life-forms such as bacteria or plankton may exist.

Working scientifically

In these activities children will:

- plan their own scientific enquiry;
- present findings in a poster form and a blog entry;
- model scientific ideas;
- use a range of sources of information;
- use scientific ideas to support or refute arguments.

Health and safety

Children should be taught that, however useful the internet and information technology, they are open to abuse. Follow school guidance on e-safety.

Exploration stage

Children's talk involves trying out their own ideas

Setting the scene

Figure 11.7 **Starship Enterprise**

Source: iStock

Show children an episode of *Star Trek* and talk about their mission to explore strange new worlds and seek new life.

Puzzle

Do children think life may exist on other worlds? Where would it be found? Could life be found within our Solar System?

> ## Talking points: true, false or not sure?
>
> ● Life may exist on Mars because it is the most Earth-like planet.
>
> ● It is too hot for life to exist on Venus.
>
> ● Life can only exist on the Earth.
>
> ● If aliens lived on Mars we would know about it.
>
> ● On a very cold planet like Neptune people could live underground.
>
> ● Life cannot exist on a planet with no atmosphere like Mercury.
>
> ● Although Pluto is very cold life may exist there.

Groups discuss the talking points and try to reach agreement on whether they think life could exist as we know it on another planet. Groups come together to share ideas. Focus discussion on their reasoning.

Scientific enquiry

Groups explore different planets to find out whether they or their moons have suitable environments to support life. Each group contributes to a large map of the solar system showing the environmental conditions on the planets and their moons. Places which have any potential for life of any kind, including microbes, could be highlighted.

Modelling

In reality manned space travel has hardly got off the ground. Scientists have sent unmanned space crafts to the ends of the Solar System, but as yet the Moon is as far as humans have travelled. Will it ever be possible for us to journey to the ends of the Solar System in search of life? How far do we need to travel and how long would it take us to get there?

● What is the furthest distance children can imagine?

● What is the longest journey they have ever made?

● How far is it to the other side of the world?

● Where does space begin?

- How far is it to the Moon?
- How long would it take to travel to the Moon?
- How does the distance to the Moon compare with the distance to Australia?

Encourage children to use their imaginations when discussing the questions. Use information sources to check their responses. The idea is to get children imagining large distances.

It is a long way to the Moon, but compared to travelling to Pluto it is a mere hop, skip and a jump. It is impossible to imagine how far it is to the outer reaches of the Solar System, but children can gain some appreciation of its vastness by using a toilet roll to make a scale model.

You will need a roll with at least 120 sheets. Work outside unless you have a space 20 metres in length. Each sheet of toilet paper represents a distance of 50,000,000km and since the Moon is approximately 400,000km away, each sheet of paper represents about 125 one-way trips. Start with a picture of the Sun on the first sheet of paper and as you roll it out children add the planets using the chart below. Children stand at appropriate distances to represent the planets. Make it clear that if the planets were drawn to scale they would be mere dots.

TABLE 11.1 Scale model of Solar System

Planet	Distance to Sun (km)	Sheets of paper
Mercury	58,000,000	1.1
Venus	108,000,000	2.1
Earth	150,000,000	3.0
Mars	228,000,000	4.5
Jupiter	778,000,000	15.5
Saturn	1,430,000,000	28.6
Uranus	2,871,000,000	57.4
Neptune	4,504,000,000	90.1
Pluto (dwarf)	5,914,000,000	118.3

How many one-way trips to the Moon are equivalent to a journey to Pluto? How many trips to Australia are equivalent to a trip to the Moon? Challenge children to work it out.

Story-telling

How do we know the planets exist? Using information sources children tell the story of how our understanding of the Solar System developed from the time of the ancient Greeks to the present day. Focus on the part played by key scientists and the use of the telescope. Produce a timeline showing key discoveries and developments. If resources are available children can construct simple telescopes like the one used by Galileo.

Figure 11.8   Galileo's telescope and the Hubble telescope

Source: Getty Images and NASA

Formative assessment

Provide opportunities for children to voice what they have learnt in the exploratory stage. Use evidence from their responses to the puzzle, talking points and other activities to assess differences between children's ideas and the scientific view. Plan how you will use the re-describing stage to help the children address their *learning needs* (see Chapter 1). You may need to modify the activities depending on the collective and individual needs of your children.

Information and teaching resources

ASE Journals:

- Primary Science 138 (May/June 2015) *Creative and tactile astronomy: Exploring the universe using all the senses* by Isabel Borges and Lina Canas.
- Primary Science 136 (Jan/Feb 2015) *Using space to inspire and engage children* by Allan Clements.

Re-describing stage

Children's talk involves making sense of scientific ideas

Teacher-led discussion

Figure 11.9 **Solar System**

Source: iStock

Use video and animations to help children picture the structure of the Solar System and how it was created. Resources can be found on the NASA website *Space place in a snap*, and there are lots of useful clips on YouTube. Talk about how the rotation of the Earth causes night and day, and the apparent movement of the Sun across the sky. Use models to demonstrate. You could also use animations and models to demonstrate how light from the Sun creates the phases of the Moon which we see on Earth.

Scientific enquiry

Since the 1960s NASA has sent a variety of unmanned spacecraft to explore the Solar System, providing remarkable images of the planets and their moons. In recent times the *New Horizons Spacecraft* reached Pluto and Charon, providing stunning photographs of these icy worlds. Children research the history of space exploration on the NASA websites and enjoy some remarkable photographs of our Solar System taken on different missions and by the Hubble telescope.

Children use their understanding of the Solar System to debate the likelihood of finding life-forms. If there is life, in what form do they expect we will find it and where? Groups should provide strong reasons for their ideas based on known environmental conditions required for life. Children should be encouraged to challenge each other's views respectfully, with evidence to support their own ideas. Assess children's progress and identify any outstanding *learning needs*.

Information and teaching resources

- NASA Space Place. *http://spaceplace.nasa.gov/search/snap/*
- The Solar System's formation. *www.youtube.com/watch?v=RT4OO0TFLHw*
- Solar System. *http://video.nationalgeographic.com/video/101-videos/solar-system-sci*
- Exploring our Solar System. *www.youtube.com/watch?v=Qd6nLM2QlWw*
- New Horizons. *www.nasa.gov/mission_pages/newhorizons/main/index.html*
- Hubblesite. *http://hubblesite.org/gallery/*
- NASA TV. *www.nasa.gov/multimedia/nasatv/index.html#public*
- Solar System animation. *www.space-art.co.uk/image.php?gallery=animations&image=solar-system-animation*

Application stage

Children's talk involves trying out scientific ideas

The *Starship Enterprise* on its fictitious journeys through the universe encountered all kinds of alien civilisations. What is the chance we would encounter alien life-forms if we travelled outside our Solar System? Are we alone in the Universe, or are there other beings living on distant planets similar to our own?

The search for extra-terrestrial life-forms has been stepped up in recent years after the discovery of Goldilocks Planets in distant Solar Systems. In 2013 astronomers reported that there could be as many as 40 billion Earth-sized planets with potential to support life in our Milky Way Galaxy.

Scientific enquiry

Figure 11.10 **Artist's image of the Kepler Space Telescope**

Source: NASA

Children explore the work of the Kepler Space Telescope and find out about the planets it has discovered. How far away are they, and what do we know about their climates? What makes scientists believe life could possibly exist on them?

Story-telling

Children imagine they are part of the crew of a spacecraft that has landed on a Goldilocks Planet. The children are space journalists and their job is to write a daily blog about life on the planet to be published back on Earth. The blog should be written in an informal style designed to interest and inform the general public. Although it should not be too technical, the blog needs to be scientifically feasible. Talk to children about their blogs and probe their understanding of the conditions required to support alien life on distant planets.

Information and teaching resources

- Kepler and K2. *www.nasa.gov/mission_pages/kepler/main/index.html*
- Kepler mission. *www.bbc.co.uk/science/space/universe/exploration/kepler_mission*

Note

1   University of St Andrews, quotations by Galileo Galilei. www-history.mcs.st-andrews.ac.uk/history/Quotations/Galileo.html

Chapter 12
Electricity

Genius is one percent inspiration, 99 percent perspiration.

Thomas Edison (1847–1931)

This chapter presents ideas for practice which can be used to teach how electric circuits work. Activities provide opportunities to construct simple series circuits using a range of components including bulbs, buzzers, motors and switches. Children progress from representing circuits pictorially to using conventional symbols. Concepts such as electric current and voltage are explored through analogy and modelling. Opportunities are provided for older children to learn about energy efficient appliances and sustainable sources of electricity.

Topics in this chapter:

- Introducing electric circuits
- Electric circuit challenge
- Saving energy

Subject knowledge to support the teaching of these topics can be found in the core book, Loxley, P., Dawes, D., Nicholls, L. and Dore, B. (2018) *Teaching primary science: Promoting enjoyment and developing understanding*, Abingdon: Routledge, Chapter 19: Electricity and magnetism.

Electricity

Imagine life without electricity. Imagine living in the dark, unable to keep warm, turn on a light or boil a kettle. Imagine relying on burning wood or coal or dung to cook, and having to breathe in potentially fatal smoke. Imagine living under the shadow of disease from rotten food due to the lack of refrigeration. This was the stark reality before the development of electrical power in the middle of the nineteenth century.

The first commercial use for electricity was lighting. In 1879 Thomas Edison developed a practical and long-lasting light bulb showing the potential of electricity to improve ways of living. Since then people's lives in the developed world have been transformed with the invention of electrical appliances such as the refrigerator, telephone, electrical heater, television, computer, mobile phone and many other devices which have exploited the potential of electricity. Unfortunately, in the developing world, billions of poor people still live in much harsher conditions because they are unable to access suitable electrical power.

There are two sources of electrical power. One is the type generated in a power station and supplied to our homes through wires which are part of the national grid. Michael Faraday was the person who discovered the principles of electricity generation in 1831. He demonstrated how electricity could be generated by moving a magnet near a coil of wire, which later led to the development of the electrical generator which creates the electricity in a power station.

The other type of electricity we use is that supplied by batteries, which is usually much less powerful than that generated in a power station. In 1800 an Italian called Alessandro Volta worked out how to produce electricity using zinc and copper discs. This discovery was the forerunner of the dry-cell battery which we use today. Volta's name lives on in the terms voltage and volts which are used to describe and measure electricity.

Dry-cell batteries are widely used for devices such as torches, toys, clocks and radios which only require relatively small amounts of electrical power to work. The voltage of a battery is indicative of the electric power it can supply to the device. For example, a lamp will shine brighter when connected to a 12-volt battery, than when connected to one of only 6 volts. Batteries are made up of cells. In common dry-cell batteries each cell has an electric voltage of 1.5 volts. 2 cells combine to make 3 volts, 4 cells to make 6 volts and so on.

The flow of electricity through a circuit is called the electrical current. Electrical current is measured in units called amperes, named after the French scientist André-Marie Ampère. A series circuit provides a single pathway down which the current can flow through the battery, through the components and back through the battery. Energy stored in the battery is carried by the electrical current to the components. Batteries only store a limited amount of energy and they 'go flat' when their energy runs out.

Switches are used to make and break a circuit and hence provide a way of controlling the supply of energy to the components. The connecting wires in an electric circuit are made from materials such as copper, which are good conductors of electricity. Metals are generally good conductors because their atomic structure aids the flow of electric current. On the other hand, materials such as plastic, wood, wool, rubber and glass are examples of insulators because their structure prevents the flow of electric current.

Today, electricity plays an increasingly important part in our lives. It lights up and heats our homes, it helps power our transport, it runs our communication systems and the media, and it keeps our industries going. It is hard to imagine how we ever managed without it.

Ideas for practice

Topic: Introducing electric circuits

Age group: 5–7 years

Introduction

The purpose of this topic is to introduce children to the concept of an electric circuit and make them aware of the dangers associated with mains electricity. The activities provide opportunities to construct simple circuits and to compare devices which are battery-powered and those which are plugged into electrical wall sockets.

Scientific view

A simple circuit is a track around which electricity flows. The flow of electricity through the bulb causes it to light up. If the circuit is not a complete loop, the electricity is prevented from flowing and the bulb will not light up. There are two sources of electricity. Some electricity is produced by batteries, while mains electricity is accessed by plugging devices into wall sockets. Electricity can be dangerous and must be used safely.

Working scientifically

In these activities children will:

- observe closely using simple equipment;
- perform simple tests;
- identify and classify;
- suggest answers to questions;
- gather and record data to help answer a question.

Health and safety

This topic provides a good opportunity for teaching children about the hazards of mains electricity and the misuse of batteries. Refer to the *Be Safe!* (2011) guidelines when planning these activities. Only use recommended battery types and sizes. Coin and button batteries are unsuitable for use by young children. Making activities will need to take account of appropriate materials, tools and supervision. Again refer to ASE guidelines.

Exploration stage

Children's talk involves trying out their own ideas

Setting the scene

Start with a torch without a battery inside. Show children the torch and ask them how it works. Listen to children's stories about torches they have at home and how they use them. Try to turn the torch on and act surprised it doesn't work. What could be the problem? Can the children help? Look inside to see what's wrong. Is there something missing? Establish that the torch needs a battery. Reinstate the battery and turn the torch on so children can see it light up. Reinforce the idea that a torch will not work without a battery. Can children explain why? Listen to their stories.

Scientific enquiry

Take the battery and bulb out of the torch and ask the children to describe them. What do they think is inside the bulb? What parts does the battery have?

In groups children explore the structure of different types of batteries and bulbs with filaments. Use magnifiers to look closely at a range of sizes of bulbs so they can clearly see the filaments. Help them identify the positive and negative parts of different batteries. Groups draw pictures showing the main parts of a battery and a bulb.

Puzzle

Show children the battery and bulb from the torch and ask whether they think it is possible to light the bulb without putting it back inside the torch. Place the bulb in turn against the positive and negative ends of the battery to see if it will light. What do the children suggest you do? There must be something else inside the torch which helps the bulb light up?

Scientific enquiry

Provide each group with a 1.5-volt cell and holder, a suitably rated bulb and holder and two wires with alligator clips. Provide all the components separately and challenge children to assembly them in order to make the bulb work. Children can draw pictures of their circuits and explain how they think they work. Does it matter which way the battery or the bulb are connected in their electric circuit? Encourage children to use the term 'electric circuit'.

Discuss whether they have solved the puzzle? How can they turn their bulb on and off? Explore children's ideas. Encourage them to connect and disconnect the alligator clips from the battery. What turned the bulb on and off in the torch? Each group explores how to connect a simple open switch to their circuits. Modify or redraw their pictures to include the switch.

Discuss talking points and children's reasons for their responses. Probe their thinking. Ask them to hypothesise about why the bulb will not light if there is a gap in the circuit.

Talking points: true, false or not sure?

- To light a bulb we only need a battery.
- The wires in a circuit connect the bulb to the battery in a loop.
- If there is a gap in the circuit the bulb will not work.
- A circuit works best when the wires are connected to the positive side of the battery.

Formative assessment

Provide opportunities for children to voice what they have learnt in the exploratory stage. Use evidence from their responses to the puzzle, talking points and other activities to assess differences between children's ideas and the scientific view. Plan how you will use the re-describing stage to help the children address their *learning needs* (see Chapter 1). You may need to modify the activities depending on the collective and individual needs of your children.

Re-describing stage

Children's talk involves making sense of scientific ideas

Teacher-led discussion

Demonstrate how a simple circuit works and talk about the need to create an unbroken pathway for electricity to flow. Illustrate how wires from the bulb need to be connected to both ends (terminals) of the battery to create a loop. Any break in the loop turns off the bulb. Demonstrate how the switch works. Use video clips to illustrate how a simple circuit works.

Modelling

Plug in a 60W lamp and turn it on. Alongside it turn on the torch. Compare the brightness of the two products. Can children explain why the lamp is much brighter than the torch? Establish that the battery inside the torch is making it glow. What is making the lamp shine so brightly? Probe children's understanding of mains electricity. Talk about the two sources of electricity, and how batteries are used for portable things like torches, mobile phones and watches. Point out that electricity which comes out of wall sockets is more powerful and more dangerous than electricity from batteries. Children use pictures to sort battery-operated products from ones which are plugged into the mains.

Arrange a collection of devices which are powered by electricity. Ask children to help you identify the ones which need to be plugged into a socket. Demonstrate how they work and talk about health and safety. Remind them that the electricity which comes out of wall sockets can be dangerous. Use video clips to help make children aware of the dangers of mains electricity. Groups can devise a safety code for using electricity. Groups come together to share their ideas, and agree on a class safety code. They can design posters to alert other children to the dangers of electricity. Refer to guidance in *Be Safe!* (2011).

Information and teaching resources

BBC Bitesize:

- Electricity. *www.bbc.co.uk/guides/z96ckqt#z8h9d2p*
- Batteries and their uses. *www.bbc.co.uk/education/clips/zpshfg8*
- Dangers of electricity. *www.bbc.co.uk/education/clips/zg84d2p*
- What would life be like without electricity? *www.bbc.co.uk/education/clips/zt2rqty*
- Electro-matic factory. *www.bbc.co.uk/bitesize/ks1/science/electricity/play/*

Other websites:

- BP Educational Services – Introducing circuits. *http://bpes.bp.com/primary-resources/science/ages-4-to-7/electricity/introducing-circuits/*

Application stage

Children's talk involves trying out scientific ideas

Household products

Listen to children's stories about their own battery-operated products. How long do the batteries last? Have the batteries ever let them down? What other problems have they had with them? With the help of their parents, children can record the battery-operated and mains-operated products in their home. Take photographs of their favourite appliances, and the ones which are used most. Back in school use the data to identify the most popular and most used products. Are they battery- or mains-operated? Use photographs along with some real products to create a display.

Children make a simple model of a household product such as a television or a washing machine using a cardboard box. They can incorporate an electric circuit with a battery, switch and light bulb to indicate when their machine is turned on.

Topic: Electric circuit challenge

Age group: 7–9 years

Introduction

The purpose of this topic is to challenge and extend children's understanding of series circuits which they developed in the previous section. You may therefore want to review parts of the previous topic before undertaking the following activities. A key part of this topic is modelling how a simple circuit works. Analogies help children talk about and picture abstract ideas like electric current, but in doing so can create misconceptions. When using models discuss their weaknesses, as well as their strengths, so children are aware that they do not behave exactly like an electric circuit.

Working scientifically

In these activities children will:

- set up simple practical enquiries;
- record findings using simple scientific language, drawings and diagrams;
- use results to draw conclusions, make predictions, suggest improvements and raise further questions;
- use straightforward scientific evidence to answer questions.

Scientific view

Conductors are materials which allow electricity to flow through them. Conductors work because electricity is there inside them, it just needs a battery to get it flowing. Insulators do not conduct electricity because there is no electricity inside them which can be made to flow by a battery. When connected in a circuit, the battery pushes the electricity inside the conducting wires around the pathway.

Health and safety

Short circuits are inevitable when children are trying out circuits so try to use batteries that can tolerate short circuits safely. Follow ASE guidance in *Be Safe!* (2011) on the safe use of batteries and check the safety of any games or models made by the children.

Exploration stage

Children's talk involves trying out their own ideas

Setting the scene

Use string instead of wire to create an electrical pathway between a bulb and a battery. Before you turn the circuit on, ask the children to guess how bright the light will glow. Do they think the string will work as well as normal connecting wires? Discuss reasons for their responses.

Puzzle

When children see the circuit will not work, ask them whether they can explain the problem. Why do connecting wires provide a good electrical pathway, while string does not?

Talking points: true, false or not sure?

- String does not allow electricity to flow through it.
- String uses up all the electricity and there is none left for the bulb.
- Electricity will only flow through metals.
- Electricity only flows through plastic.
- Connecting wires are made from metal.
- Connecting wires are made from plastic.

Discuss children's responses. Introduce the terms conductor and insulator, and define in terms of electrical pathways. Conductors provide good pathways, while insulators do not.

Scientific enquiry

Provide children with a range of objects which they can use to try to connect the bulb with the battery. For example, they could use aluminium foil cut into strips, ribbon, shoelaces, paper clips linked together, long metal nails, pencils sharpened at both ends. Record results and start to compile lists of conductors and insulators. Children extend the enquiry by designing a circuit for testing whether an object is an insulator or conductor. Look for patterns between materials and identify those which make good electrical pathways. Groups present and compare their results. Discuss what they learnt from the activity. Can they now predict whether a material is a conductor or an insulator?

Design and make

Challenge children to make a pressure switch (pad) which can be used as part of an alarm system. The switch can be used to turn on a buzzer and/or a flashing light when someone walks on it, or puts pressure on it in some other way. The task involves the choice of suitable insulating and conducting materials.

Formative assessment

Provide opportunities for children to voice what they have learnt in the exploratory stage. Use evidence from their responses to the puzzle, talking points and other activities to assess differences between children's ideas and the scientific view. Plan how you will use the re-describing stage to help the children address their *learning needs* (see Chapter 1). You may need to modify the activities depending on the collective and individual needs of your children.

Information and teaching resources

- How to make an electronic pressure pad. *www.youtube.com/watch?v=wMRiWKWZ4EE*

Re-describing stage

Children's talk involves making sense of scientific ideas

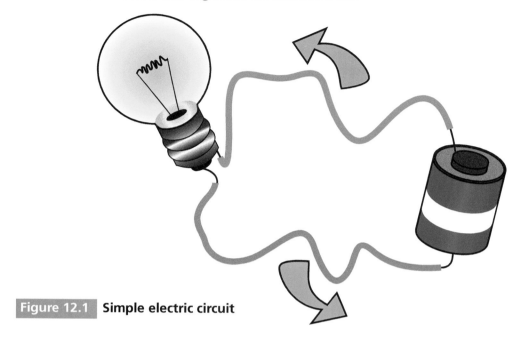

Figure 12.1 **Simple electric circuit**

Teacher-led discussion

Use a picture of a simple circuit and trace the electric pathway from the positive part of the battery around the circuit to the negative part to reinforce the idea of a complete circuit through which electricity can flow. Children may think that the battery stores electricity, which will eventually run out when the battery goes flat. This is a common misconception. Use the following activities to move children's thinking towards a more viable model by comparing the battery to a pump which pushes electricity around the circuit.

Modelling

The purpose of modelling is to provide something concrete which children can talk about as they work on developing their understanding of how electric circuits work. Talking about the strengths and weaknesses of the model is just as important as doing the modelling.

Children begin the modelling process by standing in a loop with their feet touching to represent a complete pathway. Make it clear to the children that they represent the connecting wires. Choose children within the loop to represent the battery, the bulb and the switch. Ask them what will happen when the circuit is switched on? Where is the electricity? What is going to move around the loop? Refer to the puzzle. Do they think they are modelling a circuit made with string or with metal conducting wires? Discuss children's responses and work on their understanding that conductors contain electricity.

Tell children that you will give each of them a 'bit of electricity' and hand each of them a tennis ball. Now that the wires are full of electricity, what is going to happen when the circuit is switched on? Children model electric current by passing the balls around the circuit from one person to the next. The child representing the bulb can produce a wide smile to signify it has lit up. Turning the circuit off can be modelled by two children breaking the contact between themselves. This model does not explain how the battery works. Respond to children's questions about the battery by talking about how it pushes the electricity around the loop. Discuss whether the analogy helps children imagine what is going on in the wires of a simple electric circuit. Can the children think of how to improve the model?

Story-telling

Ask children to imagine they were really tiny, so tiny that they could fit inside the wires of an electric circuit. What would they see? What do they think electricity looks like? Tell them that nobody really knows so they are free to use their imaginations. Children tell their stories through words and pictures, travelling around an electric circuit from the positive side of the battery, through the connecting wire to the bulb, through the bulb and back to the negative side of the battery. What would they see and do along the way? Would it be more difficult to travel through the bulb than the connecting wires? What happens to the electricity inside the battery? Children can create cartoons to illustrate their stories. Probe children's thinking behind their stories.

Scientific enquiry

To further develop their understanding of how electric circuits work, children can explore solutions to the following challenges:

The first challenge is to light a bulb without using holders for the bulb and battery. Children first draw a picture of how they will connect the bulb to the battery and trace the electrical pathway with their fingers. After they construct a working circuit they should again trace the pathway and compare it to their picture. Children can use magnifiers to explore how the filament is part of the electrical pathway.

The second challenge is to light a bulb with only one connecting wire. Provide children with just one connecting wire, a bulb and a battery and ask them whether they can get the bulb to light. Again they should draw a picture of the circuit first and trace the pathway with their fingers. When they have constructed a working circuit ask them to explain why a second wire is not necessary by tracing the electric pathway. Children discuss and decide what they have learnt from the challenge.

The third challenge is to compare circuits with more than one bulb. Children use connecting wires to light a 1.5V rated bulb with a 1.5V battery, then light two 1.5V bulbs with the same battery. Compare the brightness of the bulbs in the two circuits. Challenge children to provide reasons for the differences. Now ask them to create a third circuit with the two bulbs and two 1.5V batteries. Compare the brightness of the bulbs in the three circuits. Children talk about and record what they have learnt from the challenge.

Talking points: true, false or not sure?

- To light the bulb there needs to be a complete pathway around the circuit.
- A bulb will light more brightly if there are two wires in a circuit.
- Bulb holders help the bulbs shine more brightly.
- The battery only needs to be connected to one part of the bulb to turn it on.
- The bulb will light when it is connected to any part of the battery.
- The filament in the bulb is part of the electric pathway.
- Connecting more bulbs in a circuit makes them glow brighter.
- To make bulbs glow brighter we need to add more batteries.
- A switch turns off the bulb because it creates a gap in the electric pathway.
- The battery pushes the electricity around the circuit.

To help reach agreement on the talking points groups can construct appropriate circuits to test their ideas. When groups present their responses to the class probe their thinking, and address any outstanding *learning needs*. Use video clips which model how electricity passes around a simple circuit to stimulate further discussion. Children can raise their own questions for further learning.

Information and teaching resources

BBC Bitesize:

- How an electric circuit works. *www.bbc.co.uk/education/clips/zq3fb9q*
- Electrical conductors.
  www.bbc.co.uk/bitesize/ks2/science/physical_processes/circuits_conductors/read/1/
- Electric circuits and conductivity. *www.bbc.co.uk/education/clips/z8chg82*

Application stage

Children's talk involves trying out scientific ideas

Thomas Edison

Thomas Edison was a tireless inventor and shrewd businessman. He was a pioneer of the electrical industry and made a fortune from his many inventions which exploited the potential of electrical power to transform work, home and entertainment. One of Edison's inventions was the ticker tape telegraph for sending information quickly over large distances. The motion picture camera was another one. Children can use information sources to explore the life and work of Thomas Edison and discover some of his inventions which helped change the world. They can present their findings in the form of a video documentary.

Figure 12.2 **Thomas Edison**

Source: iStock

Words along wires

With the help of a mobile phone, sending words over large distances is quick and easy. Of course, in the past it was not always that way. Before the invention of the electrical telegraph in the middle of the nineteenth century, long distance messages were mainly sent by post which in some cases could take months to arrive. An alternative was to set up optical telegraph systems using smoke, flags or reflected light to relay signals over large distances. Optical systems were often used by the military.

Groups can explore different ways words can be communicated non-verbally, and consider the advantages and disadvantages of the methods regarding long-distance communication. Children work collaboratively to invent ways of sending messages from one place to another using flags, light and sounds. For example, they could use a different flag for every letter of the alphabet, or develop their own code similar to the semaphore alphabet. Regarding light and sound, they could create circuits with switches and bulbs or buzzers, which could be used to send coded messages similar to the Morse code.

Children could try sending messages over wires. How far could they send a message over wires using a 1.5V battery, 1.5V bulb and a switch? Could they send a message from one end of the classroom to the other? Groups will need long lengths of conducting wire for this experiment. They determine the maximum possible length of the circuit. What is the effect of adding more 1.5V cells? Children calculate how many cells they would need to send a message from their classroom to the head teacher's office. Groups discuss the advantages and disadvantages of sending messages through wires. Challenge them to choose the best route to set up an electric telegraph between their classroom and a school in Melbourne, Australia, using the least amount of wire. They need to consider the practicalities of laying the cable when choosing the route. Groups should present and justify their ideas.

Words along wires is a project developed by Siemens and full details are available on the STEM Centre website.

Design and make electrical products

Following in Edison's footsteps children think of ways of using electric circuits to create products.

1   What sort of light will work for you?

    There are many reasons children use torches, so the prospect of designing their own is likely to appeal to them. If not, they could always design and make a working light for some other reason. Full details of this Nuffield project can be found on the STEM Centre website.

2   Design and make a game.

    Children start by researching ideas on the web. A good starting point is the BBC Bitesize video clip called *Using circuits to make games and activities.*

Information and teaching resources

BBC Bitesize:

● How an electric circuit works. *www.bbc.co.uk/education/clips/zq3fb9q*

● Using circuits to make games and activities. *www.bbc.co.uk/education/clips/z7k3cdm*

Other websites:

● Words along wires. *www.stem.org.uk/elibrary/resource/35126/words-along-wires*

● Power for the world. *http://practicalaction.org/power-for-the-world-1*

● Info on LEDs. *http://bpes.bp.com/primary-resources/science/ages-9-to-11/electricity/electricity-topic-starter/*

● What sort of light will work for you? *www.stem.org.uk/system/files/elibrary-resources/legacy_files_migrated/2837-light_col-1848.pdf*

Topic: Saving energy

Age group: 9–11 years

Introduction

This topic builds on previous work by exploring modern day developments in the design of light bulbs and batteries, and examines how electricity is generated. Activities include the use of analogies and role-play to help children picture how electric current in a simple circuit carries energy from the battery to the bulb. Opportunities are provided in the application stage for children to extend their knowledge of electricity in real-life situations.

Scientific view

Electric current refers to the movement or flow of electricity. Connecting wires are usually made from copper which contains electric particles (electrons) which are free to move. The battery creates the electric current by pushing the electric particles through the wires and hence creating a flow of electricity around the circuit. Batteries store energy, not electricity. As the electric current flows through the circuit it carries energy from the battery to the components making them light up, move or create a sound.

Working scientifically

In these activities children will:

- plan scientific enquiries to answer questions;
- record results using scientific diagrams;
- use test results to make predictions and set up further tests;
- report finding from enquiries including conclusions and causal relationships in oral and written form.

Health and safety

Follow the ASE guidelines in *Be Safe!* (2011) for all activities. Only use PAT tested equipment bought from reputable school suppliers. Teach children not to stare into bright sources of light. Teach children how to deal with broken bulbs and leaking batteries. Make sure any models produced by the children are safe.

Exploration stage

Children's talk involves trying out their own ideas

Setting the scene

Start by reviewing the work from the previous topic and talk about the work of Thomas Edison. Although he didn't invent the first light bulb, he did produce the first commercially viable one.

Figure 12.3 **Edison's light bulb**

Source: Alamy

Edison's light bulb was the forerunner of the filament light bulbs still in use today. In recent times, new types of light bulbs have been developed which are longer lasting and more energy efficient than incandescent bulbs. Create a display of light bulbs of different types, shapes, sizes and colours. Include energy efficient lights bulbs such as LEDs (light-emitting diodes), CFLs (compact fluorescent lamps) and halogens.

Puzzle

Filament bulbs are inefficient because they create a lot of heat as well as light. Since their primary purpose is to light up a room, the heat they produce is wasted. New types of bulbs are more efficient, but by how much? The puzzle is, which is the most energy efficient type of bulb on the market today?

Scientific enquiry

Children explore the different types of light bulbs which are now available and use information sources to compare their performance with the standard filament bulb which they have replaced.

Children observe, compare and contrast the features of the different energy efficient light bulbs and sort them into groups according to their similarities and differences. Provide PAT tested lamp stands so children can compare the brightness of the bulbs. Light meters can be used to provide a measure of the light energy which they emit. Do the bulbs with the highest power ratings in watts emit the most light? Children use the data to find the most efficient bulb. Tests need to be fair and carried out safely. Teach children how to use the lamps safely, and warn them not to touch or stare at the lights when using them. Make children familiar with the ASE safety code for using electricity which is published in the booklet *Be Safe!* (2011).

Scientific enquiry

Different types of lights are used for different reasons. Task children with surveying the types of lights used in their homes, gardens and their neighbourhood generally. Are they energy efficient considering their uses? Children report and discuss their findings in groups, and make recommendations about whether more energy efficient lights could be used. Each group can blog about their findings.

Teacher-led discussion

Return to the puzzle and talk about how different types of bulbs use energy. Compare the energy used by a 60W traditional filament bulb with that used by an 18W CFL which produces similar amounts of light. Discuss where the energy comes from. Use video clips to show how electricity is generated in a power station, and how using energy efficient light bulbs can reduce the use of fossil fuels and cut down pollution. Show children how electricity bills are worked out, and challenge them to calculate how much they save by using energy efficient bulbs in every room in their house.

Formative assessment

Provide opportunities for children to voice what they have learnt in the exploratory stage. Use evidence from their responses to the puzzle and other activities to assess differences between children's ideas and the scientific view. Plan how you will use the re-describing stage to help the children address their *learning needs* (see Chapter 1). You may need to modify the activities depending on the collective and individual needs of your children.

Information and teaching resources

BBC Bitesize:

● Electricity produced by generators. *www.bbc.co.uk/education/clips/z63fb9q*

● How electricity is made. *www.bbc.co.uk/education/clips/zxp6n39*

● The dangers of electricity. *www.bbc.co.uk/education/clips/z8x2tfr*

● Where does electricity come from? *www.bbc.co.uk/education/clips/zkys34j*

Other websites:

● Comparison of light bulbs. *www.which.co.uk/energy/energy-saving-products/guides/how-to-buy-led-cfl-and-halogen-bulbs/five-tips-for-choosing-the-right-light-bulb/*

ASE Journals:

● Primary Science 135 (Nov/Dec 2014) *The 'red and blacks'*

● Primary Science 135 (Nov/Dec 2014) *Teaching the big ideas of electricity* by Steven Chapman

Re-describing stage

Children's talk involves making sense of scientific ideas

Teacher-led discussion

Focus on the idea that there are two forms of electricity. One type is supplied by power stations as discussed in the exploratory stage and the other is supplied by batteries. Recap on the idea that power stations provide energy in the form of electricity which we use to power appliances in our homes. Batteries are normally used for portable things such as mobile phones and torches, which only need small amounts of energy. Use video clips which show how we use batteries and mains electricity in our daily lives.

Story-telling

Children may be surprised to find that batteries have been around since the eighteenth century when Italian scientist Alessandro Volta (1745–1827) made the first electric cell (battery) using metal discs. Children use information sources to tell stories about his life and the methods he used which led him to discover how to produce electricity. Groups can present their findings in the form of a drama, in which they act out a scene from Volta's life.

Scientific enquiry

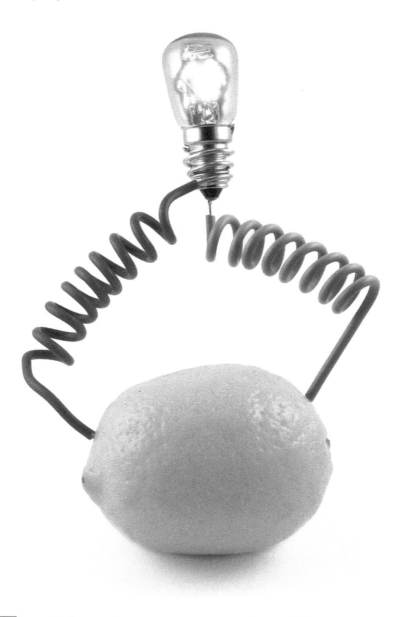

Figure 12.4 **Simple lemon battery using wires of two different metals**

Source: iStock

Groups can adapt Volta's ideas to make simple cells using objects such as potatoes, limes, lemons and even cola. The challenge is to create a battery which can light the most LEDs. Lots of information can be found on the web for these types of activities.

Children complete this activity by exploring the range of batteries which are available today. They can sort them in different ways including by type, voltage ratings, size and uses. Batteries can then be added to the display of bulbs.

Modelling

When batteries run out of energy they 'go flat' and are no longer able to supply energy to the circuit. Children may think of a battery as a container that stores electricity, like a bottle stores water. Consequently, when it 'goes flat' they imagine it has run out of electricity and may expect the 'empty' battery to be lighter. This is a common misconception.

To help address this misconception, children imagine how a battery works by comparing an electric circuit with an energy transport system. As the trucks travel around the circuit they collect energy from the battery and transport it to the bulb. The voltage of the battery denotes how much energy each truck collects. In a 1.5V single cell circuit the trucks collect just enough energy to light a 1.5V rated bulb to normal brightness. If two bulbs are added to the circuit they have to share the energy and hence they do not shine as brightly. Explain that the trucks represent the electricity as it travels around the circuit. Children can role-play this delivery analogy by taking on the role of the electric particles (trucks) which transport the energy. A full explanation of this model can be found in the core book, Loxley *et al.* (2017).

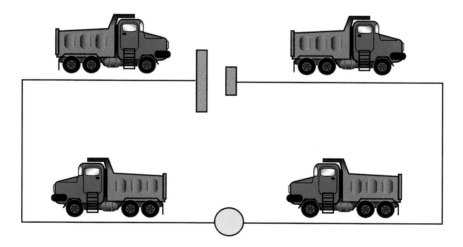

Figure 12.5 **Energy transport model**

Children use the analogy to explain why components have voltage ratings. They can also use it to explain why batteries eventually become 'flat' because they run out of energy, not electricity. Are there things about the behaviour of a simple electric circuit which the analogy cannot help explain? Can children think of a different analogy?

Teacher-led discussion

Connect a circuit with two 1.5V bulbs and one 1.5V battery, and compare to a circuit with just one bulb. Why do two bulbs in a simple circuit shine less brightly than one bulb alone? Continue to add extra bulbs to the circuit so children can see how each time they become dimmer. Ask children to use the transport analogy to explain why. Assess their understanding of the model and address any outstanding *learning needs*.

Scientific enquiry

Provide children with two 1.5V bulbs, two 1.5V batteries and connecting wires so they can explore how to light two bulbs to the same brightness as one. Children record their circuits using standard symbols for the components.

Extend the enquiry by providing other components such as bulbs with higher voltage ratings, buzzers, flashing bulbs, LEDs and magnetic reed switches with which children can create circuits containing a number of components. For each circuit they should produce an annotated circuit diagram which includes the voltage rating of the devices and the total voltage of the battery which was needed to make them work. Children should always start with one cell and add more cells until they get the component(s) to work. Each group presents their findings to the rest of the class and explains the effects of adding more cells to a circuit.

Information and teaching resources

BBC Bitesize:

● Batteries and their uses. *www.bbc.co.uk/education/clips/zpshfg8*

● Circuits, batteries and power sources. *www.bbc.co.uk/education/clips/zxp6n39*

Other websites:

● How to make your potato battery. *www.youtube.com/watch?v=nol7TmspMrM*

● How potato batteries work. *www.kidzworld.com/article/4726-how-potato-batteries-work*

● Potato batteries. *www.how-things-work-science-projects.com/potato-battery.html*

Application stage
Children's talk involves trying out scientific ideas

Story-telling

Children use information sources to discover how the way we live has been influenced by developments in electrical technology since the time of Volta. Old technologies such as coal- and oil-fired power stations can be compared to cleaner, and more sustainable, ways of producing electricity such as solar panels, and wind and wave-powered generators. Use the outcomes of the research to create an eye-catching and informative display. Children can explore the types of jobs available in the field of electrical engineering and technology. Invite a STEM ambassador to talk about developments in power generation and associated job opportunities.

Power for the world: A Practical Action project

Figure 12.6 **Solar panels in Turkana, Kenya**

Source: Practical Action/Andy Heath

This project is about bringing electrical power to poor communities in the developing world. Children can learn more about the world in which they live, as well as developing their understanding of electricity and technology. Full details and teaching resources can be found on the Practical Action website. Resources include a teacher's pack, a PowerPoint presentation to use in class, a case study of how renewable energy is used in Kenya and a 'Power for the world' certificate for the children.

Design and make models of machines

Children design and make models of machines which rely on electricity and add them to the display. Each model should be controlled by an electrical circuit. The STEM Centre website has some good ideas including a project called *Super sucker* which involves making a model vacuum cleaner and *How fast should your buggy be?* which involves making an electric car. The BP Educational Resources website provides information about building a model helicopter.

Information and teaching resources

BBC Bitesize:

- Discovering the work of Michael Faraday. *www.bbc.co.uk/education/clips/zyfpyrd*
- A comparison of two Peruvian villages with and without electricity. *www.bbc.co.uk/education/topics/z2882hv/resources/1*
- Wave power, hydroelectricity and wind farms. *www.bbc.co.uk/education/clips/zyjd7ty*

Other websites:

- How fast should your buggy be? *www.stem.org.uk/elibrary/resource/25794/how-fast-should-your-buggy-be*
- Super sucker project. *www.stem.org.uk/elibrary/resource/35625/super-sucker-designing-a-machine-to-clean-up-litter*
- Design an electric helicopter. *http://bpes.bp.com/primary-resources/design-technology/ages-9-to-11/design-and-technology/design-an-electric-helicopter-activity/*
- Power for the world. *http://practicalaction.org/power-for-the-world-1*
- Electrical engineering jobs. *https://targetjobs.co.uk/career-sectors/engineering/294506-what-jobs-can-you-do-with-an-electrical-engineering-degree*

Chapter 13

Forces and magnetism

Millions saw the apple fall. Newton was the only one who asked why?

Bernard Baruch (1870–1965)

It would be astonishing to see someone move an object by simply pointing at it. Then why are we not astonished when we see things fall to the ground without knowing what pulls them down? Of course gravity is the answer, but gravity is just a word. Nobody really knows for sure how it works. It's a mystery, and the more we think about it the more mysterious it becomes. This chapter presents *ideas for practice* which help children explore the effects of gravity and magnetism. The first topic provides activities which help younger children explore the effects of everyday forces. Subsequent topics help children develop an understanding of the bigger picture of gravity, including the role it plays in maintaining life on Earth.

Topics in this chapter:

- Forces in action

- Gravity and magnetism

- What has gravity ever done for us?

Subject knowledge to support the teaching of these topics can be found in the core book, Loxley, P., Dawes, D., Nicholls, L. and Dore, B. (2018) *Teaching primary science: Promoting enjoyment and developing understanding*, Abingdon: Routledge, Chapter 19: Electricity and magnetism and Chapter 20: Forces and motion.

The mysterious force we call gravity

Isaac Newton was born on Christmas Day 1642. It was the same year in which another great scientist, Galileo Galilei, died. Newton was a difficult and antisocial man. His childhood was anything but happy, and his life was full of petty jealousies and vindictive attacks against people who challenged him. Throughout his life Newton was determined not to be beaten, be it by a school bully, or by other academics. He always had to come out on top.

Figure 13.1 **Statue of Isaac Newton by Eduardo Paolozzi (1995) outside British Library, London**

Source: Alamy

Isaac Newton is probably best known for discovering gravity, although imagining gravity is probably a better way of describing what he did. According to a friend, the notion of gravity came into his mind as a result of watching an apple fall from a tree. The friend reported that they were reminiscing over a cup of tea when Newton told him how he worked out his theory of gravity.

Why should that apple always descend perpendicular to the ground, thought he to himself. Why should it not go sideways or upward, but constantly to the earth's centre? Assuredly, the reason is, that the earth draws it; there is a power, like that we here call gravity, which extends itself thro' the universe.[1]

It would not have been the first time Newton had seen an apple fall from a tree, but on this occasion he saw it in a totally new way. In a thought experiment he wondered whether the force of gravity that pulled the apple down towards the Earth could reach as far as the Moon. If it did, this would mean that the Earth and the Moon were joined together by the same invisible force.

Newton came to realise that this mysterious force, which we call gravity, could travel unaided through space and was responsible for holding the Solar System together. It not only stopped the Moon from flying off into space, but it also controlled the motion of the planets around the Sun. The planets orbit the Sun because they are joined to it by the force of gravity which reaches out through millions and millions of miles of space.

Understanding gravity was not Newton's only triumph; he also worked out how forces control motion. He discovered how forces make objects go faster, or slower or change direction. Objects do not need a force to keep them going at the same speed. They will move in the same direction forever unless a force changes their motion. That is why it is possible to send spaceships such long distances out into space, because there is nothing out there to slow them down. Newton worked this out nearly four hundred years ago when people still travelled by horse and cart. That's why he was a genius!

Ideas for practice

Topic: Forces in action

Age group: 5–7 years

Introduction

Children experience forces in action when playing with toys or taking part in outdoor games. The purpose of this topic is to add to those experiences and provide opportunities for children to talk about them in scientific ways. In the *application stage* children develop their learning at home, and apply their understanding to design and make a simple game.

Scientific view

A force is a push, pull or a twist. Forces can make things start to move, speed them up, slow them down, make them stop and change their direction. The bigger the force, the bigger the change of movement it can bring about.

Working scientifically

In these activities children will:

- perform simple tests;
- identify and classify different types of forces;
- use their observations and ideas to suggest answers to questions;
- record findings in ways which help answer questions.

Health and safety

For activities involving gymnastics and movement, follow your school policy on safety and supervision in PE. Use mats where appropriate. When planning the design and make activities refer to *Be Safe!* (2011) for H&S guidance.

Exploration stage

Children's talk involves trying out their own ideas

Setting the scene

Figure 13.2 **Tug of war**

Project a cartoon depicting a tug of war. Ask the children to describe what they think is happening. Draw out the rules of the game. Talk about children's experiences. Have they ever played the game? What can they remember?

Talking points: true, false or not sure?

- The person who can pull hardest will win.
- The strongest one will win.
- The one who can pull with the greatest force will win.
- The biggest person will win.
- The person who can push hardest will win.
- Whoever has the biggest hands will win.

Discuss the talking points. Encourage children to provide reasons and elaborate on their responses. Talk together about the effects of forces. Ask them to explain the difference between a pulling and a pushing force. Ask two children to mime a tug of war. Freeze-frame the mime, and ask children to describe their actions. Establish whether pulling or pushing forces are used in a tug of war.

Scientific enquiry

In the hall or outside set up a circus of activities which involve using pushing and pulling forces to make things move. Here are some suggestions:

- Riding a skateboard/scooter.
- Trying to sink a balloon in a tank of water.
- Bouncing on a trampoline.
- Skipping with a rope.
- Spinning a hoop.
- Kicking, bouncing and throwing a ball.
- Pushing a pram.
- Pulling a trolley.
- Pulling a suitcase on wheels.

Children talk about the types of forces they are using and ways of making the forces bigger. Encourage them to relate the magnitude of the force to the movement of the object. Help them establish that bigger forces can make things move faster.

Groups can demonstrate an activity and talk about the forces. Take photographs to record the activities. Use the photographs in a display classifying and illustrating how forces affect movement.

Puzzle

Show children a plastic bottle with a screw-on top. Ask them whether they could help you open it. What type of force would they use? Would they use a push or a pull, or another type of force? Discuss children's responses, and explore different words which describe the action of the force required to open the bottle. Help them distinguish between pushing, pulling and twisting forces.

Formative assessment

Provide opportunities for children to voice what they have learnt in the exploratory stage. Use evidence from their responses to the puzzle, talking points and other activities to assess differences between children's ideas and the scientific view. Plan how you will use the re-describing stage to help the children address their *learning needs* (see Chapter 1). You may need to modify the activities depending on the collective and individual needs of your children.

Re-describing stage

Children's talk involves making sense of scientific ideas

Teacher-led discussion

Help children summarise what they learnt about forces in the exploratory stage. Remind them of the three types of forces. Children can mime using pushing, pulling and twisting forces. The BBC Bitesize video clip *Pushes and pulls* shows different types of forces in action. Children can watch the clip and try to identify the different types of forces.

Modelling

How many ways can children move? They can hop, jump, crawl, slide, roll, twist, run and change direction. What else can they do? How many ways can they demonstrate using forces? What types of forces are they using? Ask them to move like different animals such as a snake, a grasshopper, an elephant and so on. Encourage children to talk about how the forces they use control their movements. Address outstanding *learning needs*. Take photographs of the children performing different movements and add them to the display.

Story-telling

Ask the children to record all the different types of forces they come across over a weekend. For example, kicking a football and being patted on the head are different examples of pushing forces. Practise at school until they get the hang of it. Children will need the help of their parents or guardians, so send a note home to explain what you are asking them to do. Children record their most unusual forces by drawing pictures or taking photographs. Back in school add the pictures and photographs to the display and listen to children's stories. Ask them to mime the actions of the forces.

Design and make a game

Blow football is a traditional game which children (and adults) have played for generations. Children can design and make their own game and explore the effect of changing the width of the straw, and the size and weight of the ball. Encourage children to explain their observations in terms of the effects the blowing force has on the ball.

Children can also make other simple games which rely on the use of forces.

Information and teaching resources

BBC Bitesize:

- Pushes and pulls. *www.bbc.co.uk/education/clips/z9dkjxs*
- Forces. *www.bbc.co.uk/education/clips/z9nkqty*
- Forces in the playground. *www.bbc.co.uk/education/clips/zvj8q6f*
- Pushes and pulls – Forces on the railway. *www.bbc.co.uk/education/clips/z489wmn*

Application stage

Children's talk involves trying out scientific ideas

Unsinkable

Figure 13.3 **Unsinkable**

Source: iStock

Present images of children playing inside water walking balloons. Find out whether any of your children have seen or used water walking balls at the seaside or in swimming pools. Listen to their stories. Can they describe how it feels when floating on the water? Why do the balloons float so well? Do they think it is possible to sink them? Discuss children's responses to the questions.

Scientific enquiry

Help children plan an enquiry to find out whether the shape and size of a balloon influences how well it floats. You will need a selection of different shaped balloons, an inflation pump, and a number of plastic tanks and/or sinks full of water.

Groups start by testing the properties of the deflated balloons.

- What are they made from?
- Are they hard or soft?
- Are they stiff or stretchy?
- Which shape is most stretchy?
- How far can they stretch them?
- Do they float? Are they hard to sink?

Talk together about the children's responses to the questions, and explore why it is important that a balloon is stretchy. Discuss the actions of the forces required to stretch a balloon. Help inflate the balloons so that each group has a range of sizes and shapes. Ask children to describe how blowing air into the balloons made them grow in size. Can they describe the action of the force created by the air? Is it a pushing or pulling force?

Each group compares how well the different balloons float in water by trying to sink them. Which balloon requires the most force to push it under the water? Does the force depend on the size or shape of the balloon? Ask children to describe how it feels when they push down on the balloon. What happens to the balloon when they stop pushing and let it go? Are balloons unsinkable? Children draw diagrams to record their observations, and compare the behaviour of deflated and inflated balloons. Can they explain why the inflated one floats best?

Can children think of other objects filled with air that might float? Let them explore different types of objects such as balls and plastic bottles.

Design and make an unsinkable boat

With adult support children make unsinkable boats/rafts using small plastic bottles. You will need a range of plastic bottles (with tops), balsa wood, sheet plastic (corrugated), lolly sticks, paper or fabric for sails, low-melt glue guns and water tanks. The challenge is to make the boats stable in the water and able to carry a load.

Design and make a model whale

Another activity is to make a model of a whale which floats just below the water. To achieve this, children will need to understand how loading their bottles with silver sand, weights or other materials will influence how they float. The challenge is to load the bottles so that they float horizontally with about half to one third of the bottle showing above the water. Using photographs as a guide children can then use appropriate materials to make a tail and turn their bottle into a whale. You could use this activity to set the scene for a topic on whales and other marine mammals.

Topic: Gravity and magnetism

Age group: 7–9 years

Introduction

This topic builds on children's understanding of forces and how they control the movement of objects. The activities provide opportunities for children to explore and compare gravity with magnetism, and to measure their effects. The application stage focuses on activities which involve the use of magnets.

Scientific view

Objects do not just fall, rather they are pulled to Earth by an invisible force called gravity. Gravity is mysterious because it cannot be seen, acts over large distances and exerts its force on objects which are not in contact with each other. Scientists describe the Earth's gravity as a force field, which is an area around the Earth in which objects experience forces. Similarly the area around a magnet is called a magnetic force field because it attracts iron and steel objects.

Working scientifically

In these activities children will:

- ask relevant questions and use scientific enquiry skills to answer them;
- set up simple practical enquiries;
- take accurate measurements using force meters;
- record data using tables;
- use results to draw simple conclusions;
- report on findings orally and pictorially.

Health and safety

Covering magnets with cling film and/or putting filings into sealed plastic bags or petri-dishes avoid problems involved in using them. Iron filings can also be purchased in sealed plastic containers. Strong magnets can jump together and pinch skin. They should not be used near electronic circuits, such as TV and monitor screens.

Exploration stage

Children's talk involves trying out their own ideas

Setting the scene

Discovery of the Laws of Gravitation by Isaac Newton

Figure 13.4 **Isaac Newton thinking about gravity**

Source: iStock

Ask the children what they know about Isaac Newton. Tell them a short story of Newton's life and why he is thought to be a great scientist. Mention he discovered gravity without going into any detail.

Puzzle

Put the question to the children which Newton asked himself. *Why does the apple fall down, and not up or sideways?*

Talking points: true, false or not sure?

- The apple falls down because it is tired of hanging from the tree.
- There is an invisible force which pulls the apple down.
- The wind blew the apple down to the ground.
- Nothing makes the apple fall; it is just something apples do.
- Birds push apples to the ground.
- The apple would fall upwards in Australia.
- The apple falls to the ground because it is heavy.
- If the apple were lighter, it would fall upward.

Groups discuss the points and try to reach agreement on what causes apples to fall to the ground. Pick up on their use of the word gravity as an explanation. Ask them to explain what they think the word means. In groups children can negotiate an explanation for the word gravity. Groups come together to share their explanations, and negotiate one on which they can all agree.

Modelling

Remind children that forces (pushes and pulls) are needed to make things speed up, slow down or change direction. What does this tell us about falling apples? Children experience the force of gravity on an apple by holding one at arm's length. Can they feel the weight? Give children something heavier to hold. Can they feel the force of gravity pulling the object down?

Scientific enquiry

Children use force meters (newton meters) to measure the pull of gravity on an apple and a range of other everyday objects. Bring in a basket of goods from a supermarket and let the children measure the weight of each item. What is the total weight of the goods?

Children can try to estimate the weight of different objects, and then test how accurate they are by weighing them. Present their results in a table. Reinforce the idea that weight is caused by the pull of gravity and hence the weight of an object is also a measure of the pull of gravity.

TABLE 13.1 Estimating the weight of objects

Object	Estimated weight (N)	Measured weight (N)	Pull of gravity (N)
1kg bag of flour		10	10

Story-telling

Children imagine themselves to be Sir Isaac Newton telling a friend about the time he discovered gravity. They should tell the story in the form of a dialogue, with the friend asking Newton questions about his discovery. They can create their own cartoons to illustrate the story.

Talk about their stories and probe their understanding of the nature of gravity. Why does the apple always fall down? What pictures of gravity do the children hold in their minds?

Formative assessment

Provide opportunities for children to voice what they have learnt in the exploratory stage. Use evidence from their responses to the puzzle, talking points and other activities to assess differences between children's ideas and the scientific view. Plan how you will use the re-describing stage to help the children address their *learning needs* (see Chapter 1). You may need to modify the activities depending on the collective and individual needs of your children.

Information and teaching resources

BBC Bitesize:

● Discovering the work of Isaac Newton. *www.bbc.co.uk/education/clips/zhmqxnb*

Re-describing stage

Children's talk involves making sense of scientific ideas

Teacher-led discussion

Start this part by addressing a common misconception. It is likely that the children will think heavier objects fall faster than lighter ones. To get them thinking, provide groups with a sheet of A4 paper and a tennis ball. Ask them to predict which will fall most quickly to the ground when dropped from the same height. Let them test out their predictions. Ask them whether their tests were fair. Suggest the paper fell slowly because it was acting like a parachute. Discuss how children can make their tests fairer. Suggest they scrunch the paper up into the size of the ball. Children repeat the test to find the two objects now hit the ground at roughly the same time. Discuss what this test may mean for the rate at which objects fall to the ground due to gravity. Do all objects fall at the same rate?

Scientific enquiry

To answer the above question, children compare the times different objects fall to the ground when dropped from the same height. Comparisons need to be made fair, and tests repeated to account for timing inaccuracies. There are H&S considerations when releasing objects from a height. Refer to *Be Safe!* (2011) for guidance.

Teacher-led discussion

Talk about what children understand by a *force field*. Children may be familiar with the term force field which is used in science fiction movies. Play a game on the children by implanting a small iron or steel rod inside an apple. Do not put it too deep, just enough so children cannot see it. Conceal a strong magnet in your hand hidden by a thin glove or tape it to a stick and camouflage it to look like a magic wand. Ask children whether they think you can make the apple move without touching it. Perform your magic and talk about children's responses. Repeat the trick showing the magnet and talk about how it works. Describe the magnet having a force field around it. What other force fields do they know about? Talk about gravity.

Modelling

Tie a paper clip to a length of thread and tape the other end to the table. Using a strong magnet lift the paper clip until the thread is vertical and taut. Ask the children why the paper clip is stuck to the magnet. What force is holding it? Ask them to predict what will happen if you lift the magnet higher until it is no longer touching the paper clip. Now slowly lift the magnet above the paper clip so they are no longer in contact. Hopefully the clip will remain suspended in the air on the end of the thread, being held there by the force of the magnetic field. Use the term 'magnetic force field' to explain the forces acting on the clip. There are two force fields involved. Gravity is pulling the clip down, while the magnetic field is pulling the other way to stop it falling. Children can explore other objects which can be suspended in air by a magnetic force field.

Use the standard demonstration with iron filings and a bar magnet to show the pattern of a magnetic force field and how its strength is concentrated at the poles. Compare to other shaped magnets. Refer to H&S advice at the start of this topic, and in *Be Safe!* (2011).

Scientific enquiry

Provide opportunities for children to raise and investigate their own questions about the properties of magnets. Unlike gravity, magnets have two poles, north and south. The convention is similar poles repel each other and opposite poles attract.

- Children can plan investigations to compare the strength of different magnets.

- Magnets have force fields but they do not attract all objects as gravity does. Children investigate which objects magnets attract and look for patterns in the types of materials.

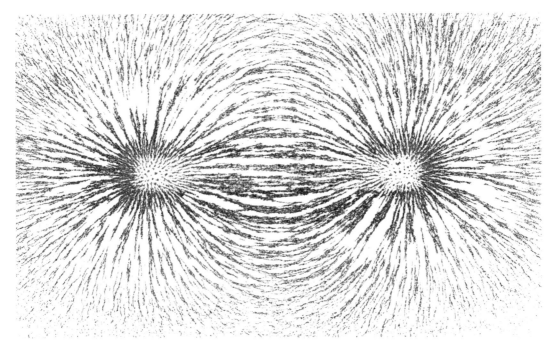

Figure 13.5 **Shape of magnetic force field**

Source: Alamy

- Magnets do not attract apples but their force field can pass through them. Children investigate and look for patterns in types of materials which magnetism passes through, and materials which block it out. Can gravity be blocked out? Encourage children to investigate.

- Children devise their own magic show involving gravitation and magnetic forces. They present the show to the class who try to explain how the trick works. Children should identify all the forces involved.

While performing their magic tricks, question the children to assess their understanding of magnetism and gravity as forces which act at a distance. Which can act over the largest distance? Use video clips to stimulate further discussion about gravity and magnetism. Address any outstanding *learning needs*.

Information and teaching resources

BBC Bitesize:

- Experiments to test air resistance. *www.bbc.co.uk/education/clips/zqshfg8*

- Gravity and its effects on a stunt artist. *www.bbc.co.uk/education/clips/zvqd7ty*

- Magnets and their invisible force. *www.bbc.co.uk/education/clips/zk9rkqt*

Application stage

Children's talk involves trying out scientific ideas

1 Designing and making games

a Treasure hunt

The game involves the search for treasure consisting of objects made from magnetic materials, which can be found with the help of a magnet. Children choose the treasure and design the game with a set of rules.

b Board games

Games in which magnets are used to control the movement of objects around a board are popular projects. Children investigate materials to use for the board and explore the best design for the objects. Objects can be made from cork with a thumbtack in them so they can be controlled by the movement of a magnet underneath the board.

2 Magnetic switches

Magnetic switches are useful devices because they enable electric circuits to be turned on remotely. Children can explore how to use them in a simple circuit and then design and make an artefact which is controlled by a magnetic switch. For example, at Christmas they could make a model of Santa whose nose lights up when he puts his hat on or his sack is brought near him (with a magnet inside).

3 Fridge magnets

Fridge magnets are a favourite project. Activities can be found on the Nuffield Foundation website or on the STEM Centre website.

4 Super-magnets

Children use the web to explore the uses of super-magnets.

Information and teaching resources

BBC Bitesize:

● Super powerful magnets. *www.bbc.co.uk/education/clips/zsg3cdm*

Other websites:

● What should be stuck to your fridge? *www.stem.org.uk/elibrary/resource/25801*

● Top ten uses for super strong magnets. *www.youtube.com/watch?v=MCsl4RcFNdl*

Topic: What has gravity ever done for us?

Age group: 9–11 years

Introduction

This topic builds on children's understanding of gravity. The purpose of the activities is to encourage children to engage with the bigger picture of gravity and develop awareness of the role it plays in maintaining life on the Earth. The application stage focuses on lifting machines designed to help us overcome the force of gravity.

Scientific view

All objects in the universe feel the effects of gravity. Here on Earth the force of gravity pulls objects on the surface towards its centre. The weight of an object is a measure of the force of gravity. Newton was the first to realise that the effects of gravity can be felt over very large distances, so large in fact that gravity is the force that holds the Solar System together.

Working scientifically

In these activities children will:

- plan enquiries to answer questions;
- take measurements using force meters;
- record data and plot suitable graphs;
- report and present findings from enquiries;
- use scientific evidence to draw conclusions.

Health and safety

When releasing objects from a height, be sure that children do not put themselves or others (below them) at risk. Refer to H&S guidance in *Be Safe!* (2011). When using pulleys be sure they are attached to a secure fixing.

Exploration stage

Children's talk involves trying out their own ideas

Setting the scene

Start with pictures and video clips from the NASA website which show astronauts 'walking in space'. Discuss what the astronaut is doing and why he/she needs to wear a spacesuit. Children use information sources to explore how the astronauts assembled the International Space Station.

Figure 13.6 **Astronaut on a spacewalk**

Source: NASA

Puzzle

Ask children to imagine what it would feel like to step outside the Space Station. What would they see beneath their feet? The Space Station is moving very fast. It travels around Earth at a speed of about 17,000 miles per hour (that's about 5 miles per second!). This means that the Space Station orbits Earth and sees a sunrise once every 92 minutes. The puzzle is, if the Space Station is travelling so fast, why are astronauts on spacewalks not left behind floating in space?

Talking points: true, false or not sure?

- Astronauts are propelled alongside the Space Station by jet packs on their backs.
- A rope is used to secure the astronaut to the Space Station.
- Astronauts inside and outside the Space Station travel at the same speed.
- There is nothing to change the speed of an astronaut outside the Space Station.
- They slow the Space Station down to enable astronauts to go outside.
- On spacewalks astronauts use a super-magnet inside their suits to fix them to the Space Station.

In groups children discuss the talking points and try to provide an answer to the puzzle. Sir Isaac Newton would have solved the puzzle straight away, because he understood that in the absence of forces objects move at a constant speed. If the astronauts are travelling at the same speed as the Space Station when they are inside, then they will continue to travel at that speed when they go outside. The chapter on forces and motion in the core book (Loxley *et al.* (2017)) provides a full explanation.

Story-telling

Sir Isaac Newton was a great scientist, but what type of man was he? Children research the life and work of Newton. Using information sources they find out about his childhood, his personality, his family life, his life at Cambridge, his adversaries, his scientific achievements and his failures. Create a display to tell his story. Debate whether Newton achieved so much because he was so cantankerous and single-minded, or whether he could have achieved even more by collaborating with other scientists.

Scientific enquiry

Newton famously said, 'If I have seen further it is by standing on the shoulders of giants.' One of the intellectual giants he was talking about was Galileo Galilei whose ideas Newton used to help develop his laws of motion. A famous legend describes Galileo dropping cannon balls from the top of the leaning tower of Pisa. He wanted to prove that regardless of their weight and size the objects would all hit the ground at the same time.

Children imagine they are assistants of Galileo charged with proving whether all objects dropped from the same height will fall to the ground in equal times. Intuitively, it makes sense to predict that the heavier objects will fall the fastest. This is a common misconception. Provide each group with a range of 'cannon balls'. Cricket balls, golf balls, tennis balls, solid rubber balls, metal balls, footballs and marbles are good substitutes. To test the effect of the force of gravity each item is dropped from the same height and the time to reach the floor is recorded. Children need to discuss timing issues, how to take accurate measurements and how to make the comparisons fair. Use force meters to measure the pull of gravity on the objects in newtons.

TABLE 13.2 Comparing fall times

Object	Weight (N)	Length of drop (m)	Time for drop (s)
marble			
golf ball			
tennis ball			
football			
others			

Children analyse their results and look for patterns. Plot the results on a graph. Was Galileo right or do the results suggest something else?

Children use force meters to measure the weight of a wide range of objects around the classroom. Challenge them to guess the pull of gravity on a range of food items such as 1kg bag of flour, 2kg bag of sugar, 200g bar of chocolate and other packaged items labelled in grams. Check their predictions by measuring the weights. Look for patterns and the relationship between the mass of an object measured in kilograms and its weight measured in newtons. Knowing that a 1kg object weighs 10N, children estimate their own weights.

Puzzle

In groups children make a list of the advantages and disadvantages of living in a gravitational force field. What would happen if gravity was 'switched off'? Debate the idea of living in a world with no gravity. How would the world be affected? Could we still survive?

Talking points: true, false or not sure?

- If gravity was switched off, nothing would change.
- If gravity was switched off, we would all float in the air.
- If gravity was switched off, the Moon would crash into the Earth.
- If gravity was switched off, the water in the oceans would flood the planet.
- If gravity was switched off, the air we breathe would float off into space.
- If gravity was switched off, the Earth would no longer orbit the sun.
- If gravity was switched off, we could not survive.

Groups present their ideas to the class and explain their reasoning. Encourage children to respectfully challenge ideas with which they do not agree. Conclude by deciding whether any living thing could survive on Earth without gravity.

Story-telling

Children use information sources to help create their own science fiction stories entitled 'Lost in Space: The day the Earth ran out of gravity.' Although the stories are fictitious, the science should still be 'believable'. Use stories to assess children's understanding of the universal nature of gravity.

Formative assessment

Provide opportunities for children to voice what they have learnt in the exploratory stage. Use evidence from their responses to the puzzle, talking points and other activities to assess differences between children's ideas and the scientific view. Plan how you will use the re-describing stage to help the children address their *learning needs* (see Chapter 1). You may need to modify the activities depending on the collective and individual needs of your children.

Information and teaching resources

- NASA astronauts conduct space walk. *www.youtube.com/watch?v=cOhkcXf416g*

- An astronaut's first space walk. *www.youtube.com/watch?v=O_iuT6uN-Is*

- How it works – The International Space Station. *www.youtube.com/watch?v=SGP6Y0Pnhe4*

Re-describing stage

Children's talk involves making sense of scientific ideas

Teacher-led discussion

Reinforce the idea that a world without gravity means a world without life. If gravity were 'turned off', we and many other objects would become weightless and as the Earth spun beneath us we would 'fly off' into space. This would include the water in the rivers, seas and oceans, as well as the air that we breathe. The Solar System would fly apart and the Earth would freeze over as it moved away from the Sun. It was gravity which helped form the Universe in the first place; without it the Universe as we know it would not exist.

Modelling

Use a globe to illustrate how we would 'fly off' a spinning Earth the way a car spins off a road when it goes too fast around a bend. Also use the analogy of a slingshot to show how objects on Earth would 'shoot off' into space when released from the force of gravity. Use animations from the web to show how gravity holds the Solar System together and model what would happen if it was suddenly 'turned off'.

Story-telling

Children paint pictures entitled 'What has gravity ever done for us?' They interpret the title in any way they like but need to be able to justify its symbolism. Examine children's thinking and their understanding of the science while they are creating the work. Address any outstanding *learning needs.*

Information and teaching resources

BBC Bitesize:

● Gravity on different worlds. *www.bbc.co.uk/education/clips/zbcpvcw*

● Earth orbits the Sun. *www.bbc.co.uk/education/clips/z6vfb9q*

Other websites:

● Newton's cannon. *http://waowen.screaming.net/revision/force&motion/ncananim.htm*

● Solar System planets. *www.youtube.com/watch?v=f6foCDF6zl0*

● Solar System video. *www.youtube.com/watch?v=z8aBZZnv6y8*

Application stage

Children's talk involves trying out scientific ideas

Lifting machines

Although we cannot live without gravity, it does at times present us with some difficulties. It would be nice to turn it off sometimes, especially when we need to lift heavy weights. Since the earliest civilisations people have learnt to use machines to lift heavy objects, the principles of which we still use today. Children research the use of lifting machines from the time of the Ancient Egyptians to the present. Create posters to show how lifting machines have changed. What has been the biggest driving force behind the change?

Children explore and compare the efficiency of three types of machines commonly used to reduce the effort required to lift a load.

1   A ramp.

2   A pulley system.

3   A lever.

A 2kg bag of sugar weighs 20N. In practice it will require slightly more than this to lift it off the ground. Children explore lifting the load straight up off the ground to a height of about half a metre. What is the least force required? They compare this with the force needed to lift it to the same height using each of the machines in the list.

Figure 13.7   **Farmer using ancient shaduf (lever) to hoist water**

Source: Alamy

Variables to consider include:

● the slope of the ramp and the type of surface;

● the number of pulleys in the system;

● the length of the lever.

Children investigate which machine can lift the load with the least effort. Groups compare their results and come to a conclusion about which is the most efficient machine.

Bridges

The Romans were famous bridge builders and one of their most famous engineers was a soldier called Vitruvius who lived in the first century BCE. Vitruvius believed that an architect should focus on three central themes when preparing a design for a building: strength, functionality and beauty.

Children imagine they are Roman bridge builders and chief engineer Vitruvius has asked them to build a scale model of a bridge to be built over a local river. The bridge needs to be strong and designed so that a horse-drawn cart could travel over it. It should also be attractive so that locals would welcome its construction. To help with their ideas children research famous Roman bridges around the world and compare their styles. Criteria for the best design should be based on Vitruvius' three design themes.

Note

1   Fara, P. (2009) *Science: A Four Thousand Year History*, Oxford: OUP.

Chapter 14
Light

Light thinks it travels faster than anything but it's wrong. No matter how fast light travels, it finds the darkness has always got there first, and is waiting for it.

Terry Pratchett, novelist (1948–2015)

The Sun is the main source of light, and without it the world would be a dark, lifeless place. Light from the Sun provides energy for plants to grow, and most animals use it to help them sense the world. This chapter focuses on the behaviour of light, and how it enables us to see objects in the world. Young children start by experiencing light and dark, and learn about animals with good night vision. Later topics explore how shadows and reflections are created, and examine how the way light travels enables us to see objects.

Topics in this chapter:

- Night animals
- Reflections and shadows
- Chasing shadows

Subject knowledge to support the teaching of these topics can be found in the core book, Loxley, P., Dawes, D., Nicholls, L. and Dore, B. (2018) *Teaching primary science: Promoting enjoyment and developing understanding*, Abingdon: Routledge, Chapter 15: Adaptation and evolution, and Chapter 21: Light.

Light

The Sun is the main source of energy on the Earth. Without light from the Sun the Earth would be a dark, cold place where life could not exist. The light we see is part of a spectrum of electromagnetic energy emitted by the Sun, much of which is blocked by our atmosphere. Light, some infrared and ultraviolet, and microwaves pass through the atmosphere and reach the Earth's surface. Of all the types of energy emitted by the Sun, light is the one that passes most easily through our atmosphere. It should be no surprise, therefore, that humans and many other animals have evolved organs (eyes) which are sensitive to light, as they have adapted to life on Earth. Although we can only see the rainbow colours of the light spectrum, some animals like bees and butterflies can see ultraviolet light as well, which enables them to forage for food in shaded areas and on cloudy days.

The Sun is not the only source of light on Earth. Fire has provided a source of light for people for many thousands of years. In some less developed parts of the world, people still burn wood and use candles or oil lamps to light their homes. In the developed world, electricity is used to power devices designed to produce light. Many of these devices contain electric light bulbs, fluorescent tubes or LEDs (light-emitting diodes).

Regardless of how it is produced, light travels outward from its source at an amazing speed of 299,792km per sec, which is an incredible 670,616,629mph. Compare this to the speed of a modern airliner which is about 600mph, and we can get a feel for how remarkable light is. Even travelling at this speed light takes about eight minutes to travel from the Sun to the Earth, which means we always see the Sun not as it is, but as it was eight minutes ago. Unlike sound, light does not require a medium (solid, liquid or gas) to travel through. Light from the Sun travels over 93,000,000 miles (150 million kilometres) through space before it arrives on Earth and finds a way into our eyes.

We may feel the heat from the Sun or a light bulb on our skin, but we don't sense the light. We cannot tell which colour of light is shining on our skin by how it feels; we have to look at it. We only sense light when it enters our eyes. As it does, it is focused on the retina, which is like the film in a camera. A signal is then passed to the brain from which an image of the light is produced in our minds. What we see of the world are our own interpretations of the images that light produces on the retina of our eyes.

We see objects either directly or indirectly. Sources of light such as the flame of a lighted candle we see directly as the light travels straight from the source into our eyes. The table on which the candle stands we see indirectly by reflected light. Light from the flame travels out in all directions, some of it strikes the table surface and bounces off again in all directions. This means people standing around the table are likely to have some of this reflected light enter their eyes and hence they will be able to see the table. We and other animals see the world mostly through reflected light.

Materials which light cannot pass through are called opaque. Opaque materials either absorb or reflect the light that shines on them. In other words, they block it out and stop it travelling in a particular direction. Because light travels in straight lines, the area 'behind' the object is deprived of light, forming a shadow. There are some transparent materials that light will pass through. Many of these materials, such as glass and different types of plastic products, are manufactured for specific uses.

Technology enables us to use light energy for different purposes. We use lamps to light up the world, cameras to record images of the world, solar cells to produce electricity and televisions to entertain us. Many of the things we use daily in our lives depend on using or producing light.

Ideas for practice

Topic: Night animals

Age group: 5–7 years

Introduction

In this topic children explore the ideas of light and dark, and focus on how owls have exceptional night vision. Opportunities are provided for children to experience darkness, and to realise that sources of light during the day and at night enable them to see. In the application stage the topic is broadened to explore how other birds of prey rely on their exceptional eyesight when hunting for food.

Scientific view

Light enables us and other animals to see and recognise different objects. Our eyes work best in the daylight, and as it gets dark at night we find it harder to see things. Animals also see better in daylight, but 'night animals' such as owls can see much better than we can in the dark. At night it is never totally dark, there are always some sources of light to help us and other animals see. If there were no light at all at night, we and all other animals would not be able to see anything.

Working scientifically

In these activities children will:

- ask questions which can be answered in different ways;
- observe closely using simple equipment;
- perform simple tests;
- use observations to suggest answers to questions.

Health and safety

Be alert to some children's fear of the dark.

Exploration stage

Children's talk involves trying out their own ideas

Setting the scene

Start by reading the illustrated version of *The owl who was afraid of the dark* by Jill Tomlinson. Ask children to imagine that Plop came to them to find out about the dark. In words and pictures children can tell their story of what the dark means to them.

Scientific enquiry

Ask the children whether they would like to be 'night animals' and go off hunting with Plop and his parents. Create dark areas underneath tables by covering them with opaque sheets. Place a variety of small, different coloured toy animals in each area. Ask for volunteers to hunt for the animals. Once inside the dark areas, children must try to identify their 'prey' by sight alone. As they come out children discuss what they could see and how many animals they could identify. Which animals were easiest to see? Once all the volunteers have experienced the dark, take away the sheets and let in some 'day light'. How many animals could they not identify in the dark? Probe children's understanding of daylight. Why is it dark at night? Why is it light during the day? Explore children's reasoning. Are they aware that daylight comes from the Sun?

Puzzle

Do the children think they would make good 'night animals'? Do they think they can see as well as owls in the dark?

Talking points: true, false or not sure?

- Owls see things we cannot in the dark.
- We need light to see.
- Owls need light to see.
- It is dark at night because there is no sunlight.
- Owls see better in the dark than in the light.
- There are lots of sources of light at night.
- Night is not totally dark.
- Owls can see at night because they have big eyes.

Use the puzzle and the talking points to get children thinking about how we need light to see. Encourage them to explain their ideas. They can practise explaining to one another in small groups, before explaining to the class. Probe the reasons for their responses.

Scientific enquiry

At the end of the story Plop flies off to go hunting in the dark with Mr and Mrs Barn Owl. Remind children that in real life owls are predators (carnivores), meaning they eat other animals to survive. Using information sources, children find out what other animals are active at night, and identify which ones owls are likely to hunt. What other predators are active at night? Do they also have big eyes? If not, how do they find their food? From the outcomes of their research children can produce simple food chains.

Formative assessment

Provide opportunities for children to voice what they have learnt in the exploratory stage. Use evidence from their responses to the puzzle, talking points and other activities to assess differences between children's ideas and the scientific view. Plan how you will use the re-describing stage to help the children address their *learning needs* (see Chapter 1). You may need to modify the activities depending on the collective and individual needs of your children.

Information and teaching resources

Book:

● Tomlinson, Jill (2002) *The Owl Who Was Afraid of the Dark*, London: Egmont.

ASE Journal:

● Primary Science 125 (Nov/Dec 2012) *The owl who was afraid of the dark* by Kevin Smith.

Re-describing stage

Children's talk involves making sense of scientific ideas

Teacher-led discussion

Ask children to close their eyes, and/or put on blindfolds and describe what total dark looks like. Ask them to explain why they cannot see anything when they close their eyes. Children observe each other closing their eyes and describe how their eyelids work. Discuss why we are able to see at night, and talk about the different things which light up the night. Use BBC Bitesize video clips to talk about different sources of light and how they provide light for us to see the world around us.

Modelling

For this activity you will need to make dark boxes which exclude the light. Use shoe boxes or cardboard boxes of a similar size. Cut out a small peep hole which children can look through, and a larger hole to represent a window to let light in. Cover the window with a movable flap to represent a curtain which can block out the light.

Provide children with a range of small objects of different colours. In turn the children put the objects inside and view them through the peephole, first with the curtain closed and then when it is open. Compare what they can see in each case. Children can use a torch to add more light to the box. Talk about the effect light has on what they can see inside the box. Ask groups to explain to each other the reasons why they see better with the curtain open. Reinforce the idea that they need light in order to see things.

Story-telling

Return to the puzzle. Show children video clips of owls hunting at night, pointing out their big eyes which enable them to see their prey. Owls can see 35 to 100 times better than humans in dim light. Children imagine they are young owls out hunting with their parents at night. They can tell their stories through words and drawings. Children talk about and present summaries of their stories. Identify and address any outstanding learning needs.

Information and teaching resources

BBC Bitesize:

- Habitats and where do different owls live? www.bbc.co.uk/education/clips/zn84d2p

- Nocturnal animals and birds. *www.bbc.co.uk/education/clips/zsshfg8*

- What is a bird of prey? *www.bbc.co.uk/education/clips/ztk4d2p*

- Where does light come from? *www.bbc.co.uk/guides/zp23r82*

Other websites:

- Night owls. *http://video.nationalgeographic.com/video/wd-ep2-owls*

- Owl video for kids. *www.youtube.com/watch?v=T-BfS_wZLiA*

Application stage
Children's talk involves trying out scientific ideas

Birds of prey

The eyesight of birds of prey such as eagles, hawks and buzzards is 4 to 8 times keener than humans. Eagles can spot rabbits from several miles away while hawks and buzzards can see small rodents on the ground from high up in the sky. And when they spot one, these birds can dive at over 100mph while keeping their eyes focused on their prey. Children can use simple binoculars to investigate what it would be like to have the eyesight of an eagle. Prepare the outside work by planting objects (toy animals) in the grounds for the children to observe. Children can compare what they can see with and without the binoculars.

Extend this activity by modelling how birds of prey swoop on their prey. Start by designing and making face masks of birds of prey. Encourage the class to choose a range of birds. The design of the masks should be researched so that the main features of a bird's face are as

Figure 14.1 **Hawk eyes**

Source: iStock

accurate as possible. Children compare the shape and size of their bird's eyes with their own. They use their masks when performing movements to music which characterise their bird soaring high in the sky while hunting for its prey.

Topic: Reflections and shadows

Age group: 7–9 years

Introduction

This topic provides opportunities for children to talk about and recognise that they need light in order to see things, and that they see objects when light is reflected off them into their eyes. In the *application stage* children use their knowledge of shadows to create their own picture story books involving a search for their lost shadow.

Scientific view

Our eyes are sensitive to light, which enables us to see and make sense of the world in which we live. We see objects because light given out by light sources bounces off these objects into our eyes. Our eyes use this light to form images of the objects. Whenever light bounces off shiny objects such as mirrors, we see images of these objects in the mirror. Shadows are formed when objects block light, creating areas of darkness.

Working scientifically

In these activities children will:

● ask questions and use different types of scientific enquiries to answer them;

● set up simple practical enquiries;

● make systematic and careful observations;

● record findings using drawings and labelled diagrams;

● report findings using simple scientific language including written and oral explanations;

● use results to draw conclusions.

Health and safety

Teach children never to stare directly into strong light sources.

Exploration stage

Children's talk involves trying out their own ideas

Setting the scene

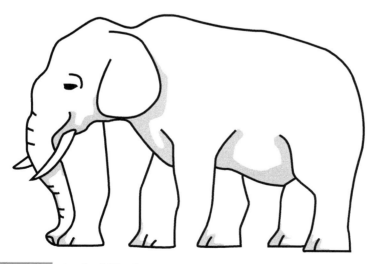

Figure 14.2 **Optical illusion**

Start with a simple optical illusion and explore what children think they see. Talk about how we see things with our eyes and our brains. Sometimes our brains find it hard to make sense of what our eyes have seen. Show and discuss a range of optical illusions from the web. Can children create their own optical illusions?

Puzzle

Figure 14.3 **Reflections in water**

Source: iStock

Show children a photograph of reflections in water. Ask them to explain what they see. Are they seeing an optical illusion? Discuss their ideas and probe their reasoning.

Children work collaboratively when discussing the puzzle and the talking points. Provide them with plain and curved mirrors so they can observe their images. The talking points are designed to raise curiosity and stimulate further questions. Ask children to question each other to find out what they know about reflections in mirrors. Each group could raise three questions which can be discussed with the class.

Talking points: true, false or not sure?

- Light is reflected off water.
- Water acts like a mirror.
- We see images inside mirrors.
- We see images in water because light bounces into our eyes.
- Mirrors remember what we look like.
- Water traps images inside it.
- Our reflection in a mirror is an illusion.

Scientific enquiry

1   Observing

Ask children how good they are at observing things. For example, how many know the colour of their eyes? Ask the children to draw one of their own eyes from memory. Then ask them to draw it again using a mirror and compare the pictures. How do they differ? What detail did they remember? What detail did they forget?

2   Looking left or is it right?

Now ask them to use the mirror to closely observe their whole face, including their teeth. Encourage them to make faces such as winking, smiling, waggling their tongue and so on. They can touch their nose with their left hand, and then their right hand. Do they notice anything strange? Is there anything different between what they do and what they see? For those who cannot work it out, stick a tiny label on their left cheek. Which cheek does the sticker appear to be on when viewed in the mirror? Children can try to write a word which can only be seen correctly in a mirror.

3   Mirror acting

Working in groups of two, children can act out mirror images of each other. Draw a line on the floor in chalk to represent the mirror. Children stand opposite each other on either side of the line pretending to look in a mirror. One child copies the other. If one child moves away from the mirror, what should the other child do to create a mirror image? Children can repeat their actions in a real mirror and check the accuracy of their mirroring.

4   Looking for the image

Next, children draw a small cartoon picture on paper. Keeping the picture flat on the table, they hold the mirror up on its edge at 90°. As they move the mirror slowly away from the cartoon, they can observe whether the cartoon appears to move in the mirror. Children speculate how far the image seems to be formed behind the mirror compared with the cartoon in front. Children can argue where the image is formed. Why can they not touch the image? Next, children draw half an object, for example half a face, or half a vase of flowers, and use the mirror to create a complete picture. What does this tell us about where the image is formed?

5   Multiple images

Children can use two flat mirrors held at an angle to each other to create multiple images of an object. They can also create multiple images by fixing two mirrors parallel to each other and placing an object in between. Let children experiment with different arrangements and see who can create most images. Is there a relationship between the angles between mirrors and the number of images produced? Children could bring in kaleidoscopes from home to share.

Thought experiment

Ask children to imagine what they are seeing when they view their own image in a mirror. If they cover the mirror with a black cloth where does their image go? Is the image trapped inside the mirror behind the cloth, or has something else happened? Children discuss the puzzle in groups, and negotiate an agreed response which can be described in words and pictures. Each group presents their ideas to the class, and explain how they arrived at their point of view. Negotiation towards an agreed point of view can continue between groups.

Formative assessment

Provide opportunities for children to voice what they have learnt in the exploratory stage. Use evidence from their responses to the puzzle, talking points and other activities to assess differences between children's ideas and the scientific view. Plan how you will use the re-describing stage to help the children address their *learning needs* (see Chapter 1). You may need to modify the activities depending on the collective and individual needs of your children.

Re-describing stage

Children's talk involves making sense of scientific ideas

Teacher-led discussion

Children may not be aware that light travels out from sources and is reflected by illuminated surfaces. Some may believe that something travels out from their eyes to enable them to see objects, or light from light sources bounces off their eyes onto objects enabling them to be seen. Focus on misconceptions and children's other *learning needs*. Start by reviewing different sources of light and how light enables us to see things around us. Use video clips to talk about and illustrate how light is reflected from objects. Review how we can see objects because light bounces off them into our eyes.

Modelling

Use the same dark boxes from the previous topic in a similar way. Children put a brightly coloured object in the box and view it in the dark with the curtain closed. Ask them to describe what they see. Next, open the curtain and shine in torch light. Children again describe what they see. Ask the children to describe in words and pictures how the light enables them to see the object more clearly. Ask them to describe what happens to the light after it is emitted by the torch. The only way the light can reach their eyes when viewing through the peep hole is by bouncing off the object in the dark box. Extend the modelling by shining different colour lights inside the box and observing their effects on the colours of the objects. Discuss children's reasons for what they observe.

Talking points: true, false or not sure?

- We see the object because light bounces off our eyes onto the object.
- We see the object because light bounces off the object into our eyes.
- We see the object because the light took the dark away.
- We see the object because it is a bright colour.

Modify the talking points to suit your children's needs. In groups, children discuss the points and try to reach agreement. Each group presents their ideas to the class for why light enables us to see things. Probe reasons for children's thinking.

Modelling

Tape a piece of black opaque paper with a slit in it across the glass on a torch so that it emits a beam of light. In a darkened classroom children can explore controlling the direction of the beam using mirrors. How many ways can they re-direct it by reflecting it using one, two and three mirrors? Children also try reflecting the beam off water and other shiny surfaces. Compare the outcomes from the mirrors with reflecting the beam off non-shiny surfaces.

Children record their results using drawings and discuss what they have found out. Which type of surface reflects light the best? Why do they think they can only see their reflection in shiny surfaces? Why are shiny surfaces shiny? Use video clips to discuss ideas related to these questions at levels appropriate to your children.

Information and teaching resources

BBC Bitesize:

- Light. *www.bbc.co.uk/education/clips/zg6r82p*
- A torch as a light source. *www.bbc.co.uk/education/clips/zb3s34j*
- Light travels in straight lines. *www.bbc.co.uk/education/clips/zyntsbk*

Application stage

Children's talk involves trying out scientific ideas

Investigating shadows

Figure 14.4 **Long shadows**

Source: iStock

To reinforce the idea that darkness is the absence of light, children can explore different materials to make shadows. Provide groups with torches, screens and a range of opaque and transparent objects which they can use to form shadows on the screen. Children record their results by drawing pictures of their shadows. Compare shadows made with the opaque and transparent objects. Listen to their explanations for why some shadows are darker than others. Create giant shadows and use data loggers to compare levels of light inside and outside the shadows. Reinforce the idea that dark shadows are formed when objects block out the light. Use words such as 'opaque' and 'transparent' when describing the different materials.

In search of my lost shadow

Working collaboratively groups of children can create their own picture story book entitled *In search of my lost shadow.* Here are some ideas to help with the plot.

1   The main protagonist has an argument with her shadow, and as a result the shadow runs away.

2   Without her shadow the protagonist starts to feel lonely, especially when she sees all the other characters happily walking around with their shadows.

3   The protagonist discovers that her shadow has gone to live in shadowland, a special place where lost shadows live.

4   After arriving at shadowland, the protagonist finds she cannot recognise her own shadow. There are so many shadows of different sizes and shapes, and of course they are all the same colour, black! As they walk around the shadows change size depending on the position of the sun, and at night they cannot be seen at all.

5   Eventually the protagonist works out how to recognise her own shadow, and after they have made up they both happily return to the real world together.

Discuss the plot with the children, and how their characters can be people or animals, or even animated objects. Before they write their story, children should spend time outside observing how their shadows change as they walk around, and at different times of the day.

Design and make a shadow theatre

Children design and make their own shadow puppet theatre and act out their story, *In search of my lost shadow*, using a narrator or by giving voice to their characters.

Information and teaching resources

BBC Bitesize:

● How do different materials affect shadows? *www.bbc.co.uk/education/clips/zsqd7ty*

● Light and shadow. *www.bbc.co.uk/education/clips/zshxpv4*

● Shadow puppets. *www.bbc.co.uk/education/clips/z87jmp3*

● Where does light and shade come from? *www.bbc.co.uk/education/clips/z8vfb9q*

Topic: Chasing shadows

Age group: 9–11 years

Introduction

In this topic children explore the nature of shadows, and use the idea that light travels in straight lines to explain how they are formed. In the application stage children create 'coloured shadows' and also look into the history of photography, which includes making their own camera obscura. The topic ends with a conference in which groups can present their research to others.

Scientific view

Shadows are formed because opaque objects create an area of darkness by blocking out light. Because light travels in straight lines the shape of a shadow can be similar to the shape of the object that created it.

Working scientifically

In these activities children will:

● plan scientific enquiries to answer questions;

● take measurements using scientific equipment;

● record data using tables and graphs;

● report findings through displays and other presentations;

● examine how scientific ideas have developed over time.

Health and safety

Remind children never to stare directly at any intense light source such as the Sun.

Exploration stage

Children's talk involves trying out their own ideas

Setting the scene

Start this topic with a puzzle. Show children a cartoon similar to the one in Figure 14.5. Ask children which part of the shadow made by the two umbrellas would be the darkest. Explore their reasons and probe their understanding of how shadows are formed.

Figure 14.5 **Double shadows**

Talking points: true, false or not sure?

- Two umbrellas block out twice the light.
- Each umbrella blocks equal amounts of light.
- One umbrella will block out as much light as two umbrellas.
- The more umbrellas the more light will be blocked out.
- Black umbrellas block out more light than white ones.
- Transparent umbrellas block out most light.

In groups children discuss the points and present reasons for their responses. Encourage groups to elaborate on their ideas by prompting them to provide examples and expand their thinking to different situations.

Modelling

Children can make small model umbrellas, and in a darkened room use torches to produce shadows. Do two umbrellas produce darker shadows than one on its own? Is there any way they can measure the 'darkness' of their shadows? Is there any reason why two shadows should be darker than one?

In an area of the school which can be blacked out, use a strong light to produce shadows using large umbrellas. Use light-meters to compare light levels outside and inside the shadows created by first one umbrella and then two. Discuss the results and compare with their predictions. Children draw diagrams to show how the shadows are formed and to explain the results. Display the pictures and encourage children to annotate one another's diagrams with positive suggestions which elaborate or provide alternative views.

Scientific enquiry

Firstly ask children to imagine they are going for a long walk starting at 9:00 in the morning and ending at 3:00 in the afternoon. Can they tell the story in words and pictures of how they think their shadow may change throughout the day? Will the size of their shadow have anything to do with the position of the Sun? Explore the thinking behind their predictions.

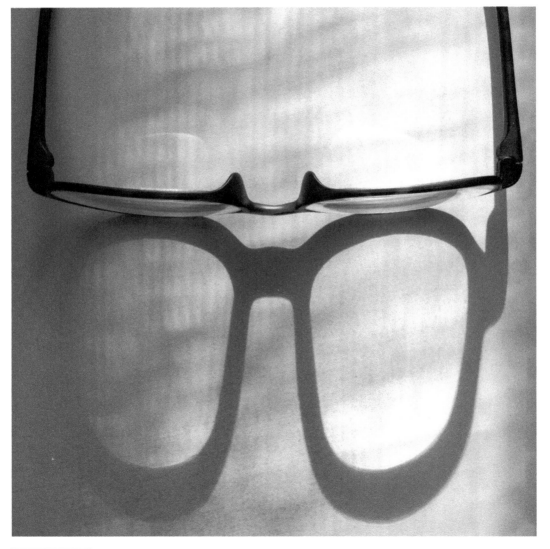

Figure 14.6 **Shadow art**

Source: iStock

Then, on a sunny day, children can record how their shadows change throughout the day. Every hour between 9:00 and 3:00 children can record the position of the Sun and draw around their shadows in the playground. They measure the length and width of their shadows and record the results for each hour on a graph. Children can also take photographs of how their shadows change. They can also take photographs of the shadows of various objects in the school grounds, including plants and possibly animals. Use the photographs to create a display.

Groups work creatively to design and photograph their own shadow art. They can search for ideas on the web.

Formative assessment

Provide opportunities for children to voice what they have learnt in the exploratory stage. Use evidence from their responses to the puzzle, talking points and other activities to assess differences between children's ideas and the scientific view. Plan how you will use the re-describing stage to help the children address their *learning needs* (see Chapter 1). You may need to modify the activities depending on the collective and individual needs of your children.

Re-describing stage

Children's talk involves making sense of scientific ideas

Teacher-led discussion

Start this part by discussing the photographic display of shadows. Challenge children to explain why shadows provide evidence that light travels away from its source in straight lines. Is there any other way it could travel and still produce shadows? Is light always on the move? Does it ever stop moving? Where does light go at night, or when the light bulb in a room is switched off? Children can work in groups to research answers to these challenging questions. While they are working, discuss with each group the characteristics of good group work. Ask them how they can help each other to learn and reinforce the value of collaboration. Groups discuss their findings, and add them to the display.

Modelling

Project light on a large screen and create shadows using your hand and fingers. Talk about how your hand forms a shadow by preventing light reaching the screen. Move your hand progressively closer to the screen so children can see how the size of the shadow changes. Try to persuade children this can only happens because the light travels in straight lines. Children use a bendy tube to look through. It is only possible to see through it when it is straight. This is evidence that light travels in straight lines.

For the following activity, you will need a well-ventilated area, or to go outdoors. Use spray paint or a water solvent dye in a spray container. Children should observe at a safe distance and the teacher should wear a face mask. Put a large sheet of white paper on the floor/ground and spray the paint or coloured dye onto it. Explain how the spray represents a light source such as a torch, and the paint presents the light which it emits. Using another sheet of paper create 'shadows' of objects using the spray. Move the object different distances from the spray and show children how the size of the shadow changes. Compare these shadows to ones created by light.

Finish the modelling by using video clips to illustrate how light travels in straight lines and how shadows are formed.

Scientific enquiry

In a darkened room children use screens, torches and objects to explore the relationship between the size of a shadow and the distance away from the light source. Record their results using suitable tables and graphs, and discuss any patterns. Children can also use drawings to show how the patterns are dependent on light travelling in straight lines. Ask children to explain their drawings. Identify and address any outstanding *learning needs*.

Information and teaching resources

BBC Bitesize:

- Light travels in straight lines. *www.bbc.co.uk/education/clips/zyntsbk*

- What are shadows? *www.bbc.co.uk/education/clips/zwh86fr*

- Seeing in the dark – reflective materials. *www.bbc.co.uk/education/clips/zs3ygk7*

Useful websites:

- Mirrors activity video. *http://bpes.bp.com/primary-resources/science/ages-9-to-11/light/light-topic-starter/*

Application stage

Children's talk involves trying out scientific ideas

Coloured shadows

Show children video clips of coloured shadows. Coloured shadows work because the object blocks out one of the three colours, leaving the other two colours to combine to make the image seen on the screen. Although explanations may be challenging for children, experimenting with combining light in this way is fascinating.

Start this activity by demonstrating how to combine the primary colours of light to make white light. Children can explore combining a range of different colours to see which colours they can create. Record their finding by producing colour-wheels. Compare with mixing different coloured paints. Finally, children can discover how to make coloured shadows.

Figure 14.7 **Coloured shadows**

Source: Alamy

Camera obscura

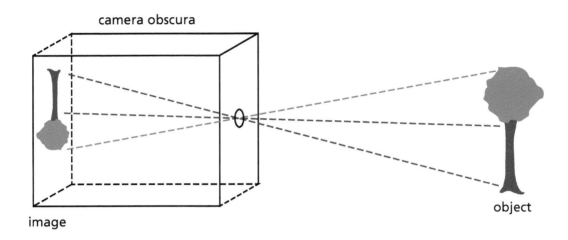

Figure 14.8 **Camera obscura**

Children will be familiar with cameras on their mobile devices, but do they know the history of them or how they can be traced back to pin-hole cameras? A pin-hole camera or camera obscura is a dark box or room with a small hole, through which light from a scene outside can pass. Because light travels in straight lines it passes through the hole and lands on the back of the box where it forms an inverted image of the scene. Show children video clips which demonstrate how a pin-hole camera works.

The history of the pin-hole camera can be traced back to the time of the Ancient Chinese and Greek civilisations, but little was written about how it was used until the time of Leonardo da Vinci towards the end of the fifteenth century. Starting with Leonardo da Vinci, groups can research the development of the pin-hole camera, and discover how it has been used for both scientific and artistic purposes. They can use pictures, photographs and video clips from the web to tell the story of how the pin-hole camera was developed into the lens cameras we use today. As part of the project, children can design and make their own pin-hole cameras. There is much helpful information on the web. Children may also want to explore the work of professional photographers and take photographs of their own.

Finish off this topic by organising a conference on the History of Photography, as part of which groups can present their research to others, including parents. Invite a science ambassador to provide the keynote speech. A common format for scientific conferences is for contributors to make an oral presentation aided by multimedia resources, followed by a discussion based on questions from their peers. Find time to positively evaluate the presentations, emphasising good practice with regard to communication skills and the effective use of digital technology.

Information and teaching resources

Websites:

- Coloured shadows. *www.exploratorium.edu/snacks/colored-shadows*
- Coloured shadows. *www.youtube.com/watch?v=q_xMoXQwAy0*
- Making a camera obscura. *www.youtube.com/watch?v=Xcv4CxQ1I-A*
- The art of camera obscura. *www.youtube.com/watch?v=-cr5YWZSId0*
- Camera obscura. *www.amazingcameraobscura.co.uk/index.htm*
- History of the camera. *www.bigshotcamera.com/fun/camerahistory/1490_obscura*

Chapter 15
Sound

Equipped with his five senses, man explores the universe around him and calls the adventure science.

Edwin Rowell Hubble, astronomer (1889–1953)

This chapter presents ideas for practice which can be used to structure children's exploration of the way sound is made through vibrations. At each level children progressively develop their understanding of the nature of sound, how it travels in different materials and the meaning of pitch and volume. From an everyday perspective children explore the problems unwanted sounds can create and look for solutions to noise pollution in both the made and the natural world.

Topics in this chapter:

- How noisy is our world?
- Elephants: the ultimate sound machine
- How marine animals use sound

Subject knowledge to support the teaching of these topics can be found in the core book, Loxley, P., Dawes, D., Nicholls, L. and Dore, B. (2018) *Teaching primary science: Promoting enjoyment and developing understanding*, Abingdon: Routledge, Chapter 15: Adaptation and evolution and Chapter 22: Sound.

It's a noisy world

Depending on where you live you may wake up to the pleasant sound of chatting birds, or if you live in a city the first thing you hear in the morning may be the roar of traffic. Sound figures largely in our world. Every day we experience noise, music and voices. We use sound to communicate and entertain. Some sounds, such as music, we can find satisfying and enjoyable. On the other hand, sounds from machines can be unpleasant and even threatening.

Be they great music or traffic noise, sounds are created by a vibrating source and propagate within a medium. Sound waves travel through solids, liquids and gases but cannot move through vacuum. Sound around us is produced when the air is disturbed by a vibrating object. Vibrations in the air are detected by our ears and converted into signals that are sent to our brains. The brain interprets these signals as sound. For example, when a drum is struck its skin moves rapidly to and fro causing the air immediately next to it to vibrate in a similar manner. Once started these vibrations are passed on through the air and are detected when they pass into a person's ear.

Survival for many animals depends on their ability to produce and detect sounds. Some bats for example have evolved highly sophisticated ways of using sound. They emit high pitched ultrasounds that produce echoes when they bounce off objects. From these echoes bats can determine the size of the objects, how far away they are and how fast they are travelling, all in a split second.

Sound is especially important for animals which live in water. Sound travels far greater distances than light under water. Seeing in the ocean can be like looking through fog on the land. Sound travels much further and about five times faster underwater than it does in air. Many marine animals rely on sound to sense their surroundings, communicate, attract mates, locate food and defend themselves. Like bats do in air, whales and dolphins use echolocation in their watery environment to navigate and locate their food. Fish produce various sounds including grunts, croaks, clicks and snaps that help them attract mates and scare off predators. Sound is vital to the survival of marine animals.

Like us, other animals suffer from the harmful effects of noise pollution. Traffic noise on land and at sea can hamper the way animals communicate. In built up environments female frogs can find it difficult to locate males from their calls, and due to traffic noise nocturnal animals such as owls and bats can have a tough time locating their prey. In the ocean, noise created by commercial shipping and off-shore drilling can confuse the navigation of marine animals such as dolphins and whales, which can result in them swimming into the shore and beaching themselves.

Although sound can cause problems in some situations, it can also be put to good use in others. Modern technology can produce ultrasounds which are used for both medical and industrial purposes. The most well known use of ultrasound is to scan for birth defects in unborn babies and to examine the health of soft tissue organs in the body.

When we are woken up by traffic noise or annoyed by loud music we may dream of living in a noise-free world. But noise is a price we pay for the benefits modern engineering and technology bring to our lives. New developments like the electric car, low noise machinery and noise-reducing building materials may help make our lives quieter in the future, and also benefit the animals with which we share this planet.

Ideas for practice

Topic: How noisy is our world?

Age group: 5–7 years

Introduction

The purpose of this topic is to make children aware of the sources of the sounds in their neighbourhood, and how sounds travel from their sources into their ears. Through the activities they can explore different sounds and distinguish between those they like and dislike. In the application stage children design and make ear muffs to block out the sounds they do not like.

Scientific view

Sounds travel from their source through the air, and we detect them with our ears. As they travel through the air sounds get fainter and become more difficult to detect.

Working scientifically

In these activities children will:

- ask questions;
- observe and use simple equipment;
- perform simple tests;
- identify and classify;
- use their observations and ideas to suggest answers to questions;
- gather and record data to help answer questions.

Health and safety

When planning work in the neighbourhood, follow ASE guidance in *Be Safe!* (2011) for risk assessment and supervision, especially near traffic. Warn children never to poke anything into their ears. No loud sound should be directed at their ears at close range. Be aware of children who may have hearing difficulties.

Exploration stage

Children's talk involves trying out their own ideas

Setting the scene

Arrive in the classroom with a big pair of ear defenders (muffs) on. Pretend not be able to hear the children. Turn it into a pantomime by refusing to hear them. 'Sorry, I can't hear you! Speak up a bit.' Have fun until you take off the ear defenders. Tell them you are wearing them because you are fed up with all the traffic noise on your way to school. Listen to children's stories about the noises which most annoy them.

Puzzle

Which are the most common noises in the school neighbourhood? Are they made by machines or animals? Discuss the puzzle with the children, and listen to their stories.

Scientific enquiry

To resolve the puzzle children can investigate the sounds in their environment using sound recorders. Start in the classroom, then explore different areas of the school and record sounds in the school grounds. Organise a walk around the neighbourhood including the local park and record the sounds. Listen for the sounds of birds. Can the children distinguish between the calls of different birds? Can they hear the birds or is there too much traffic noise?

Display the results of the enquiry in the classroom showing the noisiest and most quiet places in your neighbourhood, in each case identifying the sources of the noises. If the traffic noise is loud in your area, ask the children to think about how it affects animals. How might loud noises affect their pets who have more sensitive hearing than us? Listen to children's stories.

Ask children to listen out for different noises where they live over a weekend. They can draw pictures of their favourite and least favourite sources of sounds. Back in school they can talk about the sounds and describe how they make them feel. Add pictures to the display.

Use the results of the enquiry to identify the most common noises in your district. Are there any areas where animal noises are the most common?

Modelling

According to research the top ten most annoying noises include:

- a knife on a bottle
- a fork on a glass
- a ruler on a bottle
- a baby crying
- an electric drill.

Start by tapping a knife against a bottle. Do the children find the sound annoying? Compare their responses to tapping a ruler on the bottle, a fork on glass and the sound of an electric drill. Are these the worst noises the children have ever heard or can they make noises which are more annoying?

Scientific enquiry

Challenge the children to make their own annoying sounds. Provide a big box of safe objects which children can use to make sounds. Do not include glass objects. In groups children explore sounds which can be made using the equipment and classify them as sounds they like or dislike. Each group can describe and demonstrate their most annoying sound, and also the sound they like best.

Modelling

Children draw pictures of themselves listening to their most annoying sound. Ask them to explain why they are able to hear the sound. Why can they not see it? How could they stop themselves hearing the sound? Probe children's reasons for their responses to these questions. Draw out their ideas about how sound travels from its source to their ears. They can draw pictures to illustrate their thinking. Expect some imaginative ideas, as this could be the first time they have ever thought about sound in this way.

Formative assessment

Provide opportunities for children to voice what they have learnt in the exploratory stage. Use evidence from their responses to the puzzle and other activities to assess differences between children's ideas and the scientific view. Plan how you will use the re-describing stage to help the children address their *learning needs* (see Chapter 1). You may need to modify the activities depending on the collective and individual needs of your children.

Information and teaching resources

BBC Bitesize:

● How to identify birds from their songs. *www.bbc.co.uk/education/clips/z43fb9q*

Re-describing stage
Children's talk involves making sense of scientific ideas

Teacher-led discussion

Young children do not normally think that sound has to travel along the path between its source and the listener. For example, they might say they heard the bottle make a noise because you tapped it.

To get children thinking about sound travelling, ask them to face away from you and close their eyes. Demonstrate sounds made by an instrument such as a drum or guitar. Ask children to describe what they hear. Establish that they can hear the sound of the instrument. Children turn around and listen again to the sounds. What did they use to hear the sounds? Establish that they use their ears. What made the sounds? Establish that it was the instruments. How did the sound reach their ears? Can sound move? Listen to children's ideas and pick up on the credible ones. Help them develop their thinking towards the idea that sound travels through the air from the source to their ears.

Modelling

It is best to do this activity in a quiet playground. Sit children in a circle with the sound sources in the middle. Ask children whether closing their eyes makes any difference to what they can hear. How about holding their noses and shutting their mouths tight? Discuss responses. What can children suggest they do to block out the noise? Try out their ideas and pick up on suggestions they cover their ears. Provide children with a range of materials they could use to cover their ears. Establish that covering their ears blocks out the sound. Challenge children to explain why and further develop the model of sound travelling out from its source and entering their ears. To achieve quiet, children need to stop it entering their ears.

Next, ask the children what they think will happen if they move away from the source. Will they still be able to hear it? Listen to children's responses and let them test out their ideas by slowly moving away from the source until they can no longer hear it. Challenge children to explain what has happened to the sound? Introduce the idea that sound gets fainter as it travels through air.

Working in the classroom, explore how sound can be blocked by things such as doors and windows. Demonstrate by taking a sound source outside the classroom so that children can hear it with the door open. Ask children to explain how closing the door might affect the sound. Test their ideas. Children can draw pictures to show what they think has happened to the sound. Probe children's thinking and address any outstanding *learning needs*.

Scientific enquiry

Working in groups, children plan an enquiry to find the quietest sound which they can hear. Can they hear a pin drop? What about a piece of cotton wool falling onto a hard surface? Provide children with a range of mainly soft objects to drop onto their tables. How close to the objects do they need to be in order to hear them fall onto the table? Which object makes least noise? Ask groups to explain why they hear better when they are closer to where the objects hit the table.

Story-telling

This topic provides opportunities to make children aware of the problems people with hearing disabilities face in their everyday lives. If possible, arrange for a person with a hearing disability to talk to the children. Make children aware of the visit in advance and organise questions which they would like to ask the visitor. Share children's questions with the speaker before the visit and plan the session together. Establish with the visitor how children will ask their questions; appropriate technology may be needed.

Children in the school with hearing disabilities may like to join in the session and talk about their own experiences.

Information and teaching resources

BBC Bitesize:

● Sound and hearing. *www.bbc.co.uk/education/clips/zk7jmp3*

● Sounds that keep us safe. *www.bbc.co.uk/education/clips/z2dyk7h*

● Where does sound come from? *www.bbc.co.uk/guides/z3wf34j*

● How are sounds produced? *www.bbc.co.uk/education/clips/zxdyk7h*

Application stage

Children's talk involves trying out scientific ideas

Design and make ear defenders

Put your ear defenders back on and tell the children they are not perfect because you can still hear some noise. Could they make a better pair? Children make ear defenders using plastic or polystyrene cups filled with cotton wool or other suitable materials. Holding the defenders to their ears they can test how well they block out different types of sounds. Use various sound sources including musical instruments and high pitched sources such buzzers and whistles. Help children organise their tests so they can discover the best types of sound-insulating materials. Distinguish between types of sound and the loudness of sounds. Talk about:

● how the different sounds are produced;

● sounds which are easiest to block out;

● how the loudness (volume) of sounds compare with and without the ear defenders;

● whether moving the sources further away makes the sounds easier to block out.

Having decided on the best materials, children design ear defenders which can be worn. They could be attached to a hat, or band that fits around their heads. Children can test their defenders in the playground. Which sounds can they no longer hear? Which sounds can they still hear? Is it possible to create complete quiet?

Children create an advertising poster for their ear defenders which describes the advantages of wearing them. When talking about the posters probe whether children understand that their ears are sound detectors and that sound travels from a source into their ears.

Topic: Elephants: the ultimate sound machine

Age group: 7–9 years

Introduction

The purpose of this topic is to provide opportunities for children to explore how sounds are made by vibrations. Children enquire into how different pitched sounds are made, and factors which influence the volume of the sound. Activities in the application stage explore and model surprising ways elephants detect sounds, and also look at problems associated with noise pollution.

Scientific view

To exist, sounds need a *vibrating source* and a medium to travel through. To hear sounds, creatures need organs to detect vibrations. Sound around us is produced when the air is disturbed by vibrations from a source and these vibrations are detected as sound in our ears. The number of vibrations produced by a source in a second is the *frequency* of the sound. The term *pitch* is used to describe how we interpret different frequencies. For example, a whistle produces a higher frequency sound than a drum, which we interpret as a higher pitch when we hear it. The *volume* or loudness of a sound depends on the strength (*amplitude*) of the vibrations. If we beat a drum softly its vibrations are not as pronounced as when we hit it hard, although the frequency and hence the pitch will be the same in both cases.

Working scientifically

In these activities children will:

- ask questions and use scientific enquiry to answer questions;
- set up practical enquiries;
- gather, record and classify data to help answer questions;
- report on findings from enquiry using scientific language and drawings;
- use results to draw conclusions and make predictions;
- use information sources to support their findings.

Health and safety

For making and testing activities always consult the *Be Safe!* (2011) booklet for choosing appropriate materials and supervision. Maintain safe levels of sound. Warn children of possible dangers to faces and eyes from overstretching wires, rubber bands, fishing lines. Eye protection may be needed.

Exploration stage

Children's talk involves trying out their own ideas

Setting the scene

Figure 15.1 **Elephants are amazing sound machines**

Source: iStock

Ask the children what they know about the sounds elephants make. Play video clips of different elephant sounds. Elephants are amazing sound machines. They produce a broad range of sounds from very low pitched rumbles to higher frequency snorts, barks, roars, cries and other types of calls. Children can explore the *Elephant Voices* website which has a comprehensive range of elephant calls in its multimedia section.

Puzzle

How do elephants make such a variety of sounds? Why do they need to make so much noise? Do the different sounds have different purposes? Discuss children's responses. Encourage them to hypothesise about the ways elephants produce and use sound.

Modelling

To solve the puzzle children will need to understand how different pitched sounds are created. Some of the children, especially the musicians, may already know quite a lot about pitch. Start with their ideas and ask them to demonstrate and explain the difference between high pitched and low pitched sounds. Demonstrate low pitched sounds by beating a drum. Place some rice on the skin of a drum so children can see it jump up and down as the skin vibrates. Now demonstrate a higher pitched sound using a string instrument like a guitar. Establish that the sound is produced by vibrations in the strings. The faster they vibrate the higher the pitch. Ask the musicians to help you explain. Establish that if something is making a sound it must be vibrating.

Scientific enquiry

Figure 15.2 *Two Boys and a Girl making Music* **by Jan Miense Molenaer (1629), bequeathed by C.F. Leach, 1943**

Source: © The National Gallery, London

In groups children can explore ways of making different sounds using a range of commercial and homemade instruments and classify them according to their pitch. Children record the different sounds and create drawings to illustrate the nature of the vibrations which produce them.

Modelling

Elephants can make very gentle, soft sounds as well as extremely powerful ones. They have long vocal chords and their trunk and huge bodies act as a resonating chamber to amplify the sound. In these activities children model elephant sounds using long vibrating string systems and tubes to represent their trunks. Focus on the words they use to talk about the sounds. Encourage them to use words such vibrations, volume (loudness), pitch and tone.

1   Modelling vocal chords using vibrating strings

Children experiment with different types of wire and string to make low pitch sounds. They explore different types, lengths and tensions of the wires and strings, attaching them to large cardboard boxes or wooden boards. Their task is to create the lowest frequency sound and then work out how to increase its volume. The challenge is how to create the lowest and loudest sound possible.

2   Modelling trunk calls using bottles and tubes

Elephants use their trunk to amplify sounds, but can also use it to make sounds by blasting air through it. An elephant's trunk is a flexible extension of its nose and upper lip. Children start by exploring the part their nose plays in making sounds. Keeping their mouths shut they make sounds which come out of their nose. Can they change the pitch of sounds by 'tweaking' their nose with their fingers? The big challenge is to make sounds by blowing air through their noses. The way to make sounds is to restrict the flow of air by squeezing their nose and upper lip together. It can work!

Of course, an elephant's trunk is a lot bigger and longer than a child's nose. Children can model increasing the size of their nose using bottles and tubes. They start by blowing air across the top of different sized bottles and recording the different sounds. Which bottles create the lowest pitch? Compare the sounds created to those produced by elephants. Children continue exploring sounds using different sizes of tubes and wind instruments in their search for a way to make sounds like an elephant. (Care should be taken by children when they use glass bottles. Make sure they are aware of the dangers and show them how to handle them safely.)

3   Communicating with elephant calls

Children imagine they are a herd of elephants living on the edge of a forest in Africa. The forest is a source of shelter and food, but is also a dangerous place, especially for baby elephants which can be attacked by lions and tigers if they stray from the group. The task is for the children to model different sounds which elephants could use to communicate, for example, warning sounds to alert the herd when a predator is near, or sounds to tell the young not to stray, and sounds to scare away predators. Each group acts out a scene from the forest, communicating with elephant sounds. The rest of the class can try to work out what the different sounds mean.

Story-telling

Extend the modelling into story-telling. Challenge children to work out how the elephants would communicate over large distances. How would they communicate with another herd? They can use information sources to find out whether elephants' low pitch or high pitch sounds travel furthest. Why would elephants want to 'talk' with other far away herds? Children use information sources to research the role sound plays in the social lives of elephants. They can then tell their stories in the form of an electronic article for a science magazine which includes links to appropriate elephant noises.

Formative assessment

Provide opportunities for children to voice what they have learnt in the exploratory stage. Use evidence from their responses to the puzzle and other activities to assess differences between children's ideas and the scientific view. Plan how you will use the re-describing stage to help the children address their *learning needs* (see Chapter 1). You may need to modify the activities depending on the collective and individual needs of your children.

Information and teaching resources

BBC Bitesize:

- Comparing humans and elephants. *www.bbc.co.uk/education/clips/zd2jmp3*
- How do elephants use their trunks? *www.bbc.co.uk/education/clips/zy2jmp3*

Other websites:

- Elephant Voices. *www.elephantvoices.org/multimedia-resources/elephant-call-types-database*

Re-describing stage
Children's talk involves making sense of scientific ideas

Teacher-led discussion

Re-visit the science children talked about in the exploration stage and discuss their understanding of pitch and volume. Although children are likely to recognise that vibrations create sound, they are less likely to explain transmission of sound through the use of vibrations. Use the activities in this stage to talk about how sound vibrations travel through the air, and how we detect them with our ears.

Modelling

1   Sound travels through air into our ears

Sound a trumpet or other wind instrument at front of the classroom and ask the children to describe how it created the sound which they heard in their ears. In groups the children work collaboratively to produce a picture of how the sound was created and how they were able to hear it. Provide large pieces of white drawing paper which can be displayed on the walls. Use the drawings to compare, discuss and assess children's ideas. Encourage them to provide reasons for their thinking and to justify their ideas. Model how sound travels using a slinky or by lining the children up, one behind the other with their arms on the shoulders of the one in front, and using them as a slinky. Demonstrate how vibrations created at one end are passed all the way down the 'human slinky' to be detected at the other end. Ask children to evaluate the analogy. Does it help them imagine how sound travels through air? Can they think of a better analogy?

2   Pitch and volume

Ask the children to hum a tune and gently hold their throat. Can they feel it vibrating? Parts of their throats vibrate when they make a sound. This is the same for an elephant, except their 'sound box' is much bigger than ours.

Next, clamp a long flexible metal ruler to the top of a table so that the majority of its length is hanging over the edge. Vibrate the ruler by pulling it down and letting it go. Ask the children whether the back and forward, or vibrational movement of the ruler can be compared to the movement of the instruments used in the exploration stage. Reinforce the idea that sounds are made when an object vibrates. This is the same for all sources of sound, be they caused by a hitting a drum, plucking a string, blowing air or the trumpet call of an elephant. In groups children can explore ways of changing the pitch of the sound produced by the ruler. Help them identify the relationship between pitch and the frequency at which the ruler vibrates.

Challenge the children to model changes in volume. Help them establish whether stronger (bigger) vibrations create louder sounds. Reinforce the point by beating a drum. Introduce the term amplitude to mean size or strength of the vibrations. Use the ruler to demonstrate changes in volume by varying the amplitude of its vibrations.

Use video clips to illustrate how sounds of different pitch and volume can be created. Use the images to start up conversations and explore the children's thinking. Children work collaboratively to construct concept maps using key terms such as volume, pitch, source, vibrations, and amplitude and so on. Use the conversations and maps to identify any outstanding *learning needs*.

Information and teaching resources

BBC Bitesize:

- Making sounds with different pitch. *www.bbc.co.uk/education/clips/ztptsbk*

- Modelling how sound travels. *www.bbc.co.uk/education/clips/ztwkjxs*

- How are sounds produced? *www.bbc.co.uk/education/clips/zcy7sg8*

- How drums make sound. *www.bbc.co.uk/education/clips/zcrkxsg*

- How string instruments make sound. *www.bbc.co.uk/education/clips/zx4whv4*

- How vibrations make sound. *www.bbc.co.uk/education/clips/zswsbk7*

- Understanding sound. *www.bbc.co.uk/education/clips/z9h6n39*

Application stage

Children's talk involves trying out scientific ideas

Elephants detect sound with their feet

When African elephants stomp and trumpet as a predator approaches, other elephants six kilometres away can get the news by feeling the ground rumble with their feet. Scientists believe that pressure-sensitive nerve endings in the elephants' feet and trunks are capable of detecting the vibrations of distant elephants. Sound travels up to 17 times faster in solids than it does in air, so elephants pick up the vibrations made by other elephants with their feet long before their calls can be heard with their ears.

In groups children investigate how well different sounds travel in solids. They can start by listening to a ticking clock which is standing on a carpet or some other soft material. They should slowly move away from it until they can no longer hear it. Talk about why the sound gets fainter as they move away. Children can draw pictures to help explain their ideas.

Next, they should place the clock on a hard surface such as a long table or a long plank of wood. Starting close to the clock children can listen to it ticking by putting their ear to the hard surface. What is the first thing they notice compared to listening to it through the air? They then move their ear slowly away from the source listening at different distances. Children interpret their results. Does sound travel better through the solid or through the air? Children explore using a range of sources, and also varying the types of solid surfaces. Try using a range of tuning forks to produce the sounds. Which sounds seem loudest? Which travel furthest? Does the pitch of the sound influence how well it travels in a solid? Help children decide how to record their results, and discuss how they can make sure their tests are fair.

Elephants detect sound with their ears and trunk

Groups explore how the size of an elephant's ears and its trunk affect how well it can hear. They start their investigations by using information sources to discover how elephants use their ears and trunk to detect sound. Children can then test out what they have learnt by building and testing suitable models. Are big ears better for detecting low pitched or high pitched sounds?

Elephants are sound machines

Elephants are the ultimate 'sound machine'. They use different parts of their large bodies to produce and amplify a wide range of sounds which can be heard up to six kilometres away. Children can apply their understanding of sound to design and make their own 'sound machine', which produces and amplifies sounds. The challenge is to produce a machine which can transmit sound the furthest. Use sound meters to compare the volume of the source before and after amplification and to detect how far it can travel.

Unusual animal sounds

Children research some of the unusual ways animals produce and detect sound, and design a web page depicting the most interesting ones. The page should explain how the animals communicate and the advantages they gain from communicating in this way. Children can include live links to relevant websites which provide audio of the noises made by the animals.

Wind sculptures and chimes

Figure 15.3 *Aeolus* **by Luke Jerram**

Children can design and make their own small wind sculptures or chimes which create pleasing sounds when the wind blows. There are lots of designs on the web from which children can gain inspiration.

Noise pollution

Many of us are annoyed by the boom, boom, boom sounds made by people who play their music too loud. Cars with their music systems turned up high can be heard from hundreds of metres away. It is usually the base tones and drums which are the loudest. Talk to the children about why the music can travel so far and why it is the low pitched sounds that are often the loudest. Share ideas and experiences. Children can talk about the problems of noise pollution and what can be done about it. They research possible engineering solutions on the web. Groups can design and make simple models of houses designed to reduce noise intrusion.

Information and teaching resources

BBC Bitesize:

● Delia Derbyshire – electronic music. *www.bbc.co.uk/education/clips/z7hxpv4*

Other websites:

● How to prevent noise pollution. *www.wikihow.com/Prevent-Noise-Pollution*

● Tips on noise pollution. *http://eschooltoday.com/pollution/noise-pollution/what-is-noise-pollution.html*

● What is noise pollution? *www.youtube.com/watch?v=O1-W7gz6Znk*

Topic: How marine animals use sound

Age group: 9–11 years

Introduction

The purpose of this topic is to provide opportunities for children to explore how sound is used in the made and natural world. Activities in the exploration stage focus on how sound travels through water and how marine animals use it to communicate. In the application stage children explore real-life uses of sound and how sound pollution can affect animals.

Scientific view

Sound travels much greater distances than light under water, and it travels about five times faster than it does in air. This is why marine animals rely on sound to sense their surroundings, communicate, attract mates, locate food and defend themselves. Animals such as dolphins find it easier to navigate in the oceans using their own in-built sonar in a similar way to bats. They bounce high frequency (high pitched) sounds off objects to locate them.

Working scientifically

In these activities children will:

● plan different scientific enquiries to answer questions;

● take measurements using data loggers;

● use test results to compare and classify materials;

● report and present findings formally and through display;

● use scientific evidence from information sources to inform their ideas.

Health and safety

Risk assess any visits to the swimming pool and follow the pool's guidance on staffing and supervision. Warn children not to shout down speaking tubes, or point sound tubes directly at others.

Exploration stage

Children's talk involves trying out their own ideas

Setting the scene

Survival for many animals depends on their ability to produce and detect sounds. .Start with pictures of different animals and ask the children to imitate the sounds which they make. Begin with well known animals. As they make the sounds ask the children to gently feel their throats (voice box) vibrating and whether the vibrations change depending on the sounds which they make. Ask the children whether they know the sounds which mammals such as dolphins, porpoises, whales, seals, walrus and sea lions make. Let them have a go at imitating them and record the results so they can be played back later.

Puzzle

Which of their senses is more important for animals that live in water? Is it their hearing or their sight? Encourage children to speculate and examine their reasoning.

Talking points: true, false or not sure?

- It is not easy for animals to see under the water.
- Marine animals have special eyes which enable them to see for miles under the water.
- Sound travels better in water than light does.
- It is too dark to see anything deep down in the ocean.
- During the day animals can see very well in the ocean; only at night is there a problem.
- It is because of pollution that animals cannot see very well in the oceans.

Groups discuss the points and present their ideas for class discussion. Talk about the problems children have experienced with seeing underwater. Listen to their experiences. Explore why sound may be more important to marine animals than light.

Story-telling

Children imagine what it would be like to be a mammal living in the ocean. What would they eat? Where would they look for their food? How would they locate and catch their prey? How deep would they need to be able to dive? How far would they be able to see? How would they know if predators were close by? How would they communicate with others of their species? Children can create annotated posters to tell their story.

Scientific enquiry

Organise a session at the local swimming pool, where children can explore what it would be like to be a marine mammal, such as a dolphin. First they need to design and make some sound sources that could be used underwater. Simple ideas include a hand bell inside a waterproof bag, shakers made from plastic bottles, metal bars to hit together, sealed metal box to act as a drum. The ideas can be tested in a water tank in the classroom before they go to the pool. Seek permission from the manager at the pool to use the sound sources.

Children plan their own enquiries at the pool to find out why many marine animals rely more on their hearing rather than their sight. Key things for children to think about include: how well sound travels through water and the difficulties of seeing over long distances in water.

Story-telling

Back in the classroom children use information sources to find out how dolphins use sound to communicate underwater. They can explore the way dolphins use echolocation to find their prey and navigate around their habitat. Compare with findings for nocturnal animals who live on land such as bats. Add the information on echolocation to their poster stories.

Scientific enquiry

In groups children investigate how sound is reflected from different types of surfaces. To begin with they will need to design and make their own sound projector which can be used to direct sound in a particular direction. Simple designs consist of an insulated cardboard box in which the sound is produced, with a tube or cone attached to emit the sound in a particular direction. Children can test different types and sizes of tubes to see which focus the sound best. Use sound meters to measure the volume of the sound emitted. Use the sound projector to 'fire' sound at different types of surfaces and use the sound meters to compare how much is reflected. Children can classify different types of materials accordingly. Can they identify any patterns?

Story-telling

Children use sources of information to continue to develop their stories of how animals use sound underwater. They can find out how different animals use sound to communicate, to keep safe and find their food. What animals use echolocation? Is it just mammals, or do some fish also have their own natural sonar?

Children report their findings by writing a science article suitable for children of their own age. The article should explain the science and include at least three amazing facts. Together with their posters the articles can be used to form a display.

Formative assessment

Provide opportunities for children to voice what they have learnt in the exploratory stage. Use evidence from their responses to the puzzle, talking points and other activities to assess differences between children's ideas and the scientific view. Plan how you will use the re-describing stage to help the children address their *learning needs* (see Chapter 1). You may need to modify the activities depending on the collective and individual needs of your children.

Re-describing stage

Children's talk involves making sense of scientific ideas

Teacher-led discussion

Figure 15.4 **Dolphins rely on echolocation to find their prey**

Source: iStock

Return to the puzzle and discuss what children discovered in the exploration stage. Reinforce the idea that sound can travel for miles under water, and is therefore important in the lives of marine animals. Use images and video clips to illustrate how dolphins use echolocation. Compare the range of sounds dolphins produce with land animals such as elephants who create much lower pitched sounds. Review the difference between high and low pitched sounds. Use information resources to explore the lowest and highest pitched sounds humans can hear. Compare with various animals.

Modelling

1   Modelling the behaviour of marine mammals

Children can model being an underwater creature that relies on sound to communicate. Each group can develop and practise their own 'call' which is unique to their species. In a clear space to represent the ocean, each group can demonstrate how they use their 'calls' to locate each other. Volunteers can use blindfolds so they are solely reliant on their 'calls'. When all the groups have demonstrated their 'calls', the whole class can come together in the space to represent how the ocean is filled with different animals. Members of groups (species) can now try to locate each other using their calls.

Things to discuss:

- Were the calls they used high or low pitched sounds?
- Did they use short or long sounds to create their signals?
- Was it easy to locate their 'own species' when they were alone in the ocean?
- Were they aware of how they used their ears to find each other?
- Was it easy to locate their species when the ocean was full of other types of 'animals'?
- Did 'noise' from other 'animals' create a problem?
- Might marine mammals experience problems locating their prey?

Discuss the children's responses and probe their understanding of how marine animals use sound. Identify any outstanding *learning needs*. The topic provides opportunities for children to further develop their understanding of how animals are adapted to their habitats.

2   Modelling how sound travels in liquids

Use video clips of scientific models to discuss how sound travels through liquids, and compare with how it travels through air. If children are aware of the particle nature of materials, they can apply their knowledge to explain why sounds travel better through liquids than through air. If each child represents an air particle, then to model air they need to stand far enough apart so they cannot touch each other. The model demonstrates the difficulty of passing on sound vibrations from particle to particle because of the distance between them. To model a liquid, children stand much closer so they are able to bump into each other. If a child starts to vibrate, then she can easily pass on the vibrations by bumping into the children around her. Children use the model to explain how sound travels through a liquid.

Information and teaching resources

BBC Bitesize:

- How sound travels through air. *www.bbc.co.uk/education/clips/ztwkjxs*
- How sound works. *www.bbc.co.uk/education/clips/zkbygk7*
- Echoes. *www.bbc.co.uk/education/clips/z6ptsbk*

Other websites:

- Echolocation. *www.youtube.com/watch?v=BYiCzWZ8cBs*

- How dolphins communicate. *https://seaworld.org/Animal-Info/Animal-InfoBooks/Bottlenose-Dolphins/Communication-and-Echolocation*

- Videos about dolphins. www.dolphins-world.com/category/multimedia/video/

- Echolocation. *www2.hawaii.edu/~zinner/101/students/YvetteEcholocation/echolocation.html*

- Various videos about dolphins. *www.google.co.uk/?gfe_rd=ssl&ei=j3UOV8ub CpCFaKyXltAH#q=dolphin+echolocation+video*

Application stage

Children's talk involves trying out scientific ideas

Detecting devices

The normal range of human hearing is between 20Hz and 20KHz. Sounds below this range are called infrasound, while sounds above the range are called ultrasound. Our ears are not adapted to detect infrasound and ultrasound. However, technology enables them to be used for a variety of medical, engineering and other purposes.

Children use information sources to compare the uses of infrasound and ultrasound in our high-tech twenty-first century world. Explore the advantages of using sound energy rather than electromagnetic energy in underwater detecting devices such as sonar, and medical devices such as ultrasound scanners. What are the disadvantages? Let children decide how they want to present the results of their research. They can also explore the range of jobs associated with different types of sound technologies. Invite a local professional or STEM ambassador to talk to the children about their work and job opportunities in their field.

Noise pollution

As described in the narrative at the beginning of the chapter, animals suffer from the harmful effects of noise pollution. Children use information sources to find out how noise pollution affects land and marine animals. Which are worst affected and where? Children present their findings to the rest of the class and together decide whether anything can be done to alleviate the problems. Design a poster campaign to develop awareness of the problem.

Information and teaching resources

BBC Bitesize:

- Ultrasound and infrasound. *www.bbc.co.uk/schools/gcsebitesize/science/edexcel/waves_earth/ultrasound_infrasoundrev2.shtml*

Other websites:

- Effects of noise on wildlife. *www.naturesounds.org/conservENW.html*
- How noise pollution affects animals.
  http://news.bbc.co.uk/earth/hi/earth_news/newsid_8305000/8305320.stm
- Noise pollution and animals: *www.sciencenews.org/article/noise-made-humans-can-be-bad-news-animals*
- Noise pollution. *www.everythingconnects.org/noise-pollution.html*

INDEX

Page numbers in **bold** refer to tables. Page numbers in *italics* refer to figures.